Margaret Debbadi
Siobhan Matthewson
Series editor:
Peter Marshman

INT...
COMPUTING
FOR LOWER SECONDARY

STAGE
9

COMPUTER SCIENCE

DIGITAL LITERACY

INFORMATION TECHNOLOGY

HODDER EDUCATION
AN HACHETTE UK COMPANY

The Publishers would like to thank the following for permission to reproduce copyright material.

Photo credits

p.4 *l* © antoniodiaz/Shutterstock, *rt* © nd3000/stock.adobe.com, *rc* © Maciek905/stock.adobe.com, *rb* © Besjunior/stock.adobe.com; **p.8** © Skiminok /stock.adobe.com; **p.9** © Panuwat /stock.adobe.com; **p.11** © Ronstik /stock.adobe.com; **p.12** © SparkusDesign/stock.adobe.com; **p.28** © Raimundas /stock.adobe.com; **p.29** © Ivan Kruk /stock.adobe.com; **p.31** © Alexandr /stock.adobe.com; **p.32** © Rh2010 /stock.adobe.com; **p.34** © TimeStopper /stock.adobe.com; **p.76** © Fatmawati /stock.adobe.com; **p.77** © Shock /stock.adobe.com; **p.79** © Oatawa /stock.adobe.com; **p.83** © Ilnur Khisamutdinov /Alamy Stock Photo; **p.84** © Daniel Ernst /stock.adobe.com; **p.92** © Viper /stock.adobe.com; **p.98** © Assemit /stock.adobe.com; **p.108** © Pictorial Press Ltd/ Alamy Stock Photo; **p.111** *t* © Marc Dietrich /stock.adobe.com, *c* © Zentilia /stock.adobe.com, *b* © Demarco /stock.adobe.com; **p.112** *t* © Vadim /stock.adobe.com, *b* © Faraktinov /stock.adobe.com; **p.114** © MicroOne/stock.adobe.com; **p.115** © Monika Wisniewska /stock.adobe.com; **p.117** © Pavlovski /stock.adobe.com; **p.120** © MclittleStock /stock.adobe.com; **p.125** *t* © Tsiumpa /stock.adobe.com, *c* © Sdecoret /stock.adobe.com, *b* © Getty Images /iStockphoto/Thinskstock/scanrail; **p.133** *t* © Andrey Popov /stock.adobe.com, *b* © Mhong84 /stock.adobe.com; **p.134** © Kanpisut /stock.adobe.com; **p.139** © Jenny Sturm /stock.adobe.com; **p.171** © Cifotart /stock.adobe.com; **p.173** *l* © Musmellow /stock.adobe.com, *r* © NikWB /stock.adobe.com; **p.175** © Andrey Popov /stock.adobe.com; **p.189** © Kolonko /stock.adobe.com; **p.201** © Melinda Nagy /stock.adobe.com; **p.206** © Redpixel /stock.adobe.com

b = bottom, *c* = centre, *t* = top, *r* = right, *l* = left

Every effort has been made to trace all copyright holders, but if any have been inadvertently overlooked, the Publishers will be pleased to make the necessary arrangements at the first opportunity.

Although every effort has been made to ensure that website addresses are correct at time of going to press, Hodder Education cannot be held responsible for the content of any website mentioned in this book. It is sometimes possible to find a relocated web page by typing in the address of the home page for a website in the URL window of your browser.

Hachette UK's policy is to use papers that are natural, renewable and recyclable products and made from wood grown in well-managed forests and other controlled sources. The logging and manufacturing processes are expected to conform to the environmental regulations of the country of origin.

Orders: please contact Bookpoint Ltd, 130 Park Drive, Milton Park, Abingdon, Oxon OX14 4SE. Telephone: +44 (0)1235 827827. Fax: +44 (0)1235 400401. Email education@bookpoint.co.uk Lines are open from 9 a.m. to 5 p.m., Monday to Saturday, with a 24-hour message answering service. You can also order through our website: www.hoddereducation.com

ISBN: 9781510482005

© Margaret Debbadi and Siobhan Matthewson 2020

First published in 2020

This edition published in 2020 by

Hodder Education,
An Hachette UK Company
Carmelite House
50 Victoria Embankment
London EC4Y 0DZ

www.hoddereducation.com

Impression number   10 9 8 7 6 5 4 3 2 1

Year   2024 2023 2022 2021 2020

Cover photo ©Golden Sikorka - stock.adobe.com

Illustrations by Aptara, Inc.

Typeset in FS Albert Regular 12/14pt by Aptara, Inc.

Printed in Slovenia

A catalogue record for this title is available from the British Library.

Contents

Introduction

About this book

This Student Book will continue to support your progression in computing and in the ongoing development of the skills needed to progress to specific curriculum areas such as IGSE Computer Science and IGCSE ICT. Building on the skills developed in the previous books in this series you will further develop the technical skills needed to engage effectively in the digital world of today. The book supports the curriculum areas of digital literacy, computer science and information technology:

- **Digital literacy** focuses on the impact of digital technology in today's society. It promotes understanding of the impact of the digital world with an emphasis on maintaining safety and well-being online.
- **Computer science** is the study of computational thinking and the creation of computer programs to solve problems. It also explores how a computer interprets and carries out instructions.
- **Information technology** looks at how to use computer programs to solve problems. It takes into consideration both usability (how well a program works) and accessibility needs (whether or not everybody is able to use the program effectively).

Units

This Student Book has six units:

9.1 Drilling down: How the processor processes introduces students to the CPU, registers and the fetch – decode – execute cycle. The concepts are illustrated using simple assembly language instructions. The role of logic gates and truth tables is explored, along with the continuing impact of advanced technology such as artificial intelligence and virtual reality.

9.2 Sorting it all out: Searching and sorting data structures introduces students to the concept of arrays and their implementation as lists in Python. For loops are introduced before moving on to the following searching and sorting algorithms: insertion sort, bubble sort, linear search and binary search. These are covered in some depth in both pseudocode and then as full Python implementations. Functions are introduced along with the concept of testing code.

9.3 HTML, CSS, JavaScript: Web-Pro Games explores more sophisticated website design for an online gaming company, with further coverage of CSS and the addition of JavaScript to enable interactive webpage elements, such as forms and buttons.

9.4 Networking: Not just a way of meeting new people explores the wired and wireless technologies that make up LANs and WANs, including the internet. This chapter also discusses how data travels across networks, error detection and how it can be encrypted. Legal issues surrounding personal data are also covered.

9.5 Designing, coding and documenting solutions covers the different roles within a software development team – project manager, analyst, designer and programmer. Students will learn about Gantt charts, wireframes, user requirements, test plans and drawing up pseudocode solutions that address a client's problem.

9.6 Choosing and using: Databases and spreadsheets focuses on a music promoter running a large music festival, with business needs that can be addressed using a combination of database and spreadsheet applications. Students will create a relational database, produce more complex queries and reports, create forms for data input, introduce macros, VLOOKUPs and pivot tables, and learn about presenting user-friendly interfaces.

How to use this book

In each unit you will learn new skills by completing a series of tasks. Each unit starts with some information followed by a list of the learning objectives that you will cover. These features also appear in each unit:

Learning Outcomes

This panel lists the things you will learn about in each unit.

KEYWORDS

Important words are emboldened the first time they appear in a unit and are defined in this panel. They also appear in the glossary.

SCENARIO

This panel contains a scenario which puts the tasks into a real-world context.

This panel suggests a simple task to check your understanding.

Do you remember?

This panel lists the skills you should already be able to do before starting the unit.

These speech bubbles provide hints and tips as you complete the tasks.

Learn

This panel introduces new concepts and skills.

Practice

This panel contains tasks with step-by-step instructions to apply the new skills and or knowledge from the 'Learn' panel.

DID YOU KNOW?

This panel provides an interesting or important fact about the task or theme.

Computational Thinking

This panel highlights tasks in the unit which involve one of the key areas of computational thinking:

Pattern recognition: the identification of repeating tasks or features in a larger problem to help solve more complex problems more easily.

Decomposition: breaking larger problems down into smaller more manageable tasks. Each smaller task is examined and solved more easily than a larger more complex problem.

Abstraction: ignoring details or elements of a problem which are not needed when trying to solve a problem.

Algorithmic thinking: providing a series of instructions which include details on how to solve an identified problem.

Generalisation: the process of creating solutions to new problems using past knowledge and experience to adapt existing algorithms.

Evaluation: the process of ensuring that an algorithmic solution is an effective and efficient one – that it is fit for purpose.

Go further

This panel contains tasks to enhance and develop the skills previously learnt in the unit.

Challenge yourself

This panel provides challenging tasks with additional instructions to support new skills.

Final project

This panel contains the final tasks of the unit which encompass all the skills developed. It can be used to support self/peer assessment and teacher assessment.

Evaluation

This panel provides guidance on how to evaluate and, if necessary, test the Final project.

Student resources are available at www.hoddereducation.com/student-resources

About the CPU

At the centre of all of the technologies we use today is a device known as the **central processing unit (CPU)**. The CPU contains all of the electronic circuitry a computer needs to carry out all of the instructions provided by the computer programs running on the device. It is the electronic circuitry inside the CPU which is used to execute programs on the electronic device. Computer programs can be written in **high-level languages (HLL)** (such as Python); these are easy for the programmer to understand but processing time needs to be spent translating these

instructions into a format that the processor can understand. Programs can also be written in **low-level languages (LLL)** (such as **assembly language** or **machine code**). Assembly language programs are designed specifically for each type of processor and less translation is needed.

The specification of the CPU can have an impact on the cost of a computer. The higher the specification, the more expensive the device will be.

> Think about the various models of PCs and mobile phones available to users today and how devices with higher processing capabilities and memory are more expensive.

In this unit you will learn:

→ about the differences between high-level language, low-level language, assembly language and machine code

→ about the main influences on processing speed of a digital device

→ about the main role of the CPU and how it fetches, decodes and executes instructions

→ the names and roles of the **registers** used when instructions are being fetched, decoded and executed

What brand of CPU do you use at home or at school?

→ how computer systems use **logic gates** and **buses** for data manipulation and transmission

→ how to draw logic gates and produce **truth tables** to illustrate the operation of a logic gate

→ how to combine logic gates to create a **logic circuit** used to support complex processes

→ to consider the impact of **artificial intelligence (AI)**, **virtual reality (VR)** and robotics on today's society

→ to consider the availability of such technologies across the world today (digital divide) and the impact they can have on everyday life.

SCENARIO

Tech-D is a new technology design company whose focus is designing technology which can be used to test young children's mathematical abilities. They have asked you to help with the development of a simple calculator which can be used in classrooms with children aged between 5 and 6 years of age. The important features Tech-D has asked you to consider when you are helping to develop the calculator include:

- how the hardware specification in the calculator can be altered to change the processing capabilities of the calculator

> The instructions to be carried out are quite simple so a high specification, high cost device is not necessary.

- what language can be used to program the calculator so that instructions can be quickly converted into a language the calculator can easily carry out

- how the instructions are carried out by the calculator. To do this you need to examine the role of the CPU in a digital device and how it carries out the fetch – execute cycle when running a computer program

> Additional components cost money so they should not be included unnecessarily.

- limiting access to only users whose biometric details, such as a finger print or retina scan, are stored on the calculating device. When a student accesses the calculator they can access data stored about any previous tasks they completed on the calculator.

KEYWORDS

logic gate: a physical device or circuit that carries out a logical operation

bus: communication line used to transfer signals from one part of a digital device to another; for example, a set of wires used to transfer data around the inside of a computer

truth table: a table which shows all possible combinations of inputs and outputs for a logic gate

logic circuit: a combination of logic gates used to carry out complex operations

artificial intelligence (AI): the use of computers to simulate intelligence displayed by humans

What are some ways AI is being used today?

virtual reality (VR): the use of technology to create an artificial environment that looks and feels realistic to the end user

Describe any VR you use.

DID YOU KNOW?

Since no two people can have the same voice, fingerprint or pattern in the retina of their eyes, biometric authorisation is becoming popular. The term biometric comes from 'bio', meaning life, and 'metric', meaning measurement.

We will look later in this unit at methods of providing biometric authorisation to hardware devices and applications.

KEYWORDS

biometric: the measurement of individuals' unique physical characteristics such as fingerprints and facial recognition

biometric authorisation: the use of biometric data to identify authorised users to an application and limit control to technology

Do you remember?

Before starting this unit, you should be able to:

✔ carry out basic mathematical calculations such as addition and subtraction

✔ enter a URL into a web browser to access a specified website

✔ access a spreadsheet application and alter the contents of a cell in a spreadsheet

✔ understand simple algorithms in the form of pseudocode or a flowchart

✔ covert simple pseudocode and flowchart algorithms into coded solutions

✔ use conditions in coding to support decision making

✔ understand the concept of repetition and its application in programming.

You should also know that:

✔ instructions entered into a computer must be converted into binary before they can be carried out

✔ you can use spreadsheet applications to model real-life situations

✔ Boolean values are values which can only be represented by TRUE or FALSE.

Inside a digital device

Learn

Any processing by a digital device is carried out by a part of the device known as the central processing unit (CPU). The CPU is connected to a special **circuit board** inside your computer. The circuit board where the CPU is located is called the **motherboard**

and the CPU is attached to the motherboard via a special socket. Most digital devices have a CPU, for example, your mobile phone, a washing machine, a microwave or your computer at home. The CPU is the component inside a digital device that does all of the work.

The motherboard is used to provide power to the CPU and all of the other components inside the digital device.

The CPU carries out all of the instructions inside a digital device, such as:

➤ controlling the operation of other parts of the digital device
➤ fetching instructions
➤ carrying out instructions in computer programs
➤ carrying out arithmetic and **logical operations**
➤ managing the input and output of data.

The main role of the CPU is to run (or execute) a set of stored instructions known as a computer program. The CPU co-ordinates all of the other parts of the computer when it is executing a program. It does this using a device called the **internal clock** or **system clock**.

Just in the same way that students' movement from one class to another during the school day can be co-ordinated by a school bell, the internal clock helps the CPU manage the execution of each instruction in a program. The CPU needs a certain number of **clock ticks** to carry out each instruction. The number of ticks carried out per second in a modern CPU is measured in MHz (megahertz) or GHz (gigahertz). 1MHz equals one million clock ticks per second. 1GHz equals one billion clock ticks per second.

The more clock ticks there are every second, the more instructions the processor can carry out in one second.

KEYWORDS

circuit board: a thin plastic plate or unit which contains electronic components

motherboard: a circuit board that houses the CPU and provides connections between the hardware components inside a computer

logical operations: instructions carried out using logical operators such as >, <, >=, <>, where the result can only be TRUE or FALSE

internal clock (or system clock): a timer which is used to control the rate instructions are carried out

clock ticks: a unit to measure time inside a computer system

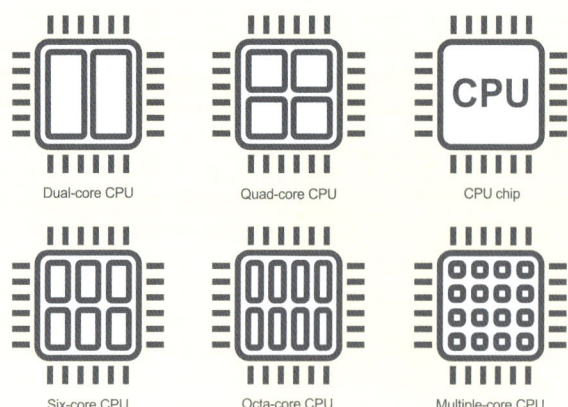

Dual-core CPU Quad-core CPU CPU chip

Six-core CPU Octa-core CPU Multiple-core CPU

The speed computers work at has continued to increase in recent years. Here are some of the other ways manufacturers have tried to increase processing speeds:

➤ Including more than one **core** (processing unit) in the CPU.

A single core can process an instruction or program on its own. CPUs can have more than one core so that more than one program (set of instructions) can be carried out at the same time.

➤ Increasing the amount of **cache** memory. Cache memory is located on the same chip as the CPU, and can be accessed very quickly. The CPU will store frequently-used instructions in cache so it has faster access to them. With more cache memory available more instructions can be accessed very quickly, which improves the speed of the computer.

➤ Increasing the amount of random access memory (RAM). RAM is used to temporarily store programs and data currently being used by the processor. RAM is placed close to the CPU (but not as close as cache memory and, therefore, cannot be accessed just as quickly). RAM is much larger than cache memory, however, and access times are still fast. The more data that can be stored in RAM, the faster it can be accessed by the CPU and the faster an instruction can be carried out. A computer with a larger amount of RAM has a higher performance than a computer with a lower amount of RAM.

CPU

1. Look in cache for data.

2. If data is in cache, send it to CPU and stop.

cache

3. If data is not in cache, fetch from RAM.

4. Send data from RAM; write it to the cache and then send it to the CPU.

RAM

If the processor can reduce the time needed to collect the instructions it is carrying out, it will also speed up processing time.

Having two cores will not mean the processor can carry out twice as many instructions as a single core, as some time and processing power needs to be spent splitting jobs or instructions between each core.

Storing data in cache is like storing data in a drawer in your house instead of outside in your garage. The drawer in your house is smaller and closer so the data is quicker and easier to find (and you don't have to go outside!).

KEYWORDS

core: an individual processing unit in the CPU; each processing unit can carry out its own set of instructions

cache: high speed memory, close to the processor, normally on the same processor chip, used to store frequently used instructions so the processor can access them quickly

Practice

When purchasing a new computer it is always important to look at the hardware specification, particularly the clock speed (processing power), cache size and number of cores.

For example, the computer below has a clock speed of 4.5 GHz, which means it operates at a speed of 4.5 billion clock ticks per second. It has 8 processing cores, 8 GB of RAM and 16.5 MB of cache.

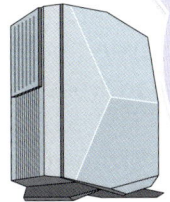

ALIENZONE GAMER (INTEL)

- Intel® Core™ i7 9800X (8-core, 16.5MB Cache, up to 4.5GHz with Intel® Turbo
- Windows 10 Home 64bit, English, Dutch, French, German, Italian
- NVIDIA® GeForce® GTX™ 1050Ti with 4BG GDDRS
- 8GB Channel DDR4 at 2666MHz
- 2TB 7200RPM SATA 6Gb/s (Standard)

$2,800.00

> 1 Hz = 1 instruction per second
> 1 kHz = 1000 instructions per second
> 1 MHz = 1000 kHz = 1 million instructions per second
> 1 GHz = 1000 MHz = 1 billion instructions per second
> Note: 'instructions' does not mean lines of code; it is the number of different tasks of any type that the processor can carry out.

Carry out the following tasks with a partner.

➤ Search the internet for a range of computer specifications (five at the most). Your search criteria could include specifications for computers with four cores (quad core), and eight cores. Look also for computers with greater than 4 MB of cache memory.

➤ Print a copy of each of the hardware specifications you have found. Look only at the number of cores, clock speed, RAM size and cache size.

   o Highlight the clock speed, number of cores, RAM and cache size in each specification.

   o Discuss which of the specifications you have found you think would be the most powerful/ fastest in terms of processing. Give a reason for your answer.

➤ Discuss why even though a processor has a clock speed of 3 GHz this does not mean the processor can carry out three billion lines of code every second.

> Think carefully about the following:
> 1. Does each instruction it carries out relate to a single line of a program?
> 2. How fast the other parts of the computer can operate – could a printer handle printing out the results of three billion instructions every second?

Inside the CPU

Practice

The CPU has three main components.

➤ **Arithmetic logic unit (ALU)** – carries out all of the calculations needed during the execution of a program.

➤ **Control unit (CU)** – issues commands to all of the other hardware components to help ensure programs are carried out correctly.

➤ Registers – store data about memory locations, instructions and data used during execution of an instruction.

  o **Accumulator (ACC)** – a register used by the ALU to store the intermediate results of processing carried out by the ALU.

  o **Program counter (PC)** – stores the address of the next instruction waiting to be executed (carried out) by the CPU.

  o **Current instruction register (CIR)** – stores the instruction currently being executed by the CPU.

  o **Memory address register (MAR)** – holds the address of the memory location being accessed either to read data from, or to write data to.

  o **Memory data register (MDR)** – any data or instructions that pass into or out of main memory must pass through the MDR.

Central processing unit   **Main memory**

Arithmetic logic unit (ALU)	Registers	Bus
	ACC	
	PC	
	CIR	
Control unit	MAR	
	MDR	

Main memory is another name for RAM, which is used to store the programs and data currently being operated on by the CPU.

Buses are sets of wires which can be used to carry a number of different signals around a digital device. These include:

➤ data (**data bus**)

➤ details of memory locations to be accessed (**address bus**)

➤ signals which tell other parts of the device what they are expected to do next (**control bus**).

Buses in computers carry the signals in the same way that we can travel from one place to another on a bus.

Address bus	Data bus	Control bus
This is like the number and destination on the front of a bus – tells the processor what location in memory will be opened to read data from or to write data to	Like the passengers on a bus – these are the data signals which move around the inside of the computer; for example, electrical signals which represent the binary code for letter R when it is pressed on a keyboard need to be carried from the keyboard to the CPU	When the bus stops a bell sound is played with a message telling passengers which stop they have reached – the control bus carries special signals which tell the processor what type of operations are being carried out

KEYWORD

control bus: carries control signals to different parts of the digital device telling them what task they need to carry out next

Practice

Complete the following diagram to help ensure you have a full understanding of the role played by each part of the CPU before we look in more detail at how the CPU carries out instructions in a computer program.

➤ Open the *Microsoft Word* document called **Understanding the CPU** provided by your teacher.
➤ Label each of the parts of the CPU by including a description of the role it plays in the fetch–decode–execute cycle.

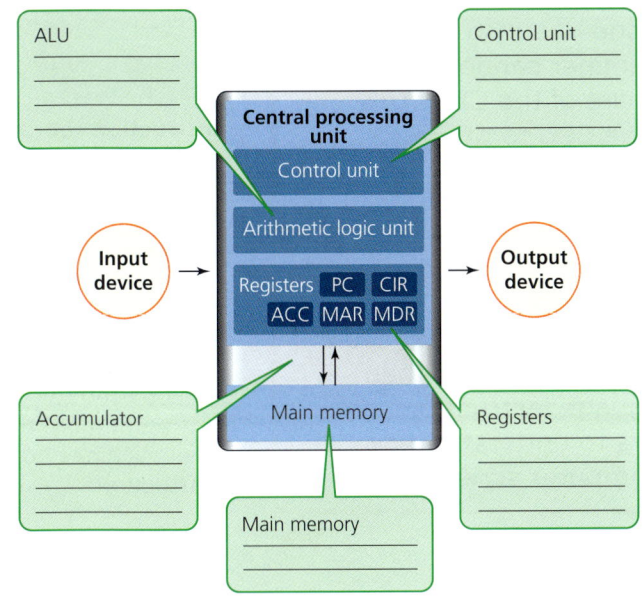

High- and low-level languages

Learn

The instructions to be carried out by a computer are provided by a computer program. Program developers use high-level languages such as JavaScript, Python or Scratch to write computer programs. However, before the processor can carry out these instructions they need to be converted into a pattern of 1s and 0s (binary) that the CPU understands.

Every CPU has its own set of binary instructions it understands. This is called its **instruction set**. The instruction set of a CPU is written in binary (also known as machine code) and is an example of a low-level language.

var1 = 0.5 If var1 > 1.3 or var1 < 0.9:	10100101010010101010101 01010101010010101010100
High-level language (HLL)	**Low-level language (LLL)**
• Easy for humans to read, write and modify. • Uses variables to identify locations in memory for storing data. • Portable, which means they can be run by any CPU.	• More difficult for humans to read, write and modify. • Identifies locations in memory using actual location addresses when storing data. • Not portable which means they can only run on a CPU with the same instruction set.

HLLs can be said to provide an **abstract** representation of how the CPU operates. This means that the programmer does not need to understand what is happening inside the CPU when they are writing their HLL program; instead, they can focus on writing a program to solve a problem. It also means that each HLL instruction will require more than one LLL instruction before it can be carried out successfully. Since one HLL instruction can represent more than one LLL, the programmer cannot always make the most efficient use of the hardware of the CPU. This means HLL instructions take longer for the CPU to process.

Experienced programmers can make use of a less abstract version of machine code, called assembly language.

Each assembly language instruction corresponds to one machine code instruction in the CPU's instruction set. The difference however is that assembly language uses a set of codes or symbols to represent each instruction rather than a group of 1s and 0s. The assembly language instructions are therefore easier for human programmers to understand, for example, to output the word 'Hi' to a computer screen:

Remember that computers only understand instructions which are written in binary.

KEYWORDS

instruction set: the set of all instructions in machine code that can be executed by a CPU

abstract: a representation that does not show all of the detail; the way a high-level language can be used to represent more than one machine code instruction

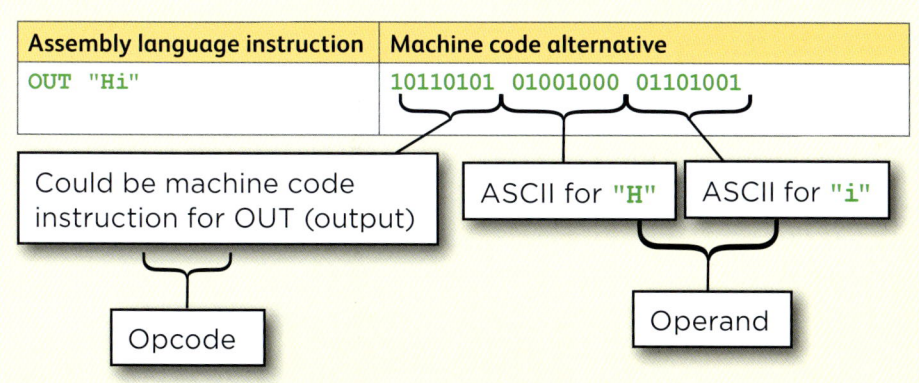

Assembly language instruction	Machine code alternative
OUT "Hi"	10110101 01001000 01101001

Could be machine code instruction for OUT (output)

Opcode

ASCII for "H"

ASCII for "i"

Operand

KEYWORDS

opcode: an instruction to be carried out

operand: a data item to be operated on or a location in memory where the data is stored

Each machine code instruction is made up of an **opcode** (the instruction to be carried out) and an **operand** (the data to be operated on or a location in memory where the data is stored).

The diagram below helps us understand the link between the CPU hardware, machine code, assembly language and high-level languages.

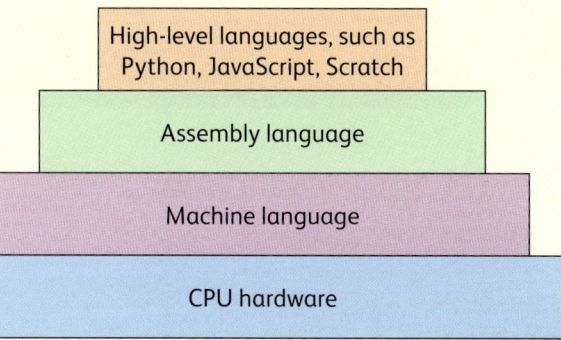

High-level languages, such as Python, JavaScript, Scratch

Assembly language

Machine language

CPU hardware

Practice

Produce an infographic which clearly illustrates to a non-computer expert the differences between high-level languages, assembly language and machine code.

Your graphic should include:

➤ a description of each type of instruction
➤ an illustration which shows the relationship between each language to the hardware of the CPU
➤ the advantages and disadvantages of each language type
➤ additional examples of high-level languages and examples of their uses
➤ an illustration of the differences between a high-level language instruction, an assembly language instruction and a machine code instruction.

Introducing fetch-decode-execute... repeat

Learn

When executing computer programs the CPU will carry out many instructions every second by going through a set of steps known as the **instruction cycle**.

An instruction cycle carried out by a processor works in three stages.

1 **Fetch** – the CPU fetches an instruction from a location in memory.

2 **Decode** – the CPU needs to work out what the instruction means, i.e. what is it telling the CPU to do.

3 **Execute** – once the CPU has figured out what it has to do it can then carry out that instruction.

This cycle is also known as the **fetch-decode-execute cycle**. The processor will continually fetch instructions from memory, decode them and then execute (or carry out) those instructions.

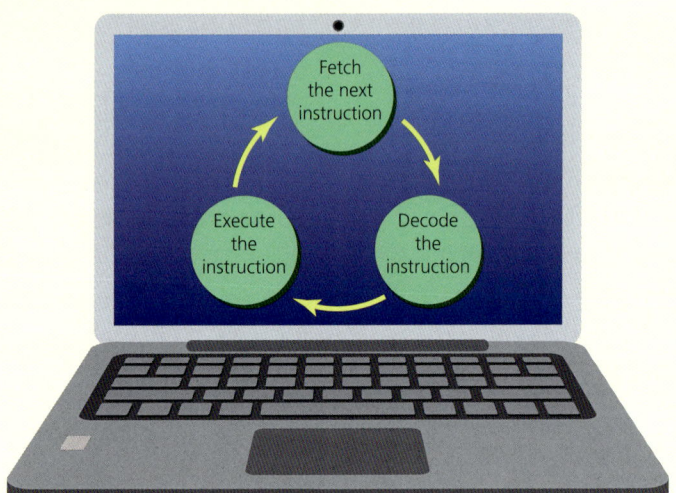

KEYWORDS

instruction cycle: the cycle carried out by the CPU as it processes instructions

fetch: the process of collecting an instruction from another location

decode: the process of working out what the instruction means, what it is telling the CPU to do

execute: the process of carrying out the instruction

fetch-decode-execute cycle: another name for the instruction cycle

Abstraction and algorithmic thinking

Using abstraction and pattern recognition you will convert a set of coded program instructions into a more English-like set of commands and then carry out the instructions represented by those commands.

Practice

When we think about the fetch-decode-execute cycle it all seems quite straightforward. The processor collects an instruction from memory, decodes it, and then carries out that instruction. The following task will help you think about some of the stages involved in the fetch-decode-execute cycle.

Your teacher will provide you with a worksheet called **Introducing the fetch decode execute cycle**. The worksheet contains two tables.

Table 1: This table is an instruction reference table. It contains a made-up assembly language instruction set for a basic calculator CPU.

Table 2: This table contains a set of memory locations with a short program (written using the made-up assembly language instruction for the calculator). It contains three additional columns for you to complete by showing the decoded version of each instruction, any updated memory location contents and any output from the program.

The worksheet contains a simple program that the calculator needs to carry out.

During this task you will work with a partner to examine each instruction in the memory locations 0-5.

To complete the task you must

➤ Read each instruction in Table 2 in turn (like a processor fetching an instruction from memory).

➤ Use the instruction references table (Table 1) to work out what each instruction is asking you to do. You should then write down the decoded instruction in the appropriate column in Table 2. (like a CPU decoding an instruction). The first has been done for you.

➤ Carry out the instruction by updating any memory location contents in Table 2 or showing any output from the program in the appropriate column (like a CPU executing the program instruction).

Table 1 – Instruction references

Instruction (opcode and operand)	Example	Description and illustration
X number	X 23	Input a number (for example, input the number 23)
Y location	Y 100	Store an input number in the memory location shown (e.g. store the input number in location 100)
Z location 1, location 2, location 3	Z 100, 101, 102	Add together the numbers in the memory locations 1 and 2 shown and store the results in location 3 (e.g. add together the numbers in memory locations 100 and 101 and store the results in memory location 102)
P location	P 102	Print / output the contents of the memory location shown (e.g. print the contents of location 102)
S location 1, location 2	S 100, 101	Subtract the contents of memory location 1 from the number in memory location 2 (for example, subtract the number in memory location 100 from the number in memory location 101)
M location 1, location 2	M 100, 101	Multiply the contents of memory location 1 and memory location 2 (e.g. multiply the number stored in memory location 100 by the number in memory location 101)

Table 2 – Assembly language program

Memory location	Instructions	Decoded instruction	Updated location contents	Output
0	X 45	Input the number 45		
1	Y 10			
2	X 217			
3	Y 11			
4	Z 10, 11, 12			
5	P 12			
6				
7				
8				
9				
10				
11				
12				

Once you have finished this task, design your own program on the blank memory locations table provided in the worksheet. Ask your partner to decode and execute it operating in the same way as a CPU completing the fetch, decode and execute cycle. For example, try writing a program which adds three numbers together and then outputs the results.

How could you amend instruction Z to help you with this?

Try adding your own assembly language instructions to the instruction decode table to make the task more complicated for your partner.

All about the accumulator

Learn

The previous practice task resulted in you converting a coded set of instructions into a format that was more easily recognisable to us as humans. You used a made-up instruction set based on letters and numbers when completing this task. The assembly language instruction set used by a CPU is a little more complicated. A more realistic set of assembly language instructions for your calculator could include the following.

Instruction	Example	Instruction meaning and example
LDA	LDA 9	Load contents of location 9 into the accumulator
ADD	ADD 10	Add contents of location 10 to the contents of the accumulator
SUB	SUB 11	Subtract contents of location 11 from the contents of the accumulator
STA	STA 12	Store the contents of accumulator in location 12
INP	INP	Place the input value typed in by the user into the accumulator (replacing any value already stored in the accumulator).
OUT	OUT	Display the contents of the accumulator to an output display

Thinking about the program you executed in the previous practice panel, the lines of code really only carried out the following high-level language instruction:

```
print (45 + 217)
```

This one single high-level language instruction represents many assembly language instructions.

In the previous practice panel you entered the first number, stored it in a memory location, entered a second number, stored it in a second memory location, and then added the contents of both locations together. However, the CPU will use an additional register called the accumulator to help with this task.

The accumulator acts almost like a short-term memory for the CPU. When it is adding two numbers together, the CPU will hold the first number in the accumulator, then add the second number to the accumulator before, for example, storing or printing the result.

By removing one level of translation (not having to convert this single high-level language instruction into many machine code instructions) processor time can be used more efficiently.

We introduced the accumulator on page 14 when looking at the registers used by the CPU.

The following short assembly language instructions allow us to place the contents of location 10 into the accumulator and then add the contents of location 11 to the accumulator.

The diagram below shows us some of the registers and part of a program stored in memory by the calculator's CPU.

Look how the contents of the accumulator change after each instruction is executed (we can ignore the contents of the other CPU registers for the moment).

1. After executing the first instruction LDA 10 (load the contents of location 10 into the accumulator), the accumulator holds the number 45.

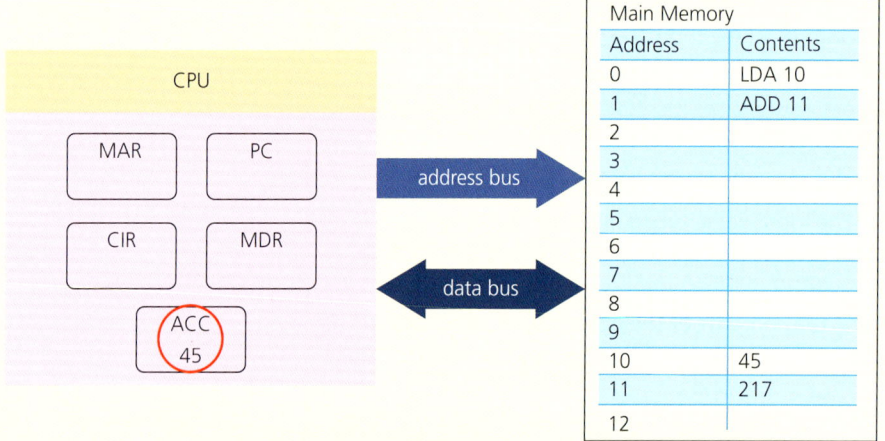

2. After executing the second instruction ADD 11 (add the contents of location 11 to the value already stored in the accumulator), the accumulator now holds the result of the ADD calculation.

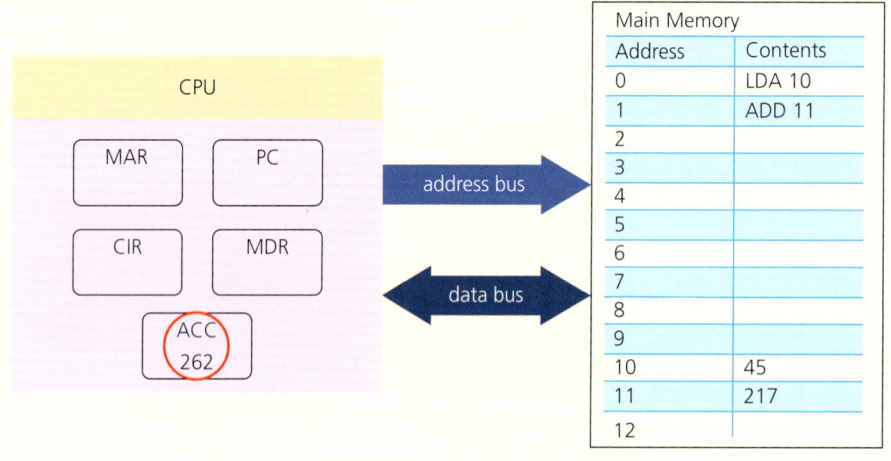

Computational Thinking

Through the process of decomposition consider the steps required by a CPU to add two numbers together and output the result of the calculation if it uses the accumulator to store the intermediate result of the calculation.

Use algorithmic thinking and our updated assembly language instruction set on page 21 to produce a short program which will allow a user to:

- ✪ input a number
- ✪ store that number in a specified memory location
- ✪ allow the user to input and store a second number
- ✪ add the two numbers together
- ✪ and output the result.

Practice

Use the updated assembly language example to rewrite your program†from the previous practice panel.†But, this time, make use of the accumulator.

Remember the program is designed to:

- ➤ allow the user to input two numbers
- ➤ store the numbers in memory locations 10 and 11
- ➤ add the two numbers together
- ➤ store the result in location 12
- ➤ output the result.

This algorithm will help you complete this task:

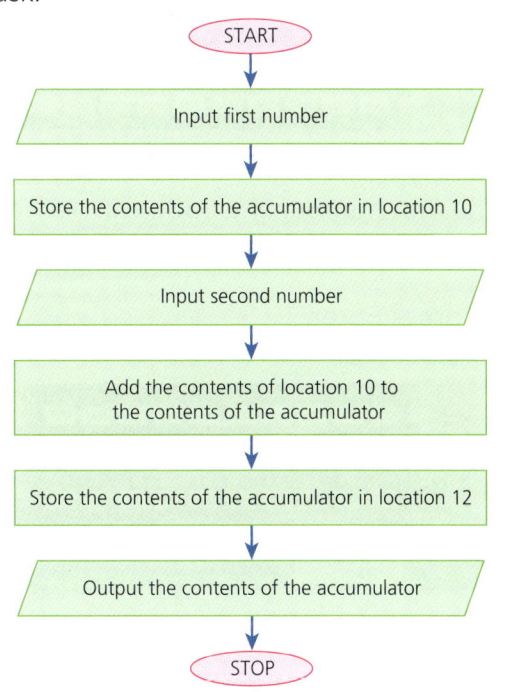

It is possible to test your code using a simulator called the **Little Man Computer (LMC)**.

- ➤ Open an internet browser, such as *Google Chrome*.
- ➤ Enter the URL https://peterhigginson.co.uk/lmc
- ➤ Enter your code into the coding window.

> **KEYWORD**
>
> **Little Man Computer (LMC):** an online CPU simulation program

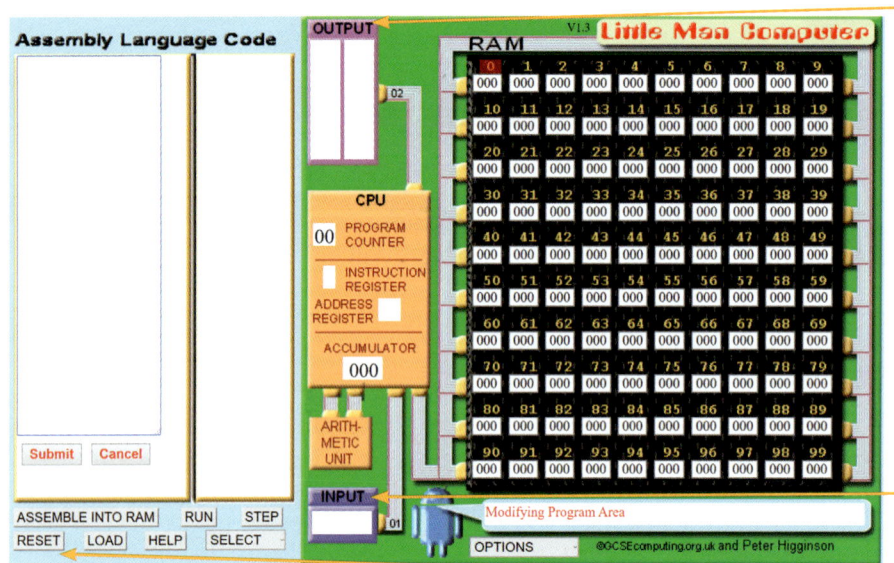

Output from the program will be displayed here

Input values can be entered here

Click here to clear the code window and enter a new program

➤ Click Submit to transfer the code into the Main Memory (RAM)

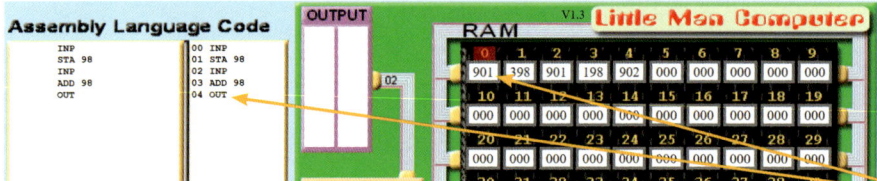

The code will be translated into machine code and placed in the first four locations in memory; for example, the machine code for the first instruction is 901.

➤ Click the Run button to execute your code.
➤ When it is time to enter the first number the code will pause and a flashing cursor will appear in the input box at the bottom of the screen.
➤ Type the first number and press Enter.
➤ The above process will be repeated.

Before you type your second number, check the location in main memory to check your number has been stored correctly in the location you specified in your second instruction; for example, in this example the number 8 was entered and stored in location 98.

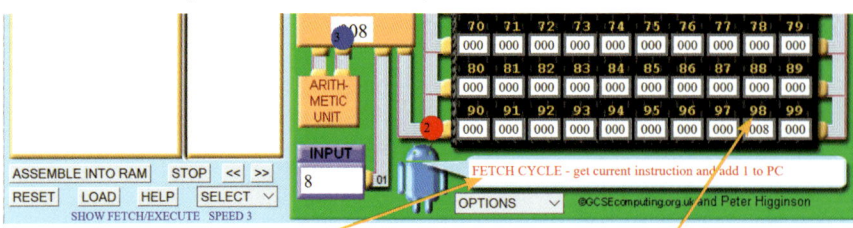

Notice how the steps of the fetch – execute cycle are being explained by 'The Little Man'!

You can increase or decrease the speed the LMC executes instructions by clicking on the << or >> buttons.

Number 8 was previously entered and the processor has now stored it in location 98.

> ➤ Experiment with the LMC by creating a more complex program. For example, one which allows the user to enter three numbers, adds them together and then stores the result in a memory location before it outputs the answer.

> Watch the contents of the registers used inside the Little Man Computer as your program is being executed. Notice how the contents change as the program is executed.

A detailed look: fetch–decode–execute

Learn

Using the LMC in the previous practice task gave you an idea of how each of the registers inside the processor are used during the fetch–decode–execute cycle.

Let us look at how the contents of the registers are used by the CPU as it executes the first line of the program shown in Main Memory in the example below.

Fetch

> ➤ The program counter contains the number 0 as this is the memory location of the first instruction to be executed.
> ➤ This means that the MAR will point to location 0.
> ➤ This address in the MAR is located via the address bus.
> ➤ There is currently nothing in the MDR, CIR or ACC.
> ➤ The contents of memory location 0 are read from main memory and sent via the data bus to the MDR.

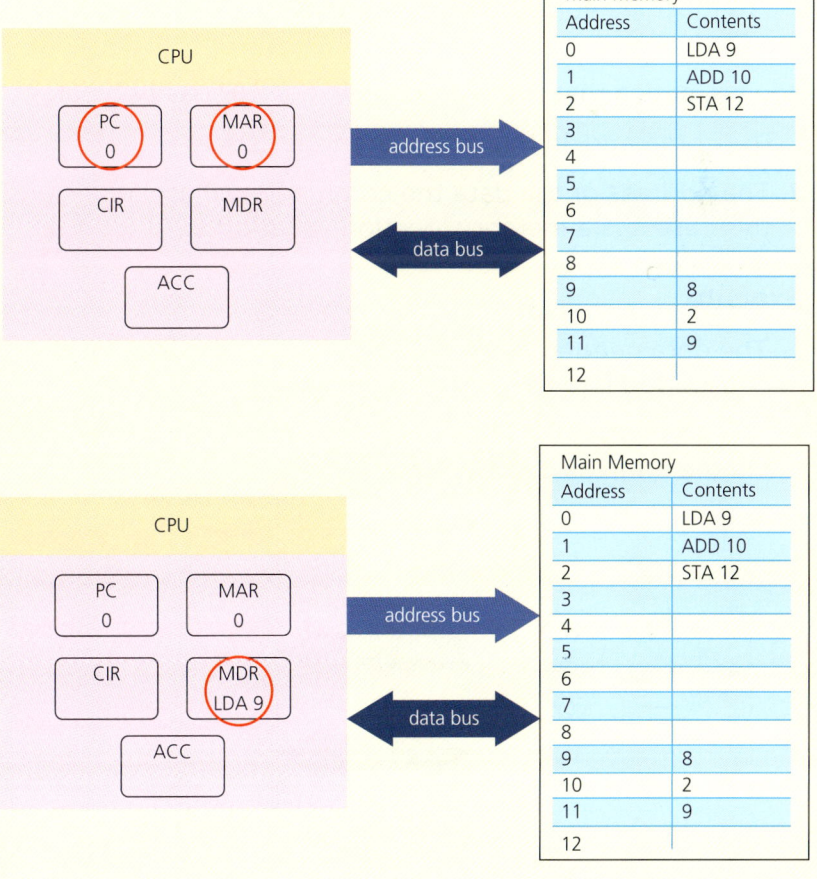

➤ Since this was an instruction it can now be copied into the CIR.

➤ The instruction has now been fetched so the PC can be increased (incremented) so that it points to the next instruction which is to be executed.

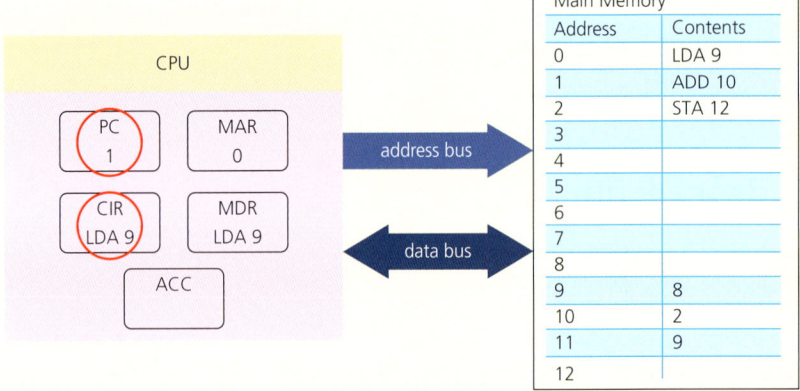

Decode

The CIR passes the instruction to the control unit (not shown in diagram) which can now decode the instruction (convert it into machine code) so that it can then be executed by the CPU.

You will notice that the instruction in the CIR has two parts.

1. The command, in this example this is LDA.

2. The address or the data the command will use: in this case it is a memory location, location 9.

> This instruction is telling the CPU it must access the contents of location 9 in memory and load the contents of that location into the ACC (accumulator) register.

Execute

➤ The data needed to execute this instruction is in location 9 so 9 is loaded into the MAR.

➤ The address in the MAR (address location 9) is now located via the address bus.

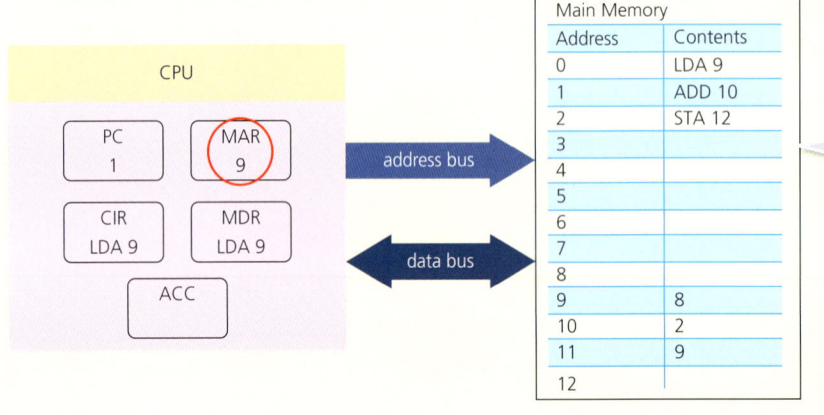

> The MAR is now pointing to the memory location we need to fetch data from and the PC is pointing to location 1 which is the memory location of the next instruction to be carried out by the processor.

➤ The contents of location 9 are read from Main Memory and sent via the data bus to the MDR, replacing what was previously stored in the MDR.

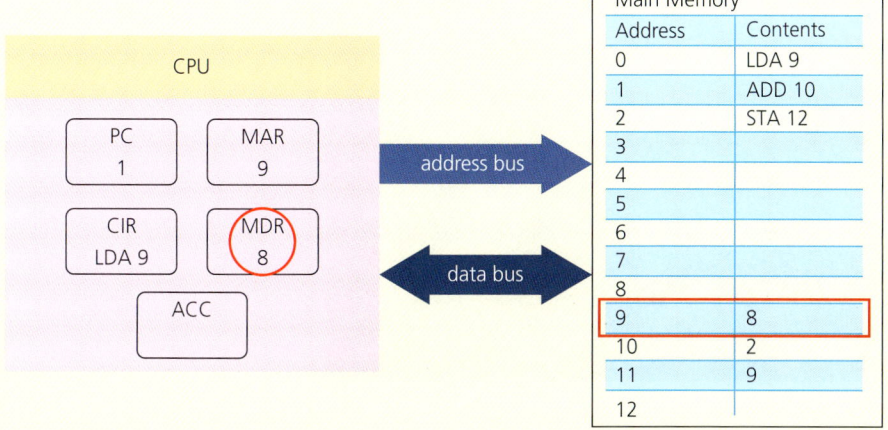

➤ The MDR now contains the number 8. The control unit previously decoded the instruction which was LDA 9. The contents of the MDR are now passed to the ACC (accumulator).

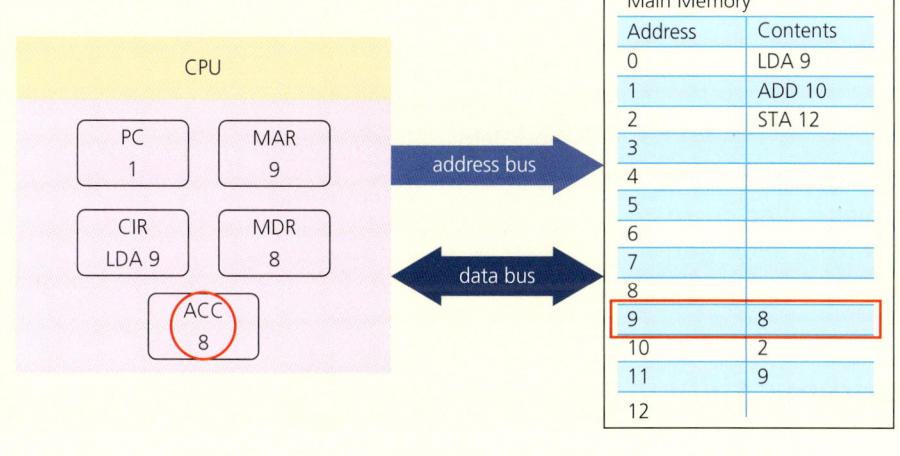

Logic gates: How it all happens, part 1

Learn

Digital devices process data using logic gates. Logic gates are **electronic circuits** that have one or more inputs which are processed to produce outputs which represent the values TRUE or FALSE.

A Boolean value is any value which is TRUE or FALSE.

KEYWORD

electronic circuit: a physical device programmed to make decisions on (process) inputs in order to produce an output signal

Input into a logic gate is in the form of an electrical signal. The signal can be altered to represent 1 or 0, hence logic gates can be used to process binary data. Large combinations of logic gates are used to carry out processing in digital devices. Computer hardware designers combine logic gates inside the CPU to allow instructions to be processed. Before a processor is created the designer will use diagrams to show how logic gates are to be combined.

Different logic gates perform different types of operations. One of these gates is an **AND gate**.

AND gates have two inputs (each of which can be 1 or 0). The AND gate will only output 1 if both inputs equal 1.

The symbol for an AND gate is:

While each logic gate is represented using its own symbol, special tables called truth tables can be used to show how each gate operates.

We will look at truth tables in more detail in the practice panel.

Abstraction and algorithmic thinking

Using abstraction consider the following real-life examples to help you understand each of the logic gate shown in the learn and practice panels which follow. Use algorithmic thinking and the rules associated with each logic gate to complete the truth table for each decision being considered.

Practice

The following real-life example can help us understand how the AND gate works:

Decision 1: Understanding AND gates

Mr X is trying to figure out if he can have buttered toast for breakfast. He can only have buttered toast if:

➤ A there is bread in the cupboard AND

➤ B there is butter in the fridge.

A represents an input telling us whether it is TRUE or FALSE (1 or 0) that Mr X has bread in his house, and B represents an input which tells us whether it is TRUE or FALSE (1 or 0) that Mr X has butter in his house.

We can use a table like the one below to examine all combinations of input and output to our AND gate.

A	B		Output
Mr X has bread	Mr X has butter	Explanation	Toast for breakfast?
0	0	There is no bread AND there is no butter	NO
0	1	There is no bread AND there is butter	NO
1	0	There is bread AND there is no butter	NO
1	1	There is bread AND there is butter	YES

> Mr X can only have toast if both statements are TRUE. There is bread AND there is butter.

If we remove the explanation column from the table we created above we now have a truth table which shows the combinations of inputs and outputs of an AND gate:

INPUTS		OUTPUT
A	B	Z = (A AND B)
0	0	0
0	1	0
1	0	0
1	1	1

➤ Open the spreadsheet file called **Using Logic Gates**. Your teacher will provide you with a copy of this file.

- ➤ Click on the tab for the worksheet called **AND gates**.
- ➤ The inputs to the AND gate have already been set to A = 0 AND B = 0, the output displayed = 0.
- ➤ Edit the inputs to show the other combinations of inputs in the truth table and complete the truth table to show the output generated.
- ➤ Save your copy of the file called **Using Logic Gates**.

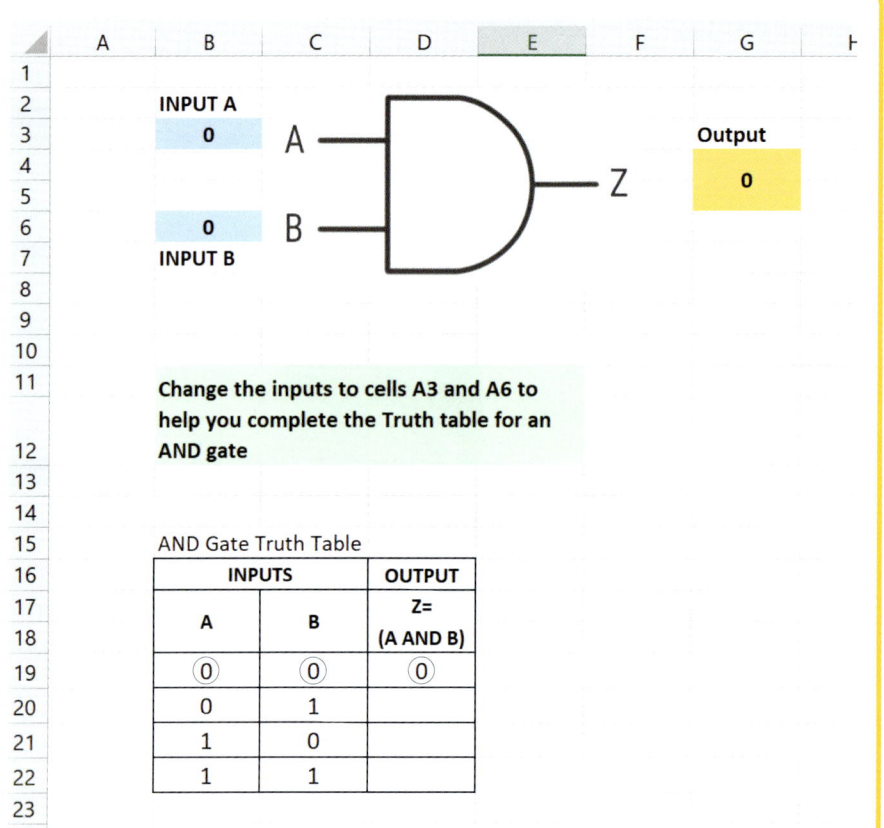

Change the inputs to cells A3 and A6 to help you complete the Truth table for an AND gate

AND Gate Truth Table

INPUTS		OUTPUT
A	B	Z= (A AND B)
⓪	⓪	⓪
0	1	
1	0	
1	1	

Logic gates: How it all happens, part 2

Practice

Logic circuits in the CPU are used to carry out very complex processing. In order to allow them to do this the logic circuit will include more than one type of gate. Some other types of gates which may be included in a logic circuit include:

Name	Description	Symbol
OR gate	OR gates have two inputs (each of which can be 1 or 0). The OR gate will output 1 if any of the two inputs equal 1	A ⟩ Z B
NOT gate	NOT gates have only 1 input (which can be 1 or 0). Output from the NOT gate will always be the opposite of the input.	A ▷o Z
XOR gate	XOR (exclusive OR) gates have two inputs (each of which can be 1 or 0). The XOR gate will output 1 if any of the two inputs equal 1 but not if both are 1.	A ⟩ Z B

KEYWORDS

OR gate: a logic gate which accepts two inputs and will output a 1 (or TRUE) value only if either of the input values equals 1

Make up an example of how an OR gate can be used.

NOT gate: a logic gate which accepts one input and will output the opposite value to the input; for example, if the input value is 1, the output value will be 0 and vice versa

XOR gate: a logic gate which accepts two inputs and will output a 1 (or TRUE) value only if either of the input values equals 1, but not if both equal 1

Abstraction and algorithmic thinking

Using abstraction consider the following real-life examples as inputs into the logic gate shown. Use the algorithmic thinking and the rules associated with each logic gate to complete the truth table for each decision being considered using the logic gate.

Practice

Decision 2: Understanding OR gates

Remember, output from an OR gate is TRUE when any or all of the inputs are TRUE.

Ms Y is meeting her friend for lunch. She arrives at the restaurant first. She can either text her friend or telephone her to tell her she is already there – either way, her friend will receive the message.

➤ A text
  OR
➤ B phone

Your teacher will give you a copy of a worksheet called **Understanding OR gates** containing a copy of the table shown below.

Use what you have learned about OR gates to help you first of all complete the table below to show if Ms Y's friend receives the message.

A	B	Explanation	Friend receives the message
Ms Y will text	Ms Y will phone		
0	0	Ms Y does not text OR phone her friend	
0	1	Ms Y can either text OR phone her friend and she will still get the message. Even if Ms Z does both, the message is still received.	
1	0		
1	1		

➤ Open the spreadsheet file called **Using Logic Gates** and click on the tab called **OR gates**.

➤ Edit the A and B input values to reflect the inputs shown on the truth table.

➤ Compare the outputs generated on the spreadsheet to the output you predicted and complete the truth table for the instruction Z = A OR B.

➤ Save your copy of the file called **Using Logic Gates**.

INPUTS		OUTPUT
A	B	Z = (A OR B)
0	0	
0	1	
1	0	
1	1	

Practice

Decision 3: Understanding NOT gates

A home owner needs to decide if he should turn the heating system on in his home.

If the temperature is above 20 °C the heating will be switched OFF (0), otherwise the heating system will be switched ON (1).

The input A is 1 (TRUE) when the temperature is above 20 °C and 0 (FALSE) when the temperature is below 20 °C.

Use the truth table below to help the homeowner decide if he needs to switch his home heating on.

INPUT	OUTPUT
A	Z
0	
1	

➤ Open the spreadsheet file called **Using Logic Gates** and click on the tab called **NOT gates**.

➤ Edit the A input values to reflect the input values shown on the truth table.

➤ Compare the outputs generated on the spreadsheet to the output you predicted and complete the truth table for the instruction Z = NOT A.

➤ Save your copy of the file called **Using Logic Gates**.

Practice

Decision 4: Understanding XOR (Exclusive OR) gates

Mrs W has gone to visit a friend at home. Her friend offers her either tea or coffee. The most polite option for Mrs W is to accept either one or the other of the two options. It would be rude to ask for both and if she does she won't receive either!

A represents coffee

B represents tea

Use the truth table below to show if Mrs W will receive a drink, depending on what she asks for.

INPUTS		OUTPUT
A	B	Z (A XOR B)
0	0	
0	1	
1	0	
1	1	

➤ Open the spreadsheet file called **Using Logic Gates** and click on the tab called **XOR gates**.

➤ Edit the A and B input values to reflect the inputs shown on the truth table.

➤ Compare the outputs generated on the spreadsheet to the output you predicted and complete the truth table for the instruction Z = A XOR B.

➤ Save your copy of the file called **Using Logic Gates**.

AI, VR and logic gates

Learn

Logic gates form the basis of all computer systems including artificial intelligence (AI) and virtual reality (VR) systems.

As we continue to harness more and more technologies the more essential technology developed which use logic gates becomes to our everyday activities. However, computer devices are not accessible to everyone. This uneven distribution of access to technology is called the **digital divide**. While the cost of technology is one reason for the digital divide, other reasons include geographical location and communication infrastructure – for instance, the internet is not available everywhere. In addition, there may be a divide along the ages of the population – not everyone is confident using modern technology.

Despite the digital divide, emerging technologies which combine the main features of AI and VR have the potential to have a dramatic impact on our everyday lives, offering advantages beyond any expectations.

KEYWORD

digital divide: the uneven distribution of access to modern technology

What are some of the disadvantages of having a digital divide?

How has AI and VR impacted upon our everyday lives?

Examples of VR	Examples of AI
• Used by schools to help students visualise mathematical solutions, take virtual field trips or take a trip back in time. • Gaming experiences are enhanced through the use of VR. It provides the user with a more immersive experience. • Used in healthcare to support training of medics in the diagnosis of illness and in the completion of medical procedures. • Architects can use VR to produce 3D models of buildings before development to allow clients to have a walk around the planned development before it is produced. • Fashion designers can also make use of VR to help visualise how their designs might look in real life. • Airlines can use VR to train pilots.	• Self-driving cars – cars plan routes, take into consideration traffic news and avoid obstacles. • Used in education to help decide on students' pathways through learning materials. • Financial markets – large amounts of data about stocks and shares can be analysed and decisions made quickly about buying and selling stocks and shares. • Individuals have access to apps on mobile devices that can be used to help them manage spending, save, and make predictions about potential changes in spending. • Medical professionals can use AI to help with diagnosis of illness, and predict the spread of epidemics. • Customers phoning larger organisations for help or advice often communicate in the first instance with an AI application that will use voice recognition to help direct their call to the correct person.

Generalisation

Using your own experience of modern technology and what you have learned about the uses of AI and VR consider how AI and VR have improved the lifestyles of individuals.

Practice

Produce a multimedia presentation on the topic of AI and VR in today's society. Your presentation should include reference to examples of how both AI and VR are used in the home and by professionals in the world today.

Use the examples provided in this unit to guide you, but also carry out your own research on the uses of AI and VR today.

In your presentation you should include:

➤ at least three potential uses for each AI and VR
➤ comments on the advantages and disadvantages of the technology in each situation
➤ illustrations of each example using a graphic or a video you have sourced from the internet.

Remember to always reference the source of the images or other content you are using in your presentation. Using content produced by someone else, without their permission and without giving credit is a breach of copyright laws.

Go further

The owner of Tech-D has asked that you design a short program in assembly language that can be used to allow the user to:

Think about storing the values in memory after they are input.

◆ Input two numbers.
◆ Subtract the second number from the first.
◆ Store the result in memory.
◆ Output number 1, number 2 and the result of the calculation.

Before you write your program, produce an algorithm to show each stage of input, transfer of data from the accumulator to memory and from the accumulator to an output device.

◆ Test your program using https://peterhigginson.co.uk/lmc/
  ❏ Enter your program into the code window for the Little Man Computer.
  ❏ Click on the Submit button to run your program.
  ❏ Make a note of the two numbers you wish to input and the result you expect from your calculation.
◆ Click the Run button to execute your program.
◆ Take a screen shot of the Little Man Computer when the program has finished executing.
◆ On the screen shot circle the output result and the input numbers stored in memory.

Logic circuits are often made up from more than one type of logic gate. In such instances, the single output from one logic gate can be used as the input to another logic gate. This is an example of **combinational logic**.

This diagram shows a logic circuit using an AND gate and a NOT gate.

Identify the type of gate used in the first part of the logic circuit, use this information to help you complete the logic statement at the top of column 3, C= A _____ B

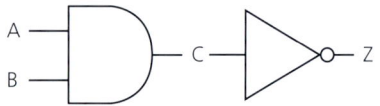

Create a trace table to show the output from the logic circuit shown below.

KEYWORD

combinational logic: the use of more than one logic gate in a logic circuit to allow complex tasks to be carried out

Inputs		C =A _____ B	Z= NOT C
A	B	C	Z
Step 1 Complete the inputs to show all possible combinations of 0 and 1 which can be input to the first logic gate.		**Step 2** Use the logic statement to work out the outputs from the first gate based on the inputs provided.	**Step 3** Use the outputs from the first gate to work out the outputs in the third column in the trace table

Challenge yourself

Working with the design team you have been asked to decide on the type of logic gates needed to complete the following tasks.

You have learned previously how CPUs are made from logic gates combined together into combinational logic circuits. This†allows computers to help with complex decision making, for example, deciding on the direction a self-drive car should turn in order to avoid an obstacle in the middle of the road.

The Tech-D calculator has to be able decide when students can move from one level of questions and tasks to the next.

You need to help the hardware designer develop a logic circuit that can help with this task.

Students can move from one level to the next only if:

➤ they have completed all tasks in their current level AND they have scored 70% or higher in a short end of level test AND

➤ they have completed an end of level check list to say they understand all of the topics covered, OR, the teacher has ticked a box to say they are happy with their understanding of that topic.

Use the following gates to help with this task:

Produce a truth table to illustrate the circuit you have designed.

> Think about the two inputs you have here – what logic gate might you use to combine these inputs to decide if the student is ready to move on?

> The outputs from the two other logic gates can be combined here.

> Think about the two inputs you have here – what logic gate might you use to combine these inputs?

Final project

Part 1

The programmer has devised a new program:

➤ It allows the user to input two numbers.

➤ It adds the numbers together and stores the result in a location 40 in memory.

➤ The user can then input a third number.

➤ The third number is subtracted from the result of the first calculation.

➤ The new result is stored in location 41 in memory.

➤ The result of the calculation is output.

Part of the program has been completed below. You have been asked to complete the program using assembly language instructions.

You should then test that the code produced will work with the CPU structure for the calculator.

Do this by copying and completing the table below to show how the contents of the program counter, accumulator and memory locations will change as the program is executed. (The first line has been completed for you.)

Use the diagram of the CPU to help you.

The user has input the number 90.

KEYWORD

trace table: a table used by programmers when testing a program; the programmer can use the table to make a note of the changes to variable values as they work through the lines of code in the program on paper

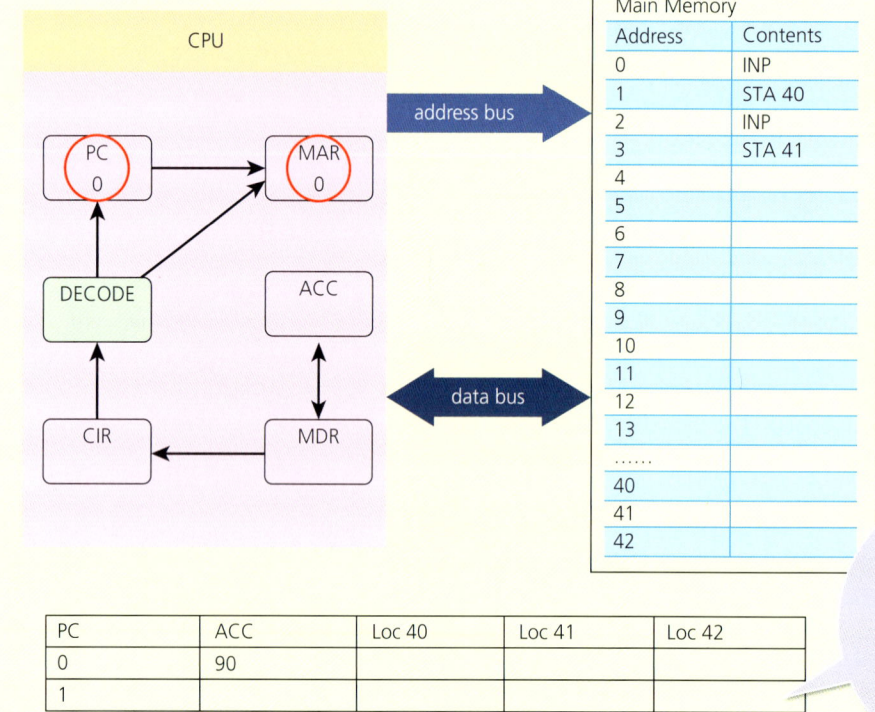

Main Memory	
Address	Contents
0	INP
1	STA 40
2	INP
3	STA 41
4	
5	
6	
7	
8	
9	
10	
11	
12	
13	
......	
40	
41	
42	

PC	ACC	Loc 40	Loc 41	Loc 42
0	90			
1				

Using a table this way to keep track of the contents of memory locations and or variables is a method used by professional programmers when they are tracing through the actions of a program. A table used this way is called a **trace table**.

Part 2

The owner of Tech-D was keen to introduce some kind of biometric security to the application. The calculators should only be accessible to the pupil whose biometric data is stored on the calculator. When a student accesses the calculator they can access data stored about any previous tasks they completed on the calculator. He is keen to use one of the following to help limit authorisation to each calculator:

➤ fingerprint analysis: where fingerprints can be stored in a database and only those whose fingerprints are stored have access to the application

➤ retina scanning: where the patterns in each person's iris can be used to decide who has access to the application

➤ facial recognition: where the shapes of individuals' faces can determine who has access

➤ voice recognition: where the pitch, tone and frequency of the user's voice pattern ca be used to determine if they have access or not.

The owner has asked that you develop a logic circuit which can be used to limit access to the application to only the pupil whose biometric data is stored on the calculator.

➤ Each calculator stores two student profiles.

➤ A student can only access their own data and tasks on the calculator.

➤ When a student logs in to the calculator they are only able to access their own learning data.

Draw a logic circuit using an OR gate and an AND gate which will

➤ use an OR gate to check first if the user is either user A or B

➤ check a file called D to ensure the users profile is correctly stored and only allow the user to progress if they have been identified as user A or B, and their profile is stored on the calculator.

Part 3

The owner of Tech-D is concerned that using biometric authorisation to provide access to the calculator might increase the price of the calculator. This could make it too expensive for some students and some schools have said they are concerned about increasing the digital divide.

They are also concerned about keeping student data secure on devices which may be shared by others.

The owner of Tech-D has asked you to produce a short report advising them on how they can bridge the digital divide with their calculator. In your report you should research and:

➤ Explain what the digital divide is.

➤ Discuss the suitability of biometric authorisation as a means of keeping data secure (give some examples where biometric authorisation is used successfully to help keep data secure).

➤ Comment on how incorporating biometric authorisation might impact on the hardware needed in the calculator; for example, RAM, number of cores, amount of cache, clock speed. How might this impact on price?

Thinking ahead to future developments and more advanced versions of the calculator, Tech-D have also asked you to consider how AI and VR could be used to support learning in the future.

➤ Describe how the calculator could use AI or VR to support student learning in future versions of the calculator.

➤ Consider how VR could be used to demonstrate mathematical processes for learners.

➤ Comment on how including AI and/or VR would impact on the cost of the device and how this might impact upon the digital divide.

> Think about digital devices we use in the home in the first instance, for example, mobile phones, laptops, tablets.

> Consider how AI could be used to assess student learning and design new learning pathways for students – what else could AI do to support learning?

Evaluation

Part 1

Ask a friend to work through your program using a trace table to ensure that the contents of the accumulator and the locations in memory are updated correctly.

They should compare the contents of their truth table to the truth table you produced.

Where your table contents are different, discuss the lines of code you have produced to determine if an error has been made.

At the end of the process you should test your program using the LMC simulation on the website https://peterhigginson.co.uk/lmc/

> Use what you learned on page 36 about creating truth tables for complex logic circuits to help you complete this task.

Part 2

Produce a truth table to show the output from your completed logic gate.

Test your truth table with the following scenarios.

➤ Student C tries to log in to the calculator. Will they be able to? If not, which logic gate will prevent them from logging on?

➤ Student B tries to log in to the calculator and access the profile for student A. Will they be able to access the profile? If not, which logic gate will prevent them from doing so?

Think through each scenario yourself before testing the logic gate. By predicting the correct outcome you can use this knowledge to test the accuracy of your complex logic circuit.

Make a note of any amendments you needed to make to your logic circuit and explain why this was necessary.

Part 3

Ask a friend to review your report on the digital divide and biometric security. When they have completed the review of your report discuss your individual thoughts and ideas on these two concepts.

From reviewing your partner's report and from your discussions in class are there any additional concerns or developments regarding the digital divide, biometric security and future development you would like to incorporate into your report? Did your partner have any concerns that you did not feel would be an issue for the digital divide or future development? Make a note of these points also and comment on why you feel they are not an issue for concern.

The importance of searching and sorting techniques

When data is collected it is important that we have a way of sorting and searching through it to find useful information. Sorting data involves placing items in a list into an ordered sequence; for example, numerical or alphabetical. For example, words in a dictionary are sorted and stored in alphabetical order. The importance of sorting is that searching through sorted data can be more efficient. In the case of the dictionary the sorted data makes it much easier to find a word. Consider what it would be like if the words were stored in a random sequence – it could take a long time to find a word.

There are a number of different methods of sorting and searching through data and each one has its own advantages and disadvantages. You are going to look at the different methods available for programmers to use and evaluate their performance.

Sorting algorithms can be evaluated in terms of:

→ the speed at which they sort large amounts of data

→ the amount of computer memory used during the sorting process

→ the number of comparisons carried out within a sort

→ the number of swaps carried out during a sort.

Searching algorithms are used to find particular items of data. They can be evaluated in terms of the number of attempts required to find an object in a list.

In this unit you will learn to:

→ use a high-level language to implement a data structure such as a list or array

→ use programming techniques like sequence, selection and repetition to manipulate the data structure

→ use sorting techniques like the insertion sort and bubble sort and consider the efficiency of the sorting techniques

→ use search techniques such as linear searches and binary searches to search through data and consider the efficiency of the search techniques

→ test a program by creating a test plan.

KEYWORDS

comparison: checking two data items against each other to determine their correct order

data structure: a variable designed to hold a number of data items together

array: a data structure which holds items of data all of the same data type

insertion sort: a method of sorting data in which the items of data are compared and swapped to their correct position one at a time

bubble sort: a method of sorting data which compares adjacent items of data and swaps them if they are not in the correct order; this process is repeated until the data is sorted

linear search: a simple search method which checks every data item in a list when searching for an item

binary search: a method of searching data which starts at the middle of a sorted list and reduces the number of items searched after each attempt

SCENARIO

You have been asked by your local running club, Spartan Athletic Club, to design, create, test and evaluate a program that will allow them to produce useful documents such as lists of members' names and lists of race times at the end of each race. Before you can do this you need to understand how to create data structures that allow you to record this data, and how to search and sort these data structures. A detailed list of what the club wants the program to do will be provided later.

Do you remember?

Before starting this unit, you should be able to carry out the following in Python:

✔ Use features of the Python programming language to create a solution to a problem.

✔ Use the **IDLE development environment** to code in script mode.

✔ Create and edit code in Python which:
  • captures user inputs
  • uses different **data types**
  • uses **arithmetic operators** and **assignment statements** to perform calculations
  • uses **built-in** Python functions
  • is easy to read and understand.

✔ Use **selection** and **repetition**.

✔ Use simple **validation** to ensure user input is correct.

✔ Test and evaluate a Python program.

KEYWORDS

IDLE development environment: integrated development and learning environment for Python; it includes the Python shell and the text editor and many other features

data types: the type of data to be stored in a variable; for example, string and integer

arithmetic operators: +, – , *, / and other symbols which can be used for arithmetic

assignment statements: a statement which assigns a variable a value; for example, $x = 3$

built-in: a function written as part of the Python language, such as print()

selection: selecting program statements to be executed based on a condition, using an IF-statement

repetition: repeating program statements based on a condition, using a loop

validation: ensuring that data entered is acceptable or satisfies criteria

What is an array?

Learn

An array is a data structure which holds a set of data items of the same data type. In a program an array has a name, a length (representing the number of data items to be stored) and a data type defined by the programmer.

For example, the running club needs to store a set of race times for 100 m runners. The values are recorded correct to two decimal places. The runner times never exceed 59 seconds. To start the process you have been asked to work with race times for only six runners.

    array name: runTimes
    data type: Float
    array length: 10

Here is a representation of the array runTimes. An individual data item or **element** is accessed by referring to the array name and the **index** of the element.

Representation of the array runTimes		
Position in array [index]	Element	Value
0	runTimes[0]	20.51
1	runTimes[1]	18.89
2	runTimes[2]	19.21
3	runTimes[3]	17.33
4	runTimes[4]	19.88
5	runTimes[5]	20.09

Key facts about arrays

➤ When an array is used, the computer reserves a set of **memory locations**, one for each element in the array. The memory locations are **contiguous** (or next to each other).

➤ In some programming languages the first element has an index of one. In other languages, the first element in the array has an index of zero. The first element in our array will have an index of zero – so the first element in this array is called runTimes[0] and holds a value of 20.51.

➤ You can assign a value to an element in an array. For example, runTimes[2]=21.45 will change the value in runTimes[2] from 19.21 to 21.45.

➤ A loop can be used to go through the entire array, one element at a time.

KEYWORDS

element: a data item identified by the array name and the position in the array; for example, runTimes[2] is the third element in the array

index: can be used to refer to the position of an element in an array

memory location: an address or physical space in computer memory for holding data

contiguous: next to each other

list: a set of objects in Python which can be edited; a list can hold objects of different data types

tuple: similar to a list, a tuple is a list which cannot be edited or changed without creating a new list

Using lists in Python

Python does not support arrays in the way other languages do. The data structures in Python are called **lists** and **tuples**. These are very similar to arrays – the main difference is that arrays can only hold data items of the same data type, whereas lists and tuples can hold mixed data types.

A tuple is a list which cannot be edited once it is created in Python code – the data in the tuple cannot be changed. The data in a list, however, can be altered at any time.

```
>>> tupleAnimals = ('dog', 'cat', 'mouse')
>>> print(tupleAnimals)
('dog', 'cat', 'mouse')
>>> tupleAnimals(2)='elephant'
SyntaxError: can't assign to function call
>>>
```

This Python code creates a tuple called `tupleAnimals` and prints the contents of the tuple onto the screen.

The code then attempts to change the name of the last animal to 'elephant', but an error occurs as the contents of a tuple cannot be changed.

Note that tuples use round brackets ( ) to enclose data.

```
>>> listAnimals = ['dog' , 'cat', 'mouse']
>>> print(listAnimals)
['dog', 'cat', 'mouse']
>>> listAnimals[2]='elephant'
>>> print(listAnimals)
['dog', 'cat', 'elephant']
>>> |
```

This Python code creates a list called `listAnimals` **and prints the contents of the list onto the screen.** The code then changes the name of the last animal to 'elephant', using the statement `listAnimals[2] = 'elephant'`.

Note that lists use square brackets [ ] to enclose data.

You are going to use lists to store the data for the running club.

The first element in the list is stored at location 0.

The last element in the list is stored at location 5 (but notice that there are 6 elements in this list. So, the final element location (5) is always equal to the length of the list minus one; in this case 6 – 1 = 5.

Position	0	1	2	3	4	5
runTimes	20.51	18.89	19.21	17.33	19.88	20.09
runnerNames	Quang	Tien	Xuan	Huy	Long	Sang

To create an empty list in Python:

```
runTimes = [ ]
```

To create a list containing data:

```
runTimes=[20.51, 18.89, 19.21, 17.33, 19.88, 20.09]

runnerNames = ["Quang", "Tien", "Xuan", "Huy", "Long", "Sang"]
```

To add an element to the end of the list, use `.append` as follows:

```
runTimes.append(21.50)

runTimes=[20.51, 18.89, 19.21, 17.33, 19.88, 20.09, 21.50]

runnerNames.append("Lee")

runnerNames = ["Quang", "Tien", "Xuan","Huy", "Long", "Sang", "Lee"]
```

To change the value of an element in the list, simply assign a new value to that element – this replaces the previous value:

```
runTimes[3]=17.88

runTimes=[20.51, 18.89, 19.21, 17.88, 19.88, 20.09, 21.50]

runnerNames[2]="Sabina"

runnerNames = ["Quang", "Tien", "Sabina", "Huy", "Long", "Sang", "Lee"]
```

To print the contents of the list:

```
print(runTimes) # prints the entire list called runTimes

print (runTimes[4]) # prints the value at position 4
```

To remove an element from a list use **.remove** as follows:

```
runTimes=[20.51, 18.89, 19.21, 17.88, 19.88, 20.09, 21.50]

runnerNames = ["Quang", "Tien", "Sabina", "Huy", "Long", "Sang", "Lee"]

runTimes.remove(18.89) # removes the value equal to 18.89

runnerNames.remove("Tien") # removes the value equal to Tien

runTimes.pop() # deletes the last element in the list.
```

Practice

➤ Look at the Python code below.

```
 1. studentNames = []
 2. studentAges = []
 3. studentNames = ["Jo", "Lan", "Maria", "Giang", "Vinh"]
 4. studentAges = [12, 13, 11, 12, 13]
 5. studentNames.append("Rafal")
 6. studentNames.remove("Lan")
 7. studentAges.pop()
 8. print(studentNames[2])
 9. print(studentAges[2])
10. print(studentNames[1])
11. print(studentAges[1])
12. studentNames[0]="Cai"
13. studentAges[3]=14
14. studentAges.append(12)
15. print(studentNames)
16. print(studentAges)
```

➤ Write down what you think the output will be from lines 8, 9, 10, 11, 15 and 16.

➤ Compare your output with a partner. Discuss the differences in what you thought would happen.

➤ Open the file called lists1.py, provided by your teacher. Run the code and check your answers with the output from the program.

➤ Now try creating your own program.

➤ Open the Python IDLE.

➤ Create a program which will perform the following tasks.

   o Create an empty list for **runTimes**.

   o Create an empty list for **runnerNames**.

   o Add the following two lines of code to the program.

   runTimes=[20.51, 18.89, 19.21, 17.88, 19.88, 20.09, 21.50]

   runnerNames = ["Quang", "Tien", "Sabina", "Huy", "Long", "Sang", "Lee"]

   o Add two further values to the end of each list.

   o Change the value of the third element in the **runTimes** list to 20.99.

   o Change the value of the first element in the **runnerNames** list to "Anna".

   o Add comments to the program to explain each line of code.

   o Save the program as lists.py.

   o Run the program and review the output to ensure it is correct.

Lists and For loops in Python

Learn

In Python, the For loop is used to repeat a statement or set of statements. The For loop can be used to move through each element in a list one at a time.

for variable in list: statement(s)	```python
	runnerNames = ["Quang", "Tien", "Sabina", "Huy", "Long", "Sang", "Lee"]
	for name in runnerNames:
	    print('Hello ' + name)
	``

	name is the variable that takes on the value of each item in the list **runnerNames** one at a time. The first time through the loop, name has the value **"Quang"**. Write down the output from this code.

A For loop can also be created using the **range** function. The range function generates a list of numbers in a given range.

47

For example, `range(0, 6)` will generate the numbers 0, 1, 2, 3, 4, 5.

for variable in range: statement(s)	```for i in range(0,6): print('Hello to you ' + runnerNames[i])```
	The For loop will count between 0 and 5. So the code will loop six times. Each name in the list will be printed. Write down the output from this code.

Here is a For loop which prints each of the elements in both lists.

```
for i in range(0,len(runTimes))

    print (runnerNames[i], runTimes[i])
```

`len(runTimes)` is the length of the list called **runTimes**. It is equal to the number of elements in the list.

Practice

➤ Open the program called lists2.py provided by your teacher.
➤ The program is supposed to output a list of the **runnerNames**. Run the program to see if it is working properly.
➤ Review the code with a partner and discuss what changes need to be made to the following line of code so that the program will print all of the runners' names:
  `for i in range(0,6):`
➤ Edit the program and make the changes you and your partner have suggested.
➤ Save and run the program to check if the program now prints all of the runners' names.
➤ Edit the program so that three further names of your choice are added to the **runnerNames** list.
➤ You can add these directly to the list by editing the line:
  `runnerNames = ["Quang", "Tien", "Sabina", "Huy", "Long", "Sang", "Lee"]`
  or you can use the append function; for example, `runnerNames.append("Jane")`
➤ At the bottom of the program, add the code for another For loop which will output the contents of the **runnerNames** list. This time use the **len** function inside the range statement.
➤ Save and run the program.
➤ Discuss with your partner why it may be better to use the **len** function in the range statement rather than entering the range of numbers to be used.

Checking out the bubble sort

Learn

Spartan Athletic Club need you to look at different sorting techniques so that you can select one for use in the new program you are going to write for the club.

You are going to learn about a bubble sort first.

The bubble sort works by comparing adjacent data items and swapping them if they are in the wrong order. In this way data items 'bubble' up through the list until they are in the correct order.

You are going to use the `runTimes` list but you will only have six values in the array so that you can see exactly how the bubble sort works.

We will use the `runTimes` list which now contains the six decimal values shown, representing 100 m run times for six members:

In this case, the list length is 6.

Problem: We need the race times to be in order starting with the smallest first.

0	20.51
1	18.89
2	19.21
3	17.33
4	19.88
5	20.09

We can do this using the bubble sort method, which is made up of numerous comparisons. Each comparison examines two adjacent elements in the array of data. If they are out of order then the code swaps their position around. One full **pass** is when each item of data has been compared to each of its neighbours once. In this list, a full pass consists of five comparisons.

The table below shows the results after one full pass through the array of data.

The two adjacent elements being compared are shaded in the table below.

Swaps are highlighted in the Swap column and are shown using arrows.

The sort process is complex and made up of a number of steps. You need to create a set of steps which will compare each element in the list with its neighbour. The table below shows how each element in the list is compared to the one beside it.

Pass 1 through the list

Comparison	runTimes[0]	runTimes[1]	runTimes[2]	runTimes[3]	runTimes[4]	runTimes[5]	Swap?
1	20.51 ⟷ 18.59		19.21	17.33	19.88	20.09	20.51 < 18.59? No. Swap
2	18.59	20.51 ⟷ 19.21		17.33	19.88	20.09	20.51<19.21? No. Swap
3	18.59	19.21	20.51 ⟷ 17.33		19.88	20.09	20.51 < 17.33? No. Swap
4	18.59	19.21	17.33	20.51 ⟷ 19.88		20.09	20.51 < 19.88? No. Swap
5	18.59	19.21	17.33	19.88	20.51 ⟷ 20.09		20.51< 20.09? No. Swap
Order after first pass	18.59	19.21	17.33	19.88	20.09	20.51	

The first comparison is between element [0] (20.51) and element [1] (18.59). The algorithm asks: is element [0] less than element [1]? The answer is no, so it swaps the contents of the two elements so that element [0] is now equal to 18.59 and element [1] is equal to 20.51.

> Remember that we want to sort the data starting with the smallest first – this determines the question that the algorithm asks.

The second comparison is between element [1] and element [2]. Element [1] is now equal to 20.51 and element [2] is equal to 19.21. The algorithm asks the question: is element [1] less than element [2]? Again, the answer is no so the two are swapped around. Element [1] now equals 19.21 and element [2] now equals 20.51.

This continues with [2] and [3], and so on, until the algorithm has compared elements [4] and [5], which is the end of the first pass.

At the end of the first pass the largest number is in the correct position. So, there is no need to include 20.51 in any future comparisons. There is one less number to compare. Next time we only need to compare five items.

Other items in the list are still out of order however, so the algorithm needs to make further passes.

Pass 2 through the list

Comparison	runTimes[0]	runTimes[1]	runTimes[2]	runTimes[3]	runTimes[4]	runTimes[5]	Swap?
1	18.59	19.21	17.33	19.88	20.09	20.51	18.59 < 19.21? Yes. No swap
2	18.59	19.21 ⟷ 17.33		19.88	20.09	20.51	19.21<17.33? No. Swap
3	18.59	17.33	19.21	19.88	20.09	20.51	19.21 < 19.88? Yes. No swap
4	18.59	17.33	19.21	19.88	20.09	20.51	19.88 < 20.09? Yes. No swap
Order after 2nd pass	18.59	17.33	19.21	19.88	20.09	20.51	

In the second pass, the algorithm again compares element [0] with [1], then [1] with [2], and so on.

At the end of the second pass the two largest numbers are in the correct position. So, there is no need to include 20.09 or 20.51 in any future comparisons. There are two less numbers to compare. Next time, we only need to compare four items.

This process is repeated, so that on the third pass, the third largest value will be moved to the third last position and there will be three less numbers to compare. And so on.

The data is considered to be sorted when a full pass through the data is completed without any swaps.

KEYWORDS

pass: one complete run through the data items in the list or array
swaps: swapping the position of two data items in the list or array

Algorithmic thinking

- ✪ Using the data in the last row of the table above, create a new table to represent a third pass through the array of data. The column and row headings will be the same.
- ✪ Create a fourth table to represent the fourth pass and check to see if the data is sorted.
- ✪ How many passes through the array are required to ensure the array is sorted?
- ✪ How many comparisons are required to sort the data?

Practice

- ➤ Here is a list containing a set of temperatures recorded in a classroom.
  `classroomTemperatures=[23, 22, 20, 18, 17]`
- ➤ Open the document called **ShowSort.docx** provided by your teacher.
- ➤ Using the bubble sort technique, sort the data smallest first.
- ➤ You must complete the tables in the document to show the order of the data after each pass through the list.
- ➤ Discuss your answers for each pass with a partner.

Creating code for the bubble sort

> Remember that the comparisons reduce after each pass through the loop. If there are six items in the list then the comparisons start at 6 then reduce to 5, 4, 3 and so on.

Learn

- ➤ Now that you have learned about the bubble sort you are going to create the code.
- ➤ The algorithm for the bubble sort will need to include:
  - one loop to do the comparisons
  - one loop for each pass through the list
  - a section of code that will swap the items in the list if necessary.
- ➤ The simplest way to swap two items is to use a temporary variable. Call this variable temp.
  - Let's say item 1 = 20, item 2 = 25
  - To swap item 1 and item 2, use temp.
    - temp = item 1
    - item 1 = item 2
    - item 2 = temp

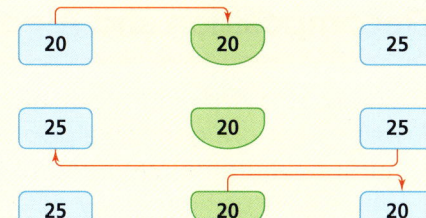

Assuming the list **runTimes** is used with six data items, the algorithm in **pseudocode** is shown below. Note that the FOR loop in the pseudocode here **(For i=0 to 5)** counts in the same way as Python. That is, it will count through 0, 1, 2, 3 and 4. This means the code inside the loop will be executed five times, once for each count.

```
FOR i= 0 to 5

  FOR j=0 to (5 - i)

    IF runTimes[j] > runTimes [j+1]

      temp = runTimes [j]

      runTimes [j] = runTimes [j+1]

      runTimes [j+1] = temp

    END IF

  END FOR

END FOR
```

This If statement checks if the items are out of order, and if so swaps the position of the two items.

This For loop compares adjacent items and reduces the number of comparisons by 1 after each pass (this is the (5 – i) term).

This For loop controls the number of passes through the list. In this example there will be 5 passes.

This algorithm is written using pseudocode rather than using a flowchart. Pseudocode is written using English-like phrases that are similar to real code but do not have to obey a precise **syntax**. When a loop is used the end of the loop is signified by the word 'end', followed by the loop type. For example, 'end For' shows that this is the end of the For loop.

Decomposition and Algorithmic thinking

The previous pseudocode algorithm will only work for six data items. A more general algorithm is needed for a list with any number of items. We need to base this on the length of the list – which tells us how many data items there are.

In the previous example, the list had six data items and the algorithm required five passes. We can generalise this to any size of list: the number of passes = length of the list – 1.

KEYWORDS

pseudocode: English-like phrases used to represent the solution to a problem

syntax: the spelling and grammar of the programming language

An algorithm for a list with any number of data items would, therefore, look like this:

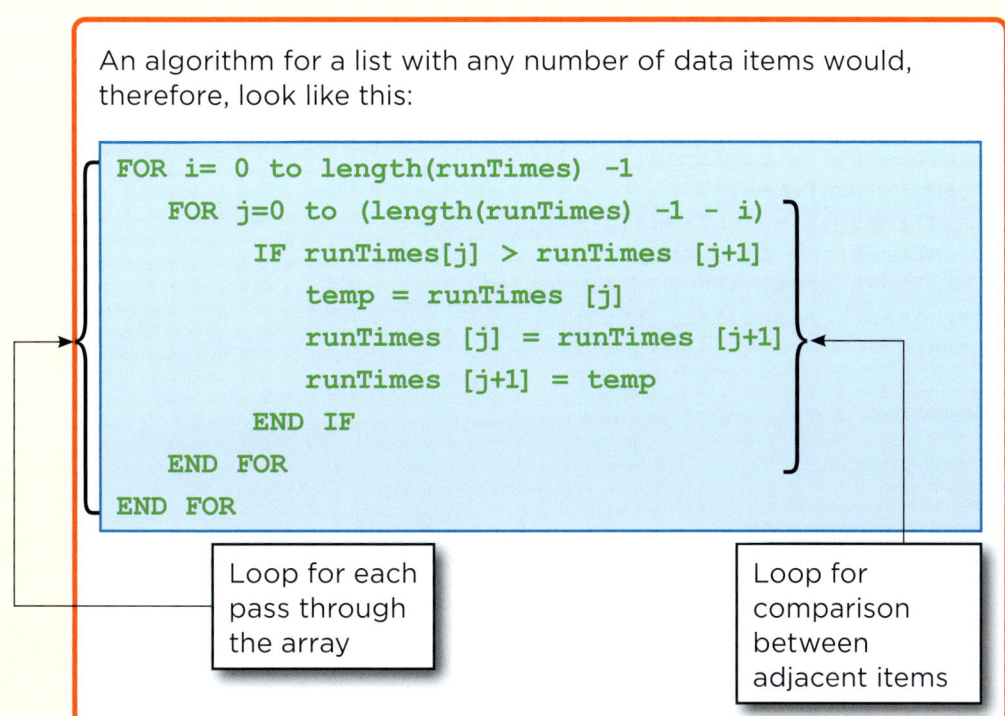

```
FOR i= 0 to length(runTimes) -1
    FOR j=0 to (length(runTimes) -1 - i)
        IF runTimes[j] > runTimes [j+1]
            temp = runTimes [j]
            runTimes [j] = runTimes [j+1]
            runTimes [j+1] = temp
        END IF
    END FOR
END FOR
```

Loop for each pass through the array

Loop for comparison between adjacent items

As before, the bubble sort uses the inner loop to move through a list comparing adjacent data items as it moves along.

If a list element **runTimes[j]** is greater than the element immediately to its right (which is labelled as **runTimes[j+1]**), it swaps them using the temp variable, as we discussed earlier.

The first time around, this process will 'bubble' the largest value to the end of the list.

If N=the number of data items in the list then after N−1 passes, the data will be sorted.

Now we have seen how the pseudocode works, let's look at the Python code for the first algorithm which sorts six data items.

```
# Programming the Bubble Sort
runTimes = [18.59, 19.21, 17.33, 19.88, 20.09, 20.51]
for i in range(0,5):
    for j in range(0, 5 - i):
            if runTimes[j] > runTimes[j + 1]:
                temp = runTimes[j]
                runTimes[j] = runTimes[j + 1]
                runTimes[j + 1] = temp
        # Print runTimes array after every pass
    print ("After pass " + str(i+1) +":")
    print(runTimes)

print ("The sorted list : ")
print(runTimes)
```

This is the output from the program:

```
After pass 1:
[18.59, 17.33, 19.21, 19.88, 20.09, 20.51]
After pass 2:
[17.33, 18.59, 19.21, 19.88, 20.09, 20.51]
After pass 3:
[17.33, 18.59, 19.21, 19.88, 20.09, 20.51]
After pass 4:
[17.33, 18.59, 19.21, 19.88, 20.09, 20.51]
After pass 5:
[17.33, 18.59, 19.21, 19.88, 20.09, 20.51]
The sorted list :
[17.33, 18.59, 19.21, 19.88, 20.09, 20.51]
```

Practice

➤ Open the program called **BubbleSort2.py** provided by your teacher.
➤ Run the program and observe the output.
➤ Try adding an additional number to the end of the **runTimes** list as follows:
    runTimes = [18.59, 19.21, 17.33, 19.88, 20.09, 20.51,19.78]
➤ Run the program and check the output.
➤ If the data is not sorted review the output with a partner and discuss why this is the case.
➤ Modify the code in the program so that the code can sort all the items in this list. To do this you need to use the length of the **runTimes** list in the loops. The code for this in Python is:

```
len(runTimes)
```

➤ Replace the references to number of data items in the two For loops with expressions that include the **len(runTimes)** code.
➤ Run the program and check the output. All data items should be in the correct order.
➤ Modify the code to output the data from largest to smallest first.

Hint: This only requires one small modification in the IF statement.

Is the insertion sort for me?

Learn

Another sorting algorithm is called the insertion sort. An insertion sort is a bit like sorting a hand (or deck) of playing cards.

Let's say you have five playing cards. To sort your cards you could:

➤ take one card and place it on the table
➤ take a second card, compare it to the first card, and place the first and second cards in the correct order
➤ take the third card, compare it to cards 1 and 2, and place it on the table, in the correct order
➤ repeat this process for cards 4 and 5 to sort your entire hand.

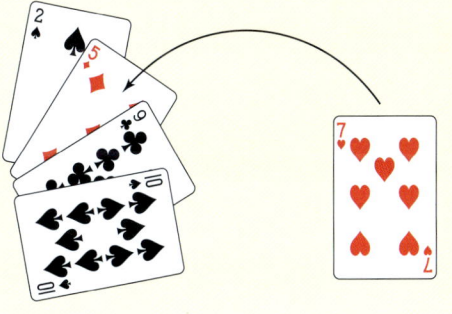

The cards on the table at each stage form the 'sorted sublist'. The cards in your hand remain unsorted. The process moves the unsorted cards into the correct position in the sorted sublist.

Now consider using the same approach with the data in the **runTimes** list:

0	20.51
1	18.89
2	19.21
3	17.33
4	19.88
5	20.09

The tables below show the results after one full pass using the insertion sort algorithm. Each comparison is between an unsorted element and an adjacent element from the sorted sublist. When a data item is swapped it is added to the sorted sublist in the correct order. At the end of one full pass the array of data is fully sorted.

Initially item [0] (20.51) is added to the sorted sublist. (A list with only one element is always sorted.) The remaining elements remain unsorted.

Comparison	runTimes[0]	runTimes[1]	runTimes[2]	runTimes[3]	runTimes[4]	runTimes[5]	Swap?
	20.51	18.89	19.21	17.33	19.88	20.09	

Item [1] (18.89) is now compared (comparison 1) with item [0] from the sorted list: is item [0] < item [1]? No, so items [0] and [1] are swapped. Items [0] and [1] are now sorted correctly and form the sorted sublist.

Comparison	runTimes[0]	runTimes[1]	runTimes[2]	runTimes[3]	runTimes[4]	runTimes[5]	Swap?
1	20.51 ←→	18.89	19.21	17.33	19.88	20.09	20.51 < 18.89? No. Swap position – Add 18.89 to sorted sublist.
	18.89	20.51	19.21	17.33	19.88	20.09	Two items are now sorted.

Next, item [2] (19.21) is compared (comparison 2) with item [1] from the sorted sublist. Is item [1] < item [2]? No, so item [2] and item [1] are swapped. We now have to compare (comparison 3) item [1] and item [0] again: is item [0] (18.89) < item [1] (19.21) ? Yes, so we leave them as they are. The first three items [0], [1], and [2] are all in order in the 'sorted sublist'.

Comparison	runTimes[0]	runTimes[1]	runTimes[2]	runTimes[3]	runTimes[4]	runTimes[5]	Swap?
2	18.89	20.51 ←→	19.21	17.33	19.88	20.09	20.51 < 19.21? No. Swap and add 19.21 to sorted sublist.
3	18.89	19.21	20.51	17.33	19.88	20.09	Check new sorted sublist. 18.89 < 19.21? Yes. No change.
	18.89	19.21	20.51	17.33	19.88	20.09	Note that the sorted sublist now contains three values.

We continue doing the same thing – next for item [3] (17.33):

Comparison	runTimes[0]	runTimes[1]	runTimes[2]	runTimes[3]	runTimes[4]	runTimes[5]	Swap?
4	18.89	19.21	20.51 ⟷	17.33	19.88	20.09	20.51 < 17.33? No. Swap and add 17.33 to sorted sublist.
5	18.89	19.21 ⟷	17.33	20.51	19.88	20.09	Check new sorted sublist. 19.21 < 17.33? No. Swap.
6	18.89 ⟷	17.33	19.21	20.51	19.88	20.09	18.89 < 17.33? No. Swap.
	17.33	18.89	19.21	20.51	19.88	20.09	Note that the sorted sublist now contains four values.

Now consider item [4] (19.88):

Comparison	runTimes[0]	runTimes[1]	runTimes[2]	runTimes[3]	runTimes[4]	runTimes[5]	Swap?
7	17.33	18.89	19.21	20.51 ⟷	19.88	20.09	20.51 < 19.88? No. Swap and add to sorted sublist.
8	17.33	18.89	19.21	19.88	20.51	20.09	Check new sorted sublist. 19.21<19.88? Yes. No change.
	17.33	18.89	19.21	19.88	20.51	20.09	Note that the sorted sublist now contains five values.

Finally, consider the last value, item [5] (20.09):

Comparison	runTimes[0]	runTimes[1]	runTimes[2]	runTimes[3]	runTimes[4]	runTimes[5]	Swap?
9	17.33	18.89	19.21	19.88 ⟷ 20.51		20.09	20.51 < 20.09? No. Swap and add 20.09 to sorted sublist.
10	17.33	18.89	19.21	19.88	20.09	20.51	check new sorted sublist. 19.88 < 20.09? Yes. No change.
	17.33	18.89	19.21	19.88	20.09	20.51	The sorted 'sublist' now contains all six values.

Practice

- In a group of four discuss how the bubble sort and the insertion sort compare in terms of:
  - the number of comparisons made during a sort.
  - the number of swaps made during a sort.
- Comment on which sorting algorithm you feel is more efficient.
- In groups, using a word processor, create a set of six large A5 cards, they can be gaming cards or simple numbers as long as they each have different values.
- Print the cards and cut them out, you are going to use them in a table exercise.
  - In your groups, set the cards out in order, largest value first. One person should note the order of the cards at the start. You can use a device to take a photograph of these.
  - Now use the bubble sort to sort the cards in order of smallest value first.
  - One person should note the order of the cards after each pass of the bubble sort. Again you can use a device to take a photograph after each pass.
  - One person in your group should count the comparisons and another person should count the number of swaps done.
  - Repeat the process using the insertion sort. Remember to set the cards in the same order as they were at the start of the bubble sort.
  - Now use the following values to decide which of the two sorts are more efficient:
    - number of swaps for each sort
    - number of comparisons for each sort.

Creating code for the insertion sort

Learn

Now that you have studied the insertion sort you are going to create the code.

The insertion sort also uses two loops:
➤ One loop to select each value as the **currentvalue**.
➤ One loop to insert the value being compared (**currentvalue**) into the correct position in the sorted sublist.

```
FOR i= 1 to 6
  currentvalue=runTimes[i]
  position=i
    WHILE (position>0 and runTimes[position-1] >
currentvalue)
        runTimes[position] = runTimes[position-1]
        position=position-1
    END WHILE
  runTimes[position]=currentvalue
END FOR
```

Loop for inserting the current element into the correct position within the sorted sublist.

Loop for selecting each element as the current value.

➤ The first element (**runTimes[0]**) is already part of the sorted sublist. So, the For loop starts at 1 this time and initially selects the second element in the array (**runTimes[1]**) as the current value.
➤ The current value of **runTimes[1]** is then compared with the element next to it in the sorted sublist (**runTimes[0]**).

If **runTimes[0]** is larger than the current value of **runTimes[1]** then **runTimes[0]** is swapped with **runTimes[1]**.
➤ When the For loop moves on to 2, it selects the third element (**runTimes[2]**) as the current value.
➤ The current value is compared to each of the preceding elements in the sorted sublist in turn. If an element is larger than the **currentvalue** then they are swapped around.
➤ In this way the While loop will compare and swap each element until it is in the correct place.

You may wonder why this loop is '1 to 6' when the loop for the bubble sort algorithm was '0 to 5'. (Both of them loop around five times.) The reason we use '1 to 6' here is that we are using the variable 'i' to refer to an element – and for the insertion sort we start with element 1 not element 0. So we need the loop to begin at 1, not 0.

Again, the algorithm as written above will only work for six data items. A better algorithm would work for any number of items. As with the bubble sort algorithm, this can be done if we can obtain the length of the list.

The pseudocode below describes a general insertion sort algorithm. The only difference from before is the use of the **len()** function in the For loop:

```
FOR i= 1 to length(runTimes)
  currentvalue=runTimes[i]
  position=i
   WHILE (position>0 and runTimes[position-1] >
currentvalue)
     runTimes[position] = runTimes[position-1]
     position=position-1
    END WHILE
  runTimes[position]=currentvalue
END FOR
```

Loop for inserting current element into the correct position within the sorted sublist.

Loop for selecting each element as the current value.

Look at the Python code for the first insertion sort algorithm which sorts six data items:

File Edit Format Run Options Window Help

```
runTimes = [18.59, 19.21, 17.33, 19.88, 20.09, 20.51]
for index in range(1,len(runTimes)):
    currentvalue = runTimes[index]
    position = index
    while position>0 and runTimes[position-1]>currentvalue:
        runTimes[position]=runTimes[position-1]
        position = position-1
    runTimes[position]=currentvalue
    print(runTimes)
print ("The sorted list : ")
print(runTimes)
```

The output from the program is shown below.

```
[18.59, 19.21, 17.33, 19.88, 20.09, 20.51]
[17.33, 18.59, 19.21, 19.88, 20.09, 20.51]
[17.33, 18.59, 19.21, 19.88, 20.09, 20.51]
[17.33, 18.59, 19.21, 19.88, 20.09, 20.51]
[17.33, 18.59, 19.21, 19.88, 20.09, 20.51]
The sorted list :
[17.33, 18.59, 19.21, 19.88, 20.09, 20.51]
>>> |
```

Practice

➤ Open the program called **ins1.py** provided by your teacher.
➤ Run the program and observe the output.
➤ Modify the program as shown below to include code that will count the number of swaps.

```
runTimes = [18.59, 19.21, 17.33, 19.88, 20.09, 20.51]

#add this new line of code
noofswaps=0

for index in range(1,6):
    currentvalue = runTimes[index]
    position = index
    while position>0 and runTimes[position-1]>currentvalue:
        runTimes[position]=runTimes[position-1]
        position = position-1

        #add this new line of code
        noofswaps=noofswaps+1

    runTimes[position]=currentvalue
    print(runTimes)

print ("The sorted list : ")
print(runTimes)

#add this new line of code
print ("The number of swaps was ", noofswaps)
|
```

- ➤ Run the program and check the output.
- ➤ Create a set of small cards containing the values in the **runTimes** list.
- ➤ With a partner, use the cards to check how many swaps are needed. Compare your value with that generated by the program.
- ➤ Try adding an additional number to the end of the **runTimes** list as follows:
  runTimes = [18.59,19.21,17.33,19.88,20.09,20.51,15.22]
- ➤ Run the program and check the output.
- ➤ If the data is not sorted review the output with a partner and discuss why this is the case.
- ➤ Modify the code in the program so that the code can sort all the items in this list. To do this you need to use the length of the **runTimes** list in the loops. The code for this in Python is:

```
len(runTimes)
```

- ➤ You need to change this line of code:

```
for index in range(1,6):
```

- ➤ Run the program and check the output. All data items should be in the correct order.
- ➤ Modify the code to output the data from largest to smallest first.

Evaluating sorting algorithms

Learn

Sort methods can be compared in terms of their efficiency. To do this we need to know:

> A comparison is when two items of data are compared to each other.

- ➤ the number of data items to be sorted (we refer to this number as N)
- ➤ the number of comparisons needed to sorted the data items
- ➤ the number of swaps needed to sort the data.

> A swap is when items of data swap their position in the list.

Look at the table below. It shows how the bubble and insertion sorts compare in terms of the number of comparisons and the number of swaps. N = the number of data items to be sorted.

Sort	Number of comparisons		Number of swaps	
	Average case	Worst case	Average case	Worst case
Bubble sort e.g. if N = 6	$N^2/2$ e.g. 36 ÷ 2 = 18	$N^2/2$ e.g. 36 ÷ 2 = 18	$N^2/2=$ e.g. 36 ÷ 2 = 18	$N^2/2$ e.g. 36 ÷ 2 = 18
Insertion sort e.g. if N = 6	$N^2/4$ e.g. 36 ÷ 4 = 9	$N^2/2$ e.g. 36 ÷ 2 = 18	$N^2/8$ e.g. 36 ÷ 8 = 4.5 (which we round up to 5)	$N^2/4$ e.g. 36 ÷ 4 = 9

The insertion sort is more efficient than the bubble sort in terms of comparisons and swaps.

Bubble sort	Insertion sort
Advantages ● Uses a simple algorithm ● Good for very near-sorted lists	**Advantages** ● Uses a simple algorithm ● Adaptive – the performance adapts to the initial order of the elements ● This algorithm may be used when the data items are nearly sorted ● Requires a constant amount of memory as the entire sort can occur in internal memory
Disadvantages ● Inefficient for sorting large amounts of data. The time taken to sort data is related to the square of the number of items (N) to be sorted ● Inefficient for sorting data that is reverse order or near-reverse order	**Disadvantages** ● Becomes less efficient as the number of items in the list increases ● The algorithm requires a large amount of shifts within the sorted sublist
Features ● The algorithm works by comparing and swapping adjacent data items until all items in the list are in the correct order ● Data items 'bubble' up through the list until they are in the correct order ● This sort method involves a number of passes through the list or list to be sorted	**Features** ● The algorithm works by comparing a single value with the elements in a sorted sublist ● Values in the sorted sublist are shifted so that the single value is put in the correct place in the sorted sublist

Practice

Look at the code in the files **BubbleSort1.py** and **ins1.py**. Evaluate each algorithm using the table below:

Sort	Number of comparisons	Number of swaps
Bubble sort		
Insertion sort		

Linear searches and binary searches

Learn

Search algorithms work with data structures such as arrays and lists, and are used to find data given certain criteria. Just as there are different sorting algorithms, there are also different searching algorithms.

When searching through large amounts of data it is important to apply an efficient search method to ensure the fastest possible return of results.

Sorting data in advance of searching can make the search more efficient.

Spartan Athletic store lots of data and need to search through it to find information about runners. You will need to select an appropriate search algorithm for the program you are writing.

The linear search

This is searching at its simplest. The list of data items is searched one by one from top to bottom to see if the **target value** exists in the list. In a linear search, the average number of attempts required to find a target value is half the number of data items. So, to find a target value in a set of 20 data items would take, on average, 10 attempts.

For example, to find the name 'Singh' in the following list.

Serial search sorted by surname			ID	Surname
1st try	↓no		003	Chang
2nd try		↓no	006	Grant
3rd try		↓no	001	Kang
4th try		↓no	013	Khan
5th try		↓no	008	Patel
Last try		↓→	005	Singh
(six tries total)			002	Smith
			019	Wilson

An effective search must indicate whether or not the target value has been found.

This can be done by using a Boolean variable. Set the Boolean variable to false initially and set it to true only if the target value is found within the array.

Here is an algorithm for a linear search through an array called `runTimes` holding six data items.

KEYWORD

target value: the number or value that is currently being searched for in the list

Remember that a Boolean variable can only be true or false.

The algorithm uses a Boolean variable called **found**.

```
1.  found = false                          set found to false initially
2.  FOR i= 0 to 5                          For loop to go through
                                           each element in runTimes
3.      IF runTimes[i]  = targetValue      if the value in runTimes[i]
                                           matches the target value
4.          found=true                     set found to true
5.      END IF

6.  END FOR
7.  IF found = true                        if the target value has
                                           been found
8.    OUTPUT MESSAGE "Target value found"  output found message
9.  ELSE
10.   OUTPUT MESSAGE "Target
      value not found"
```

The for loop in a linear search will compare every element in the list to the target value. This type of search is inefficient as each element in the list is checked against the target value so there is a high number of comparisons.

Practice

In pairs, play 'Think of a Number'. Ask your friend to think of a number between 1 and 20. Now you must try and guess the number. Your friend should tell you whether to go lower or higher. Write down the number of guesses you make. Discuss what you did when you were making each guess. Did your friend help you by saying 'go higher' or 'go lower'?

KEYWORD

search space: the number of items in the list that are currently being checked for the target value

Learn

The binary search

Binary search is a more complex algorithm which only works on data that is already sorted.

➤ Start by finding the middle location in the list.
➤ Compare the value in the middle location to the target value. If the target value is not found, reset the search area by:
  • recalculating the middle location
  • recalculating either the start location or the end location.
➤ This process is repeated and the number of items being searched through, the **search space**, is decreased until eventually there is only one item to be searched through.

log is short for logarithm. This is a mathematical operation that tells us how many times the base (2 in this case) is multiplied by itself to reach another number. For example, log to the base 2 of 8 is written like this: $\log_2(8)$. It tells us how many 2s we need to multiply to get 8. $2 \times 2 \times 2 = 8$. The answer is 3, i.e. $\log_2(8) = 3$.

In a binary search, the maximum number of attempts required to find a target value is $\log_2$(number of items).

So, to find a target value in a set of 20 data items, the maximum number of attempts would be 4.

Compare this number to the average number of attempts in a linear search of 20 data items.

Now consider the array **runTimes** which now contains 10 numbers sorted in numerical order.

The target value = 21.09.

Advanced: How is this calculated for 20 data items? Calculators do not normally have a $\log_2$ button but they do have a $\log_{10}$ button, so we'd like to convert our $\log_2$ formula to $\log_{10}$. We can do this using a special mathematical formula:

number of attempts = $\log_2$(number of items) = $\log_{10}$(number of items) ÷ $\log_{10}$(2)

number of attempts:
= $\log_2(20)$
= $\log_{10}(20) \div \log_{10}(2)$
= $1.30102 \div 0.30102$
= 4.32

This is rounded down to four attempts.

To find $\log_{10}(20)$ enter 20 then press $\log_{10}$ on a calculator. The result is 1.30102. To find $\log_{10}(2)$ enter 2 then press $\log_{10}$ on a calculator. The result is 0.30102.

runTimes

location	0	1	2	3	4	5	6	7	8	9
value	17.33	18.89	19.21	19.88	20.09	20.51	20.66	21.09	21.44	21.56

To find 21.09:

Find the mid-point location:

start_location = 0

end_location = 9

mid = start_location + (end_location – start_location)/2

mid = 0 + ((9 – 0) ÷ 2) = 4.5

Use location 4.

Floor division is used. The result of the division is truncated. This means the whole number part of the result is used as the mid and the part after the decimal point is ignored.

location	0	1	2	3	4	5	6	7	8	9
value	17.33	18.89	19.21	19.88	20.09	20.51	20.66	21.09	21.44	21.56
	Start				Mid					End

Is the value in location 4 = to the target value? No

Is the value in location 4 < target value? Yes. (This means we know the target value must be somewhere in locations 5–9.)

Calculate a new start_location:

Start_location= mid + 1 = 4 + 1 = 5

end_location remains the same = 9

Find the new mid-point location again to start searching for the second time:

start_location = 5

end_location = 9

mid = start_locaton + (end_location – start_location) ÷ 2

mid = 5 + ((9 – 4) ÷ 2) = 7.5; use 7

The search space has been decreased. It is now from location 5 to location 9 and includes only five data items.

location	5	6	7	8	9
value	20.51	20.66	21.09	21.44	21.56
	Start		Mid		End

Search again.

Is the value in location 7 equal to the target value? Yes.

The target value has been found after two attempts. This is much more efficient than applying a linear search which would have taken eight attempts.

Practice

➤ Try searching, through **runTimes**, for the target value 20.51 using the binary search method.

runTimes

location	0	1	2	3	4	5	6	7	8	9
value	17.33	18.89	19.21	19.88	20.09	20.51	20.66	21.09	21.44	21.56

➤ You can do this by completing the following steps.
  1. Start by finding the middle location in the list.
  middle location = start_location + (end_location – start_location) ÷ 2
  2. Compare the value in the middle location to the target value (20.51).
  If the value in the middle location < target value (20.51)
  o New start_location = middle location + 1
  o end_location remains the same
  o middle location = start_location + (end_location – start_location) ÷ 2
  OR
  If the value in the middle location > target value (20.51)
  o start_location remains the same
  o New end_location = middle location – 1
  o middle location = start_location + (end_location – start_location) ÷ 2
  OR
  If the value in the middle location = target value then the value has been found.
  3. Repeat step 2 while the target value is not found and the start_location <= end_location

➤ What if the target value is not there? Try searching for 21.00?
  When does the search stop?
  The search must stop when the start_location is greater than the end_location.

Learn

Here is the pseudocode algorithm for a binary search through an array which has already been sorted in descending order. It also handles the situation when a number is not found.

```
start _ location =0
end _ location=  length(runnerNames)-1
found = false
WHILE (start _ location <= end _ location)   AND (found = false)
      mid = start _ location +(end _ location-start _ location) / /2
      IF runnerNames[mid]==target
        found=true
      ELSE
       IF (target > runnerNames[mid])
        start _ location = mid + 1
       ELSE
        IF (target < runnerNames[mid])
            end _ location = mid - 1
         END IF
       END IF
        END IF
END WHILE
IF found = true
OUTPUT MESSAGE "Target value found"
ELSE
   OUTPUT MESSAGE "Target value not found"
END IF
```

This condition makes sure that the program stops searching when the start location becomes greater than the end location.

Every time a search attempt is made, the middle location must be recalculated using the new start or end location.

If the target value is greater than the value in the middle location the new **start _ location** will be 1 above the middle location.

If the target value is less than the value in the middle location the new **end _ location** will be 1†below the middle location.

Here is the Python code for a binary search of a list that has already been sorted. Comments are included to help explain what is happening.

```python
target=input("Enter the name of the runner you want to find")
#set the start value to 0 the position of the first element in the list
start=0

#set the end value to the position of the last element in the list
#this is equal to the length of the list minus 1
end=len(runnerNames)-1

#set the boolean variable found equal to false
#this indicates that the target name has not yet been found
found=False

#this is the code to carry out the binary search
while((start<=end)and found==False):
    #calculate the mid position
    mid=start+int((end-start)/2)

    #check to see if the name in the mid position equals the target name we are loooking for
    if runnerNames[mid]==target:
        #set the boolean variable found equal to true if the target name is found
        found=True
        #output a message to let the user know that the target name has been found
        print("Runner name found")
        #print the name of the runner and the runner's time
        print(runnerNames[mid], runTimes[mid])
    elif target > runnerNames[mid]:
        #if the target name is alphabetically after the name in the mid position
        #calculate a new start point for the search
        start = mid + 1
    elif target < runnerNames[mid]:
        #if the target name is alphabetically before the name in the mid position
        #calculate a new end point for the search
        end = mid - 1
#if the target name is not found output a message to the user
if(found==False):
    print("No such runner")
```

Practice

- ➤ In pairs make a set of 10 small cards using paper. Each one should contain a surname.
- ➤ Place the surnames in a random order on a table.
- ➤ Ask your partner to select a surname and count the number of attempts that have to be made before the surname is found.
- ➤ Now sort the surnames into alphabetical order and repeat the exercise using the binary search.
- ➤ Discuss which of the two options are most efficient and provide numerical data to support your conclusion. Use words such as 'target value' and 'search space' in your discussion.

Go further

You are now going to create a section of code which will output the race report for the Spartan Athletic Club.

Blocks of code can be written as functions or procedures in Python.

A function is a block of code that has been designed to carry out a particular task. Functions help break the program code up into smaller more manageable chunks as the program gets larger. Functions can be re-used and called over and over again in a program.

You have already used many of Python's built-in functions such as **print()** or **input()**.

A user-defined function is made up of:
◆ keyword 'def' which is at the start of the function header
◆ a function name
◆ parameters which are used to pass values to a function; *these are optional*
◆ a colon (:) to show the end of the function header
◆ a set of indented Python statements which make up the function body
◆ an optional return statement which can allow the function to return a value.

A function which does not have a return statement is called a procedure.

In this exercise we will use a simple procedure which does not include the optional parameters or return statement.

Here is a simple procedure called **printwelcomemessage** which will print a welcome statement when the Spartan Athletic program is opened.

```python
def printwelcomemessage():
    print("Welcome to Spartan Athletic Software")
    print("This software will output the race report for you")
```

Function or procedure body – there is no return statement so this is called a procedure.

Function or procedure header – there are no parameters in this procedure header.

Once a procedure or function has been defined, we can call it from anywhere within the program. To do this we simply use the procedure or function name and include any parameters.

This is how we call the procedure **printwelcomemessage** from somewhere else in the program:
◆ Open the program called **GF.py**, provided by your teacher.
◆ Create a procedure header for a procedure called **printracereport**.
◆ The **printracereport** procedure should print a heading for the report and the contents of the two lists **runTimes** and **runnerNames**.
An example of how this might look is shown below:
RACE REPORT
Xuan 17.33
and so on ...

- Add code to the procedure which will carry out this task.
- Add a statement to call `printracereport` after the code which sorts the lists.
- Save and run the program.

Now add a procedure called `calculateaverage` which will calculate and output the average run time for members.

- To do this you will need to add the procedure header.
- Then add code to the procedure which will calculate the total value of the `runTimes` and divide the total by the length of the list (that is, the number of data items).
  An algorithm for this task could be:

```
total=0
average=0.0
FOR i= 0 to length(runtimes)-1
  total=total + runtimes[i]
END FOR
average=total/length(runTimes)
print(average)
```

- Add a statement to call `calculateaverage` after the statement which calls the `printracereport` procedure.

Challenge yourself

Testing the solution

Remember that a solution must always be tested before it is released.

The Spartan Athletic club need a good quality program which processes the data and outputs the correct results. You have been asked to carry out testing to:

➤ improve the quality of the program
➤ ensure the program is bug free
➤ ensure the program operates efficiently.

A test plan is a document which lists in details the data to be used when carrying out testing. You should include:

➤ valid data - that is, data that is acceptable
➤ erroneous data – data which is not acceptable to the program, for example data in runTimes should be greater than 0 but less than 60
➤ null data – when no data at all is entered, for instance – entering no data by just pressing the Enter key
➤ extreme data – data that is at both ends of a range; for example, 0 and 60 would be two examples of extreme data for runTimes.

DID YOU KNOW?

White box testing involves detailed testing of the internal logic of a section of code.

The tester needs to know how the code works and the internal structure of the code.

White box tests are carried out on units of code.

Test data should be used so that every statement is executed at least once.

White box testing identifies errors in syntax, logic and dataflow within the code.

Black box testing focuses on inputs and outputs. The unit of code being tested is viewed as a black box and the tester cannot see inside the box. This type of testing identifies errors in data structures, errors in reports or unexpected behaviour errors.

Open the file called **CY.py** provided by your teacher.

Run the program and examine the code.

This program asks the user if they want to add more names to the lists. The section of code printed below allows the user to do this.

(Note that the run times have decimal places so this needs to be converted to the 'float' data type.)

```python
#loop to enter runner names and times
#ask the user if they want to add names to the list
answer=input("Do you want to add names to the list?")

#loop to run while the user wants to enter names into the list
while (answer=="Y"):
    # loop to input and validate runner names
    newrunnername=input("Enter player name " + str(i+1))
    while(newrunnername==""):
        newrunnername=input("Enter a valid player name for player "+ str(i+1))
    runnerNames.append(newrunnername)

    #loop to input and validate run times
    #use float to convert the newruntime as it has decimal points
    newruntime=float(input("Enter player" + str(i+1) +"'s time "))
    while(newruntime<0 or newruntime>60):
        newruntime=float(input("Enter a valid time (0-60) for player "+ str(i+1)))
    runTimes.append(newruntime)


    answer=input("Do you want to enter another runner?(Y/N)")
    #loop to validate the answer entered by the user
    #it must be Y/N
    while answer not in ("Y", "N"):
        answer=input("Enter Y on N please ")
    # i is used to increase the position of the element in the list
    # every time a name and time is entered, the list position is increased by 1
    i=i+1
```

This section of code contains nested While loops.

A nested loop is when one loop has another loop inside of it. In this case there are four While loops. Three While loops are nested inside the main While loop.

Think about creating a test plan for the code below which validates the variable called newruntime. A valid run time value is in the range 0–60.

```
#loop to input and validate run times
#use float to convert the newruntime as it has decimal points
newruntime=float(input("Enter player" + str(i+1) +"'s time "))
while(newruntime<0 or newruntime>60):
    newruntime=float(input("Enter a valid time (0-60) for player "+ str(i+1)))
runTimes.append(newruntime)
```

A test plan for this code could be organised in the following way:

Test number	Reason for test	Test data	Expected output	Observed output	Does observed and expected match?
1.	Valid data for newruntime	31	Accepted	Accepted	Yes
2.	Invalid data for newruntime	-13	Rejected and error message	Rejected and error message	Yes
3.	Null data newruntime	Press the enter key	Error message	Error message	Yes
4.	Extreme data for newruntime	0	Accepted	Accepted	Yes
5.	Extreme for data for newruntime	60	Accepted	Accepted	Yes

➤ With a partner create a test plan which will check all aspects of the program **CY.py**. This should include sets of tests for:
  • adding new runners
  • the sections of code which validate **newrunnername** and **answer**
  • making sure the sort works after new members have been added to the list
  • making sure the binary search is working correctly.
➤ Test the program by using the data in your test plan. When you enter the data, complete the 'Does observed and expected match?' column.
➤ Evaluate the program's performance based on the results of the testing.
➤ Make the changes to the code that you noted above.
➤ Test the program to ensure it is still working effectively.

Final project

A local charity has heard about your good work with the running club. The chairperson has approached you to help them with data they need to collect about members of the charity and their donations. The charity needs to produce summary data about donations for this year.

Part of the program has been created for you. Open the file called **charity.py** provided by your teacher.

➤ You need to add code to the program which will:
  - set up a list called memberNames which will hold the names of 15 members. You can choose the names of the members.

    For example: `memberNames=["John Lee", "Jo Chang", etc.]`
  - set up a list called `memberDonations` which records the donations for each of the 15 members. You can decide on the amount for each member but it must be between 10.00 and 20.00.

    For example, `memberDonations=[12.00, 14.50, etc.]`
  - allow the secretary to input more member names and donations.
    - Member names cannot be blank. In the program **charity.py** this validation loop has been completed for you.
    - Donations can only be in the range 10.00–20.00 and are taken in dollars. You must add code to the program which will allow for the input and validation of a new donation. The code should add the new donation to the `memberDonations` list using the `append()` function.

> Look back at the code in the file **CY.py** and examine the loops used to validate the data.

➤ Sort the data, from lowest to highest, on the basis of members' donations.

➤ To do this you will need to review the code for the Go further exercise where names and run times were sorted together based on the run times of members.

> If you need to swap a value in the `memberDonations` list, you will also have to swap the corresponding value in the `memberNames` list so that each donation amount stays matched to its relevant name.

➤ Print a member donations report using the sorted lists. An example of what this might look like is shown below.

Member Donations Report

John Green $12.00

John Lee $14.50

and so on ...

➤ Create a procedure called `averagedonation` which will process the data in the list `memberDonations` so that the average donation, the minimum donation and the maximum donation is calculated and output. An example of how these three results should be output is shown below:

> When the list is sorted, the minimum donation will be in position[0] of the list and the maximum will be in the last location.

Minimum donation = $10.00

Maximum donation = $19.50

Average donation = $14.00

➤ Use the code for the binary search to allow the chairperson to search members over and over again.

➤ You will be working with two lists as follows:

memberNames

Position	Value
0	John Lee
1	Jo Chang
....	
....	

memberDonations

Position	Value
0	12.00
1	14.50
....	
....	

So, memberNames[0] is John Lee and memberDonations[0] is $12.00. Therefore, John Lee has donated 12 dollars.

➤ Test your program to ensure that it runs correctly.

Evaluation

➤ Ask a partner to run your program and enter a set of test values for your program.

➤ Ask them to comment on:
  o the sort method you have used in terms of efficiency; they should refer to: swaps and comparisons
  o the validation that you have used to ensure values entered are acceptable.

Combining HTML, CSS and JavaScript

To add interactivity to websites, developers will often use a programming language called JavaScript. JavaScript was first developed in 1995 with the intention that it be used to add a bit more glamour and style over and above any presentation possible using HTML. Fast forward to today and companies like Google and Facebook are developing complex web applications using JavaScript. JavaScript has evolved to the point that it is one of the most commonly used languages by developers of server-side applications. One of the key points leading to the success of JavaScript is the continual update in its functionality. The ongoing development of new and exciting features and library functions means it continues to offer developers new options. The Facebook Ads app makes use of the React JavaScript library for example. Provided the JavaScript development team can continue to develop libraries of code for its loyal users, JavaScript popularity will continue to soar.

Many online users today expect websites to be interactive. Users are able to use interactive websites to look up information, send information to other organisations and perform other tasks such as play games.

HTML defines the content and structure of a web page and CSS is used to define how the content is presented. JavaScript is used to define how the user can interact with that content.

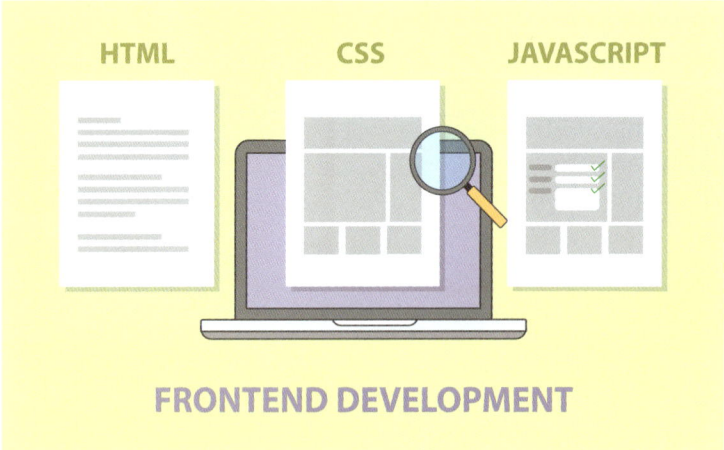

▲ HTML, CSS and JavaScript can be combined to create well presented, interactive content on web pages.

In this unit you will learn to:

→ access and use a library of CSS styles provided by w3schools

→ use containers to group items on a web page to ensure all elements are styled in the same way

→ control the display of elements on a web page so content can be displayed side by side

→ use CSS to alter the way images are displayed on a web page

→ use existing CSS styles to create a navigation bar

→ use HTML to create anchors which allow users to jump between content on a single web page

→ explain the difference between **client-side processing** and **server-side processing**

→ use HTML to create a form for user data entry

→ use CSS to create interactive elements which allow users to interact with web pages

→ use JavaScript to validate data entered into a form on a web page

→ continue to practise and further develop your knowledge of HTML and CSS.

KEYWORDS

client-side processing: refers to the situation where a program or script is processed within the client's web browser; the code is often embedded in the HTML of the web page being viewed or it may be called as an external file; a common example of client-side processing is the validation of data entered into an online form before it is submitted by the user

server-side processing: when a web page is posted back to the web server, the script is processed on the web server and returns feedback to the user's web page. A common example of server-side processing is saving data to a web based database, navigating to a new web page or validating a user's login to a website

SCENARIO

Web-Pro Games is a computer game development company. It is trying to encourage young people to consider careers in computer game development. The company has launched an international Pro-Games Development Competition which is

open to young people from the ages of 11–14. Web-Pro Games has asked you to help it complete a new website which will be used to launch the competition.

The website will have three pages.

• The first page will contain information about the Web-Pro Games organisation, the competition and the rules of the competition.

• The second page will contain an application form to be completed in order to enter the competition. The form should be submitted online using an email link.

• The third page will contain:
  • a sample game plan
  • tutorials for potential gamers to complete to produce a simple game
  • a task for potential coders to complete before they can enter the competition.

- Each page should have a contact us link in the navigation bar to allow young people to email Web-Pro Games for more information about the competition.

Web-Pro Games has asked that all of the web pages are consistent and professional. The company wants you to design a theme for the web pages. The theme should appeal to 11–14 year olds, should be interactive and include accessibility elements.

> You should already be familiar with accessibility and this will be further developed in this unit.

Do you remember?

Before starting this unit, you should be able to:

✔ use HTML to add structure and content to applications displayed using web browsers; for example:

- multimedia content (text, images, sound, video)
- internal and external hyperlinks, and hyperlinks to launch an email application.

✔ apply inline and internal CSS styles to amend the presentation of a web page

✔ create and link an external CSS file to amend the presentation of multiple pages in a website

✔ use ids and classes to create and apply CSS styles more than once

✔ analyse pseudocode to assist in the creation of a coded solution to a problem

✔ use If statements to evaluate conditions to determine which branch of code is to be executed.

HTML: A quick review

Learn

HTML is used to produce the structure for a web page while CSS provides the presentation or styling for web page content. Every web page presented on the internet uses the same HTML tags to add text, images, video, sound and other content; yet they all look totally different.

Some commonly used HTML tags and their functions include:

HTML tag	Function of HTML tag
`<html> </html>`	Defines the start and end of an HTML document
`<head> </head>`	Contains information about an HTML document e.g. the title
`<title> </title>`	Identifies a title for an HTML document. May be displayed in the browser tab
`<body> </body>`	The start and end of the main body of the HTML document. What will be displayed in the browser window
`<h1> </h1>`	Heading styles. Can range from h1 to h6 with h6 being the smallest.
`<p> </p>`	Used to define a paragraph of text
` `	Used to represent a break in the display of text in the browser window
`<b> </b>`	Embolden text displayed on the browser window
`<i> </i>`	Italicise text displayed on the browser window
`<u> </u>`	Underline text displayed on the browser window
`<ol> </ol> / <ul> </ul>`	Ordered list or unordered list
`<li> </li>`	Defines individual items on a list displayed in a browser window
`<img src >`	Displays an image in the browser window from a location specified
`<audio> </audio>`	Used to insert a audio file into an HTML document
`<video> </video>`	Used to insert a video file into an HTML document
`<a href>`	Adds a hyperlink from one HTML document to another page, file or web page
`<table> </table>`	Defines the start and end of a table in an HTML document
`<tr> </tr>`	Shows the start and end of a row in a table
`<th> </th>`	Identifies an item in a table as a header
`<td> </td>`	Describes data in a table as being added to a cell in a table
`<!-- -->`	Used to comment or explain HTML code in a source file
`<style> </style>`	Used to add CSS to an HTML document
`<div> </div>`	Used to divide an HTML document into sections or divisions

Practice

The owner of Web-Pro Games has provided you with the following information to be included on the company website.

Web-Pro Games is based in Stockholm, Sweden. It was founded in 2005 by game programmer and graphics designer Alex Phillips. Alex is from Stockholm and started developing computer games from the age of 12. Alex started with the block programming language Scratch before progressing to creating games using Python and Java.

Web-Pro Games see the world wide web as being the ideal platform for young people to share and play games. It sees the web as being a way of reaching a worldwide audience.

Since winning the game developer of the year award, Alex Phillips has organised a competition every year which attracts entrants from all over the world. The competition aims to encourage young people to consider a career in electronic game development.

Alex's advice for young game developers is:

➤ develop your maths skills
➤ build up your programming skills in a range of programming languages
➤ build a portfolio of games you have developed or helped create
➤ join after-school programming clubs where you can learn from others and share ideas
➤ don't give up!

Computational Thinking

A storyboard for the first page of the website has already been created. Using abstraction, extract the necessary information from the text provided to produce content that will match the following layout for the index page of the Web-Pro Games website.

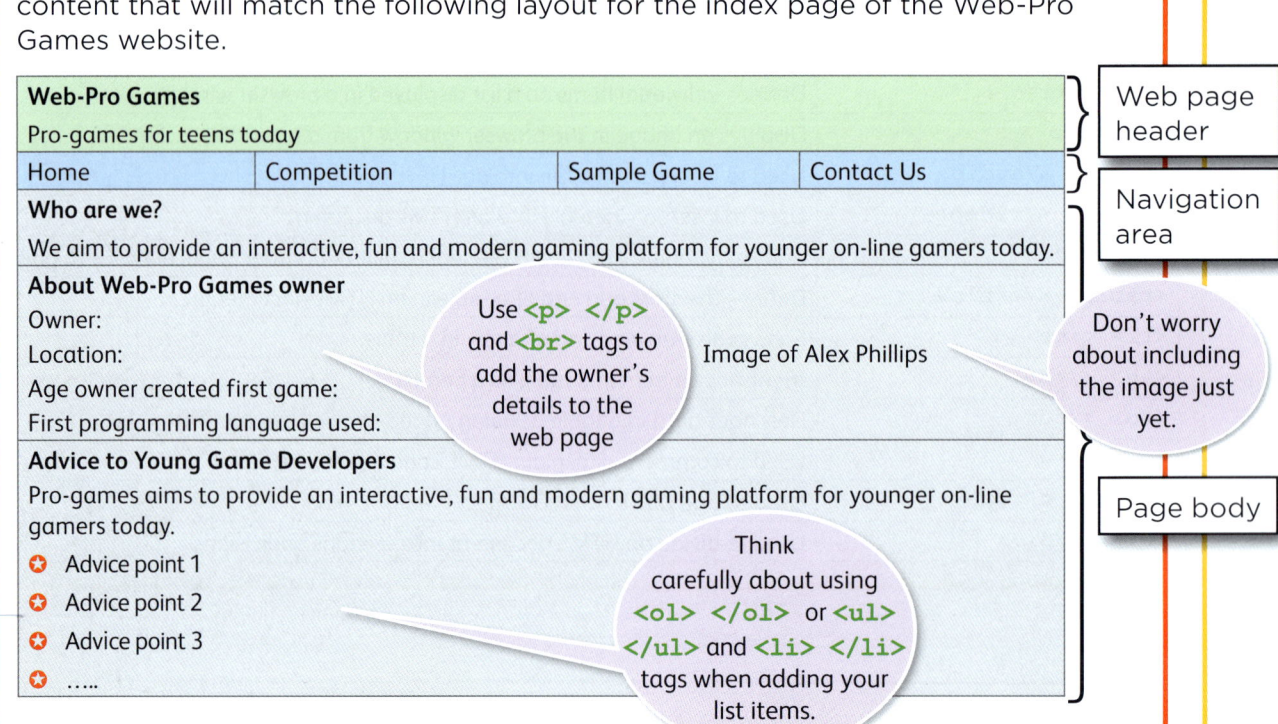

Your teacher will provide you with a folder called **MyWeb**.

It contains three incomplete web pages: **index.html**, **competition.html**, and **sample.html**.

Use the HTML tags you are already familiar with to add content to the page called **index.html**.

➤ Open NotePad++

➤ Open **index.html**.

➤ Edit the HTML to include the following content under the comments as shown in the image below:

  o Add information about the owner.

  o Add advice for young game developers.

  (The advice to young gamers should be presented in a list as shown in the storyboard on the previous page. Think about how you could use the following HTML syntax to add a numbered list to this web page.)

```
<ul>
    <li>list item </li>
    <li>list item</li>
</ul>
```

You can present your list as an unordered list using **<ul> </ul>**, or as a numbered list using **<ol> </ol>**.

You can edit the presentation of a list by applying a style to the <ul> tag; for example, **<ul style= "list-style-type:square;">** will display your list with square bullets.

To review the HTML tags used when creating ordered and unordered lists, visit www.w3schools.com/html/html_lists.asp. Experiment with different list styles until you are happy with the way your list is presented.

Add navigation links later.

Advice to potential young gamers should appear here as an ordered list.

Extract details from information provided about Alex Phillips and include them here. Text should be presented as Owner: Alex Phillips, and so on ...

Don't forget the title 'About Web-Pro Games owner'

➤ Save your file **index.html** once all data has been added.

w3schools for CSS: container class

Learn

What makes one website look different from another is not the HTML code used to produce the content but the CSS code used to style it.

CSS can be used to style the presentation of navigation elements in addition to the content displayed on web pages. Developers can create their own CSS to change the presentation of their web pages. CSS can be inline (included in the main body of the HTML document alongside the HTML tags), it can be internal to the HTML document (within the header section at the beginning of the document) or it can be accessed by linking to an external .css file. Since CSS can be an external file this means that the CSS being used can be stored anywhere provided that file location can be accessed by a web address.

Website developers will often create their own style definitions and apply them to different HTML elements in the document they are creating. This can prove to be quite inefficient, especially if the same styles are being used over and over again. This can also lead to problems if the developer needs to edit style definitions at a later stage; it can be difficult to locate all of the style definitions in a large HTML document.

To combat this problem developers are able to create and reuse style definitions by using a special feature of CSS known as a **class**. A class is used to assign a name to and create a style definition which can be used again and again. Once that style has been defined it can be applied again and again to different HTML elements in a web page.

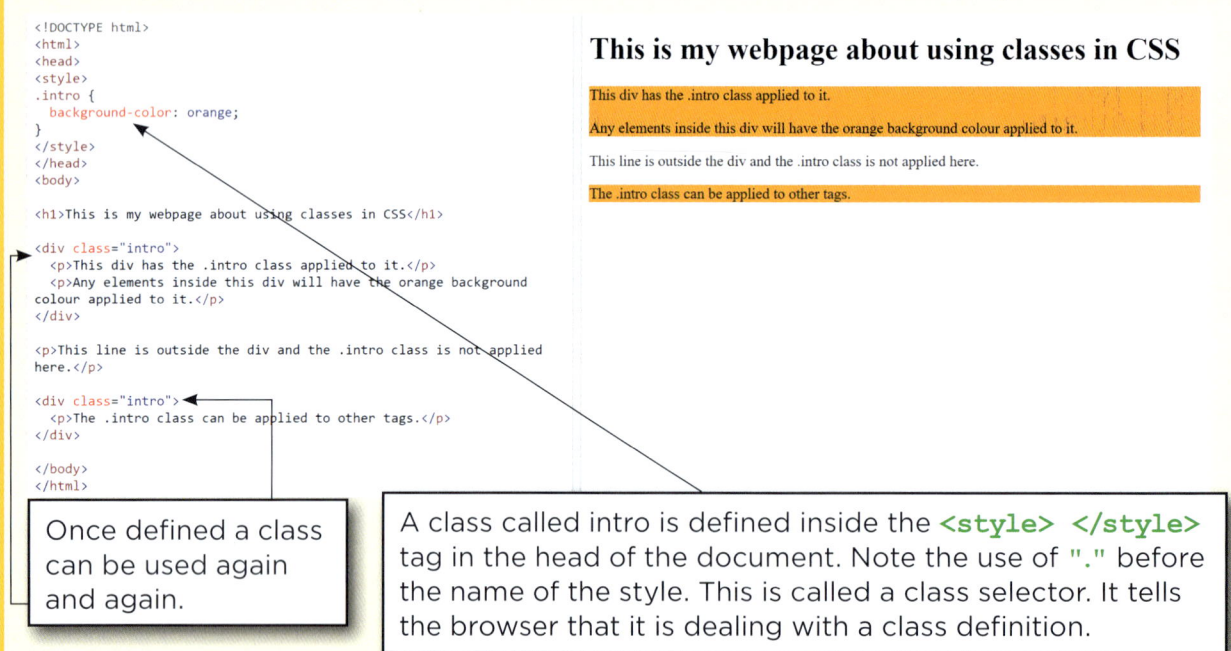

```
<!DOCTYPE html>
<html>
<head>
<style>
.intro {
  background-color: orange;
}
</style>
</head>
<body>

<h1>This is my webpage about using classes in CSS</h1>

<div class="intro">
  <p>This div has the .intro class applied to it.</p>
  <p>Any elements inside this div will have the orange background
colour applied to it.</p>
</div>

<p>This line is outside the div and the .intro class is not applied
here.</p>

<div class="intro">
  <p>The .intro class can be applied to other tags.</p>
</div>

</body>
</html>
```

This is my webpage about using classes in CSS

This div has the .intro class applied to it.

Any elements inside this div will have the orange background colour applied to it.

This line is outside the div and the .intro class is not applied here.

The .intro class can be applied to other tags.

Once defined a class can be used again and again.

A class called intro is defined inside the **<style> </style>** tag in the head of the document. Note the use of "." before the name of the style. This is called a class selector. It tells the browser that it is dealing with a class definition.

Class definitions can be stored and shared online. The w3schools website has made a wide library of CSS classes available for web developers to use license-free.

You can use some of the **w3schools CSS** classes to style your web pages.

The w3schools library of CSS classes can be accessed and used directly from their website by providing a link to the w3css stylesheet at www.w3schools.com/w3css.

> We will look in this chapter at how to use CSS files which are stored on a different server to the actual web page using it.

One of the predefined CSS classes we can use from w3schools library is the **container class** (that is, the class called 'container'). The container class can be used, for example, to set the **margins**, **padding** and alignment for any HTML element defined inside that container. Any HTML element inside a defined container to will have the same margins, padding and alignment.

KEYWORDS

w3schools CSS: a CSS library provided by w3schools which is free to use

container class: a CSS class which can be used to group HTML elements together so they can all be styled the same way

margins: space around the top, right, bottom and left of an HTML element

padding: provides space between any HTML element and any borders around it

Practice

You will use the container class to add additional styles to the page **index.html** for the Web-Pro Gaming website.

➤ Open NotePad++
➤ Open **index.html**.

Before you can use w3.css in your web page you need to add a link to the w3schools style sheet.

> In the same way you can link to your own external style sheet.

➤ Add a link, as shown below, to the w3schools w3.css style sheet in between the **\<head> \</head>** tags of the web page.

```
index.html
1   <!\DOCTYPE html>
2   <html>
3   <head>
4   <title> About Web-Pro Games </title> <!-- browser title -->
5
6   <link rel="stylesheet" href="https://www.w3schools.com/w3css/4/w3.css"> <!-- link to w3.css -->
7   </head>
8
```

➤ Once the w3.css file is linked, you can reference it (use the definitions it contains) within the HTML.
➤ This can either be done from within an HTML tag; for example:

\<h1> class="w3-container" Heading Text\</h1>

➤ Or, as part of **\<div>\</div>** tags; for example:

"\<div class="w3-container">

> The **\<div> \</div>** tag can be used to separate (or divide) the content of an HTML document into sections. The benefit of combining css with **\<div>\</div>** tags is that all content contained within the tags can be styled in the same way.

➤ Edit the HTML for the banner section as shown below.

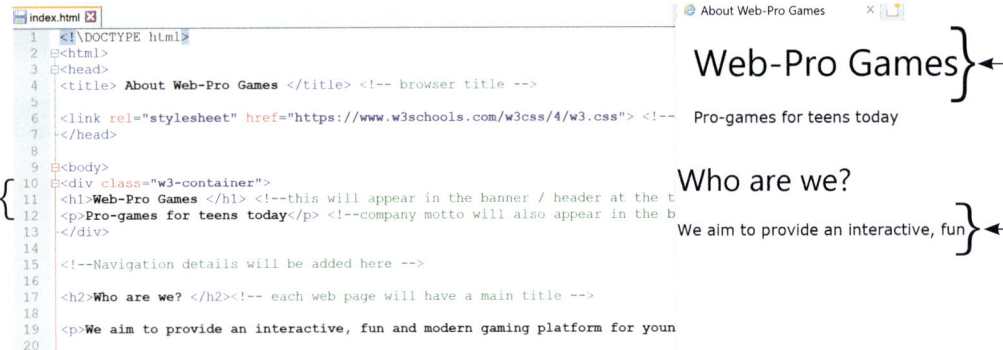

The container class is not applied to this line of text – this text is not indented from the side of the page.

Use the `<div>` `</div>` tags to separate the banner information from the rest of the page. Then add the w3-container class to the opening of the `<div>` tag.

The container class has been applied to this text within the `<div></div>` tags – note the text is indented from the side of the page.

➤ Save index.html and preview the page by clicking on Run and selecting the name of the browser you wish to use.

w3schools for CSS: classes

Learn

You have explored the w3 container class. However, w3schools have defined many more classes that that can be applied to your HTML.

For instance:

➤ **w3-color class** – this defines the background colour.

➤ **w3-text-color class** – this defines the text colour.

➤ **w3-cell class** – this allows, for example, text and images to be presented side by side, or for text and images to be combined.

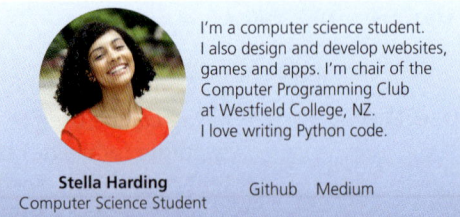

I'm a computer science student. I also design and develop websites, games and apps. I'm chair of the Computer Programming Club at Westfield College, NZ. I love writing Python code.

Stella Harding
Computer Science Student   Github   Medium

The w3schools classes provide developers with many complex tools to use to help improve the layout of their web pages. Developers can combine classes and apply more than one class to an HTML element to produce complex web page layouts.

It is possible to add more than one class to a single `<div>` tag at any one time simply by listing each class inside quotation marks after the style definition. For example, `<div class = "w3-container w3-light-blue">` would allow us to set the background colour of this division to light blue using a w3-color class.

KEYWORDS

w3-color class: a css class predefined by w3schools which can be used to add colour to any HTML element

w3-text-color class: a css class predefined by w3schools which can be used to change the colour to any HTML text element

w3-cell class: displays blocks of HTML content side by side in a browser window as though presented inside a table

Practice

You can add colour to the container by adding the w3-color class to the container.

➤ Select and apply your own colour to the web page header of **index.html**.

➤ Use w3-text-color to edit the colour of your heading 1 (h1) text in the web page banner.

> w3 provide a wide range of named colour and text styles for use when using CSS. Have a look on www.w3schools.com for more information.

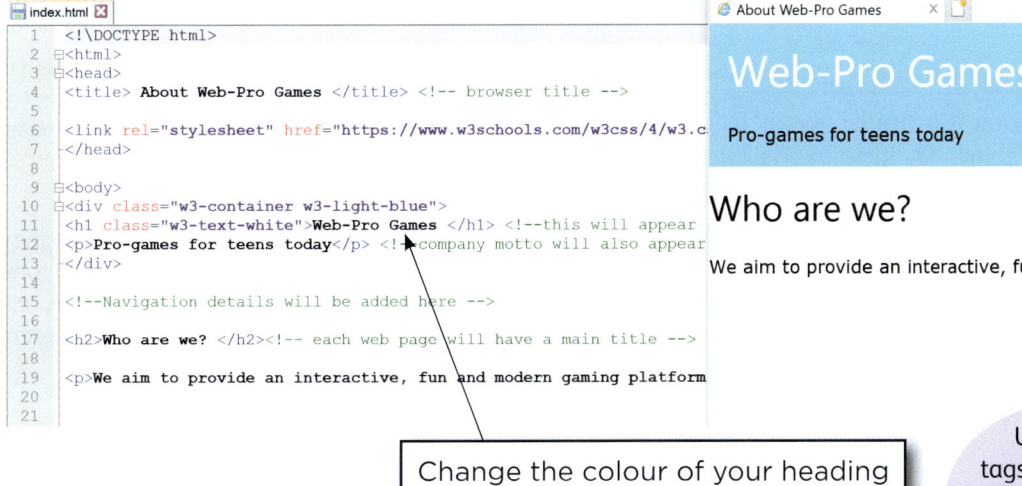

```
 1   <!\DOCTYPE html>
 2   <html>
 3   <head>
 4   <title> About Web-Pro Games </title> <!-- browser title -->
 5
 6   <link rel="stylesheet" href="https://www.w3schools.com/w3css/4/w3.c
 7   </head>
 8
 9   <body>
10   <div class="w3-container w3-light-blue">
11   <h1 class="w3-text-white">Web-Pro Games </h1> <!--this will appear
12   <p>Pro-games for teens today</p> <!--company motto will also appear
13   </div>
14
15   <!--Navigation details will be added here -->
16
17   <h2>Who are we? </h2><!-- each web page will have a main title -->
18
19   <p>We aim to provide an interactive, fun and modern gaming platform
20
21
```

Change the colour of your heading

> Remember to place the class inside the container you wish to apply the style to.

➤ Use the **`<div> </div>`** tags and the w3schools classes you have investigated to improve the rest of the content in index.html.
Try using the following to make each **`<div></div>`** look different:

  o the w3 container class

  o the w3 color classes

  o the w3 text color classes.

➤ Save and test **index.html** after each amendment to the HTML.

➤ Continue editing the content and styles until you are happy with how the page looks.

> Use <div> tags to separate the navigation area from the main body of the page.

> Consider making further improvements to the presentation of the text on **index.html**. For example, you might use **<b> </b>**, **<i> </i>**, **<u> </u>** to highlight important content.

Practice

The storyboard for **index.html** (on page 80) requires an image of Alex Phillips to be displayed alongside his profile on the web page. To lay out the page content in this way we can use another w3-container class called the w3-cell class. This will display blocks of HTML content side by side in the browser display window.

➤ Open NotePad++

➤ Open **index.html**.

➤ Edit the HTML content to include the following HTML definitions which will display two w3-cells side by side in your browser window.

```
19   <p>We aim to provide an interactive, fun and modern gaming platform for younger on-line
20
21
22
23
24   <!--Add information about the owner -->
25   <div
26   <div class="w3-container w3-sand w3-cell">
27   <p>info</p> <!-- add Alex Phillips information here in a list format-->
28   </div>
29
30
31   <div class="w3-container w3-light-gray w3-cell">
32   <p>image</p> <!-- use <img> tag to add a photograph of Alex Phillips here-->
33   </div>
34   </div>
35
```

Hyper Text Markup Language file   length : 1,134   lines : 46   Ln : 8   Col : 1   Sel : 0 | 0

Web-Pro Games

Pro-games for teens today

Who are we?

We aim to provide an interactive, fun

info   image

This will add two cells side by side where Alex Phillips' details and images can then be inserted.

The w3-cell styles tell the browser to display the sand coloured and light grey containers side by side in the browser window.

Now that we have created containers for the text and image of Alex Phillips we can add additional HTML tags to the container to include the content described in the storyboard on page 80.

➤ Edit the HTML in the first **<div>** to display information about the owner as shown in the storyboard.

➤ Edit the HTML in the second **<div>** to include an image of the owner Alex Phillips.

Display the information as an unordered list.

Algorithmic thinking

w3CSS provides CSS classes which allow images to be displayed as circled images or with borders.

About Web-Pro Gaming

- Owned By: Alex Phillips
- Location: Stockholm, Sweden
- Age owner created first game: 12
- First programming language used: Scratch

KEYWORDS

w3-circle class: will display an HTML element inside a circle shape when it is presented in a browser window

w3-border class: displays a border around an HTML element when it is displayed in a browser window

With a friend, discuss how you could add **w3-circle** and **w3-border** classes to the following HTML code so the image of Alex Phillips displays like the picture above.

```
<img src="assets/alex.jpg" alt="Image
of Alex Phillips">
```

You can add your class definitions here.

Go to www.w3schools.com/w3css/w3css_images.asp and investigate other w3.css image classes which can be used to control how images are displayed in a browser window.

Experiment with the w3.css image classes shown on the w3schools website. Use these to experiment with the way the image of Alex Phillips is displayed.

When you are happy with how your **index.html** page looks save the page and exit from NotePad++.

> Look back at the HTML examples on page 85 for help with adding more than one class to a `<div>` tag.

> You could add hover effects to your image or add colour effects to the images using some of the example styles provided in the w3 style definitions.

CSS and HTML: buttons, bars and anchors

Learn

Websites provide users with a range of ways to navigate from one web page to another. You should already have some experience adding **text-based hyperlinks** to HTML documents. Most websites however provide users with a **navigation bar** (often presented across the top of the web page) to allow a user to navigate using buttons or images.

For example, the Hodder Education website uses a combination of text-based hyperlinks and navigation buttons all presented in a navigation bar across the top of the web page.

Text-based hyperlink

Navigation button

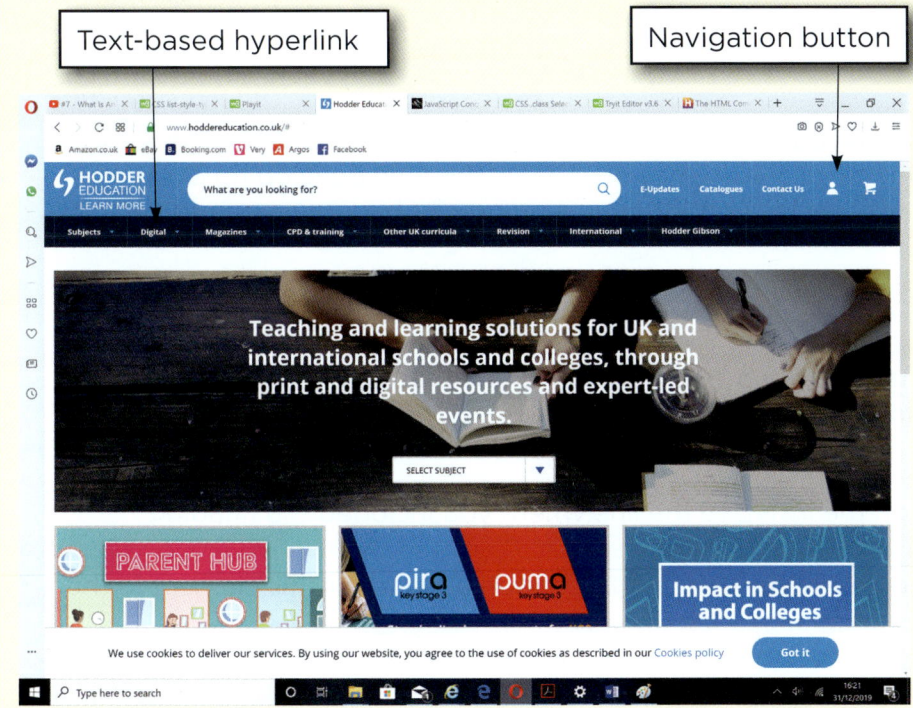

KEYWORDS

text-based hyperlink: a word or words which have a hyperlink embedded to provide users with a link to additional content or pages in an application

navigation bar: a section of an interface which provides users with a method of accessing other content or pages in an application

anchor: a hyperlink which provides a link to content or headings further down a web page

Sometimes, if an individual web page is very long, the developer will include a hyperlink within the page which allows the user to jump to another section of the page. A hyperlink used this way is called an **anchor**.

To create an anchor and hyperlink on a page in this way a web developer will use a special HTML attribute called an **id attribute** to assign a name to the content to be accessed in another position on the HTML document.

Each of the blue text elements represents a hyperlink to a section of the page further down the screen. The user can click on any hyperlink in order to 'jump' to that location on the web page. This is particularly useful on web pages which have a lot of content or for web pages which are being developed for presentation on smaller screens.

An id attribute will be used to place a name beside the publications content in the HTML document.

A hyperlink will be added here which will link to the id attribute for the publications section of the web page.

Home / Shortcodes / Anchors

Anchors

Anchors are jump links that link to headings farther down the page.

On this page:

↓ Publications

↓ Travel

↓ Biography

↓ About Us

↓ Coming Up

Publications

Lorem ipsum dolor sit amet, consectetur adipiscing elit. Mauris feugiat pellentesque massa, sit amet bibendum mi vestibulum a. Aliquam interdum neque dolor, ullamcorper malesuada erat dapibus vitae. Nam sit amet nisl quis quam accumsan dictum sodales quis est. Nulla varius diam quis eros lobortis pharetra. Proin a gravida mi, eleifend sagittis nisi. Suspendisse sed consectetur felis. Vestibulum condimentum at lectus id malesuada. Curabitur et tristique enim. Sed tempus varius lorem, nec placerat nibh tristique eget. Ut sodales luctus posuere. Sed lorem nulla, condimentum malesuada augue vitae, pellentesque dignissim lorem.

Travel

Morbi faucibus magna tellus, eget porta nunc sollicitudin vel. Suspendisse ultricies bibendum enim et molestie. In feugiat nulla nec cursus mattis. Proin sed eros placerat, ullamcorper urna ut,

KEYWORD

id attribute: a method of applying a name or unique id to an HTML element

Practice

Users accessing the home page for Web-Pro Gaming may not want to view Alex Phillips' profile and image, or the images of staff working on developing computer games. Instead they may be looking for advice on how to become a game developer.

Anchors can be used to allow users to jump to content on a different part of a web page.

Before you can do that, you need to include an id attribute to one of the HTML elements in the section of the page you wish to link to.

➤ Open **index.html**.

➤ Scroll down through the HTML to the line where you included the heading Advice For Young Game Developers.

➤ Add an id attribute beside the heading to provide a name for this element in the document.

```
49
50   <!--Add advice for young game developers -->
51   <h3><a id="advice"></a>Advice For Young Game Developers</h3>
52
```

➤ Add a text-based hyperlink at the top of the HTML page and link this hyperlink to the id attribute you have just created. The text 'Click here for some advice if you want to become a young game developer!' will appear on the web page underlined. It will provide the user with a hyperlink to the section of the page containing the identifier 'advice'.

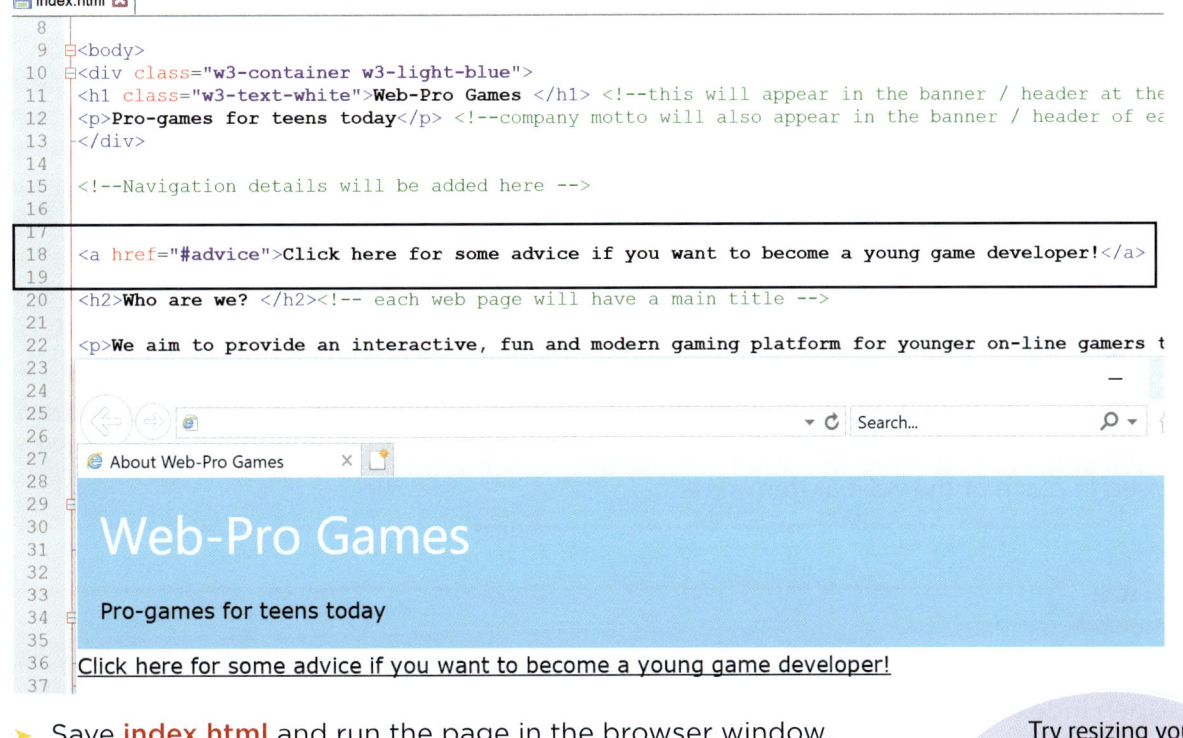

➤ Save **index.html** and run the page in the browser window.
➤ Click on the hyperlink which now appears at the top of the page.
➤ It should now display the section of the page with the heading 'Advice for Young Game Developers'.

> Try resizing your browser window so you cannot see the section of the page with the heading 'Advice for Young Game Developers' before you test your anchor.

The storyboard on page 80 for **index.html** shows that the web page should contain a navigation bar with four navigation buttons.

The buttons should provide links to each of the web pages in the website. In addition, there is a Contact Us button which users can click on to automatically send an email to the owners of Web-Pro Games.

The w3schools CSS definitions provide styles for developers to use which can help them create button bars which can be used as navigation tools such as the one shown.

In this example, the developer has used two additional w3schools class definitions to create a horizontal navigation bar.

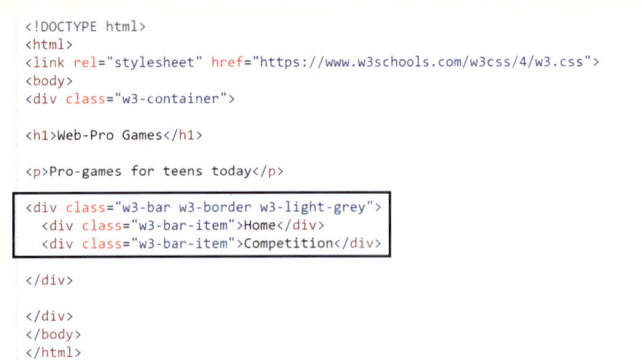

```
<!DOCTYPE html>
<html>
<link rel="stylesheet" href="https://www.w3schools.com/w3css/4/w3.css">
<body>
<div class="w3-container">

<h1>Web-Pro Games</h1>

<p>Pro-games for teens today</p>

<div class="w3-bar w3-border w3-light-grey">
  <div class="w3-bar-item">Home</div>
  <div class="w3-bar-item">Competition</div>

</div>

</div>
</body>
</html>
```

Web-Pro Games

Pro-games for teens today

Home   Competition

KEYWORDS

w3-bar: a class which groups HTML elements together and displays them across the screen in a web browser

w3-bar-item: a class used to define the individual items which will appear inside a w3-bar container

w3-button: a w3 class used to define a button style element which can be used for navigation bars on web pages

The **w3-bar** class is combined with w3-border and w3-light-grey to create a horizontal navigation bar on this HTML document.

The **w3-bar-item** class is used to add two text-based elements to the†navigation bar. In the practice panel which follows we will see how hyperlinks can then be added to each bar item using the **<a> </a>** tag.

For those who prefer graphical navigation elements, the **w3-button** can be used in place of the w3-bar-item class.

Practice

➤ Open NotePad++.

➤ Open **index.html**.

➤ Under the comment **<!--Navigation details will be added here -->** add the following to insert a button class which will eventually contain a hyperlink to the Home for the Web-Pro Games website.

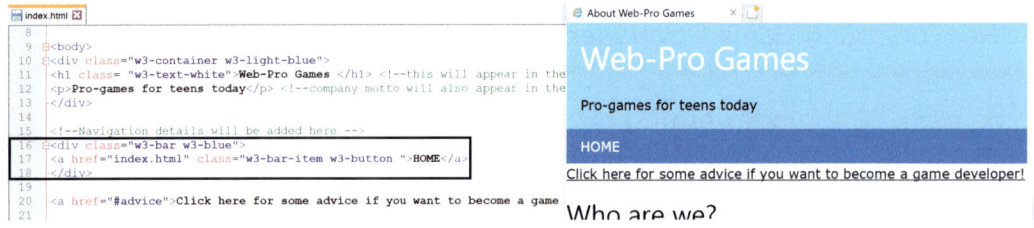

➤ With a friend discuss the role of each of the following CSS styles:

    o w3-bar and how you might change the colour of the bar

    o w3-bar item

    o w3-button.

➤ Discuss with a friend how you could amend your HTML to include links on your navigation bar for the pages called **competition.html** and **sample.html**.

➤ How would the link on the button for Contact Us differ from the other hyperlinks? Alex's email is alex@webprogames.com

Look back at page 85 for a reminder of how to use the w3schools color definitions.

You should have some experience of including the mailto link in HTML documents. This is a fictional email address created for the purposes of this exercise.

Generalisation and Algorithmic Thinking

Generalisation involves the application of previously acquired skills and knowledge in the development of a solution to a problem. Using skills you have acquired in the use of CSS amend the colour schemes, styles and button colours used in your navigation bar to ensure it fits in with the style and colour scheme of the remainder of your web page.

There are a range of classes available to allow you to style your navigation buttons in a way which suits you and the style of your website. Visit www.w3schools.com/w3css/w3css_navigation.asp to investigate the range of button styles you can apply to your website. Use algorithmic thinking to help you consider how the HTML tags required can be combined to allow you to create and style the buttons needed for your version of the Web-Pro Games website.

Consider how you can edit index.html to do the following:

➤ add colour to your navigation buttons

➤ add borders to your navigation bar

➤ change the size of your navigation bar.

You can also change the appearance of individual buttons in the navigation bar for example by adding borders:

```
10  <div class="w3-container w3-light-blue">
11    <h1 class= "w3-text-white">Web-Pro Games </h1> <!--this will appear in t
12    <p>Pro-games for teens today</p> <!--company motto will also appear in t
13  </div>
14
15    <!--Navigation details will be added here -->
16  <div class="w3-bar w3-blue">
17    <a href="index.html" class="w3-bar-item w3-button w3-border">HOME</a>
18    <a href="competition.html" class="w3-bar-item w3-button ">COMPETITION</a
19    <a href="sample.html" class="w3-bar-item w3-button ">SAMPLE</a>
20    <a href="mailto:alex@progameweb.com" class="w3-bar-item w3-button ">CONT.
21  </div>
22
```

Pro-games for teens today

HOME   COMPETITION

Click here for some advice if

Who are we?

We aim to provide an interac

Find out more about button styles by going to www.w3schools.com/w3css/w3css_buttons.asp

Apply additional button styles and colours to your navigation bar until you are happy with the appearance.

➤ Ensure all buttons have been linked correctly to the other web pages stored in MyWeb.

➤ Save **index.html** and close NotePad++.

HTML: Forms for user input

Learn

Many organisations use web pages to collect information from users. One way they do this is through the use of data input forms. Forms provide users with headings which prompt them to enter their data into text boxes or select pre-determined options.

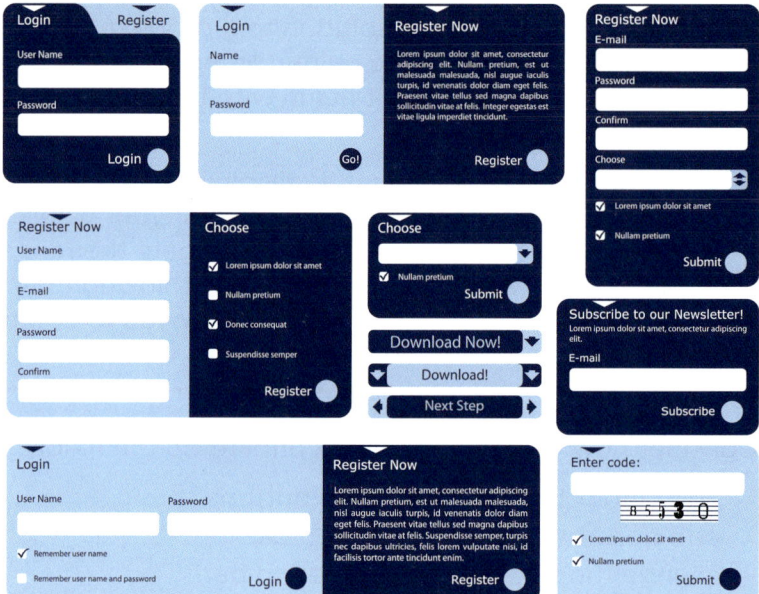

Forms can be added to HTML documents using the `<form> </form>` tags. Often developers want the section of an HTML page which contains the form content to stand out from the rest of the page; placing the form inside a new `<div> </div>` tag will allow this portion of the HTML document to be styled differently from the remainder of the page.

For instance:

```
<div>

<!--create a new div section which can be used to contain the form -->

<!--classes or styles can be added to the div in the normal way -->

<!--this can help make the form stand out from the rest of the web page -->

<h3>Headings and other html elements can be added as normal</h3>

<form> <!-- the form tags are used to create the input elements in the form -->

First name: <input type="text" name="firstname"> <!--text input fields can be added using the input type tag-->

<form action="mailto:inputform@mywebsite.com" name="submit">

<!-- the form action tag can be used to create a submit button so the contents of the form can be emailed to the recipient -->

</form>

</div>
```

Practice

Alex Phillips has provided you with a storyboard for the second page of the Web-Pro Games website.

Web-Pro Games				
Pro-games for teens today				} Web page header
Home	Competition	Sample Game	Contact Us	} Navigation area
Young Game Developer Competition			Image of tween gaming	
Do you think you have what it takes to be a game developer with Web-Pro Games?				
Let's see if you have what it takes. Enter our competition by filling out the form below. We will send you an information pack.				
This competition is only open to young people aged under the age of 15!				
You must have an adult's permission to enter!				
Competition Application Form				
First Name:				
Second Name:				
Gender:	Male ◦	Female ◦	Other ◦	
Adults Telephone:				
(Enter the telephone number of an adult who has given you permission to enter this competition)				
Email Form to Alex				

(bracket) Page body

Computational Thinking

You now have experience in the use of a wide range of HTML tags. You are also familiar now with a wide range of CSS definitions made available through the w3schools website. Use this knowledge to develop the HTML and CSS on the web page called **competition.html** to include the text for the web page header and the body of text called Young Game Developer Competition. Using algorithmic thinking you should also be able to combine multiple CSS definitions when applying them to HTML tags.

Some comments have been included in the file to help you complete this task.

✪ Open NotePad++.

✪ Open **competition.html**.

✪ Add the correct HTML to the `<head>` tag to ensure an appropriate title appears for the page when it opens in the browser window.

Use `<title>` `</title>`

✪ Add an appropriate link to the head tag so the web page links to www.w3schools.com/w3css

✪ Use the same CSS styles for the heading and navigation and body parts of **competition.html** to ensure it is styled in the same way as **index.html**.

✪ Use HTML to add the following from the storyboard on page 93.

  o The heading, Young Game Developer Competition.

  o Text underneath the heading Young Game Developer Competition. Add this as an unordered list.

> Look back at **index.html** to help you remember the CSS styles you used previously.

> Look carefully at how you used the w3-container and w3-cell classes to organise the information about Alex Phillips in **index.html**.

> With a friend, investigate how you could use the classes in w3.css layout to help improve how the content in these two containers is displayed.

➤ Underneath the comment `<!-- add application form here -->` add a new div with the w3 container class applied. This will be the container for the application form.

➤ Add the heading 'Competition Application Form' to this container.

➤ Add a colour class to this container. You can also add any other classes to this container to style it in a way to suit your website. For example, you may wish to change the colour of the container or the text inside the container.

➤ File and save **competition. html** and run it in the browser window to make sure all of your code is working correctly.

➤ HTML uses the **form element** `<form> </form>` to create a form which will be used to collect user input. Add the form element to your container as shown.

```
32        <li>This competition is only open to young people a
33        <li>You must have and adults permission to enter! <
34
35   </div>
36
37   <div class="w3-container w3-light-gray w3-cell">
38   <image src="assets/gaming.png" alt="tween gaming image'
39   </div>
40
41
42
43
44   <!-- add application form here -->
45
46   <div class="w3-container w3-pale-yellow">
47
48   <h3>Competition Application Form </h3>
49   <form>
50
51
52
53
54   </form>
55
56   </div>
57
58
```

Add the `<form>` element to create a form.

You can change the colour of the container or the text inside the container.

KEYWORD

form element: an HTML element which tells the browser that a form for data entry is to be displayed in a browser window

➤ HTML uses the input element to collect information from the user.
➤ Add the following HTML between the **<form> </form>** tags on competition.html; this will create:
  o a text box called 'firstname' with a label 'First name'
  o a text box called 'secondname' with a label 'Second name'
  o a radio button input with a 'Gender' label and the option 'Male'.

```
47
48    <h3>Competition Application Form </h3>
49    <form>
50
51    First name:   <input type="text" name="firstname"> <br>
52    Second name:  <input type="text" name="secondname"> <br>
53
54
55    Gender:
56    <input type="radio" name="gender" value= "Male"> Male
57
58
59
60
61    </form>
62
```

• Let us see if you have what it takes! t the form below. We will send you an i
• This competition is only open to youn
• You must have and adults permission

Competition Application Form

First name: [   ]
Second name: [   ]
Gender: ○ Male

These add form elements with a label that gives instructions to the user to let them know what data needs to be entered into the form. Remember to use **
** to ensure the second form element appears on a new line.

In HTML we can use the radio input type to provide the user with options to select from.

➤ Now add two more gender options, by including radio buttons for 'Female' and 'Other'.
➤ Use **
** to space out the form elements on competition.html.

Developing the form further

➤ Add a label and input text box to the form to allow the user to enter their age.
➤ Add a label and input text box to the form to allow the user to enter an adult's telephone number. This is how the organisers will confirm the entrants have an adult's permission to take part in the competition.
➤ Use the **<p> </p>** tag to add an instruction underneath the telephone label and input text box, as shown in the storyboard for this page on page 93.
➤ Save competition.html and run it in the browser window to ensure the form is displaying correctly.
➤ Close NotePad++.

KEYWORD

radio button: a graphical control element used to provide users with options to choose from when entering data; only one option can be selected

JavaScript: Submitting and validating forms

Learn

When data is entered into an input form by the website user, they need to be able to send the data recorded in the form fields to the organisation that owns the website. One of the simplest ways of doing this is to use a mailto form. A mailto form allows the user to click on a submit button which opens the user's email application to display a new message containing all of the details they wish to send to the organisation. The mailto: tag can be added at the bottom of a form to create a button the user can click on to submit the completed form.

The mailto: tag must have a matching action attribute which is associated with the opening form tag. This is used to tell the web browser what to do with the form once it is submitted by the user. In the example below the contents of the form are to be emailed to someone. The action attribute can also however be used to link to a special script file which can be used to handle the data recorded on the form.

A web page that uses the mailto form action will open a software program called *Microsoft Outlook Express*. It will then attach the contents of the form as a text file to an email which can then be sent to the email recipient. If the input form contains the fields: 'Name', 'Address' and a submit button, the data submitted in the email attachment will look something like:

```
1 Name=Harry Potter&Address=Hogwarts
Castle&Submit=Submit
```

Some of the downsides of using the mailto: approach include:

➤ form data is sent as an attachment which has to be opened and stored by the recipient (this may involve the recipient having to add the data to a database application)

➤ the user of the website must be using Outlook Express in order for mailto to work effectively.

It is unrealistic to assume that everyone accessing a website will be using or have access to the two applications required by the mailto: approach so many organisations today use specialised script forms which are saved with their HTML pages on their web server. These scripts are known as form mail scripts and are linked to in the same way as a CSS file but instead of styling a web page displayed using a web browser the form mail script collects the data from the form fields and sends it to a specified email address.

form   form mail script   email

web server

KEYWORDS

mailto form: HTML which allows the user to click on a submit button which then opens an email application

action attribute: an HTML attribute which will provide details of where to send data from an input form when the submit button is clicked by the user

form mail script: a specially written script file which is stored on a web server with a website; the script is linked to from within an HTML document and is used to collect data recorded on an HTML form before sending it to a specified email address

DID YOU KNOW?

Many different programming languages can be used to produce form mail scripts. Some examples include Perl, PHP, ASP.

Practice

Competition entrants need to submit their application form to Alex so he can check with an adult that they have permission to enter the competition.

Alex has asked you to set up a mailto: form so he can see in the first instance what the form will look like on his website; form mail script is not needed at this stage.

➤ At the bottom of the form HTML enter a **submit input type** (`input type="submit"`) to add a button for the user to click on when they have completed their form.

KEYWORD

submit input type: an HTML form element which provides users with a button to click when they have completed a data entry form

```
63    <br><p>Enter the telephone number of an adult who has given you permis
64
65    <input type="submit" value="Email Form To Alex">
66
67
68   </form>
```

Enter the telephone number of

Email Form To Alex

➤ Save **competition.html** and run the page in your browser window.
➤ Click on the 'Email Form to Alex' button.

Nothing will happen at this stage as you have not told the browser what you want it to do when the button is clicked on by the user.

➤ We need to include an action attribute to tell the web browser what to do with the form once it is submitted by the user. The action is included within the opening **<form>** tag. Edit the opening form tag to read:

<form action="mailto:alex@webprogames" name=submit>

This will include an action attribute which provides an instruction to mail the form to alex@webprogames when the submit button is clicked.

```
46   <div class="w3-container w3-pale-yellow">
47
48   <h3>Competition Application Form </h3>
49   <form action="mailto:alex@webprogames.com" name="submit">
50
51   First name:   <input type="text" name="firstname"> <br>
52   Second name:  <input type="text" name="secondname"> <br>
53
54
55   Gender:
56   <input type="radio" name="gender" value= "Male"> Male
57   <input type="radio" name="gender" value= "Female"> Female
58   <input type="radio" name="gender" value= "Other"> Other
59   <br>
60
61   Age:   <input type="text" name="age"> <br>
62   Adults Telephone:   <input type="text" name="telephone">
63   <br><p>Enter the telephone number of an adult who has given you permis
64
65   <input type="submit" value="Email Form To Alex">
66
67
68   </form>
```

• You must have and adults permission to enter!

Competition Application Form

First name: [   ]
Second name: [   ]
Gender: ○ Male ○ Female ○ Other
Age: [   ]
Adults Telephone: [   ]

Enter the telephone number of an adult who has giv

Email Form To Alex

This allows us to apply the action attribute to the submit button added to the bottom of the form earlier.

➤ Save **competition.html** and run in the browser window.
➤ Click the 'Email Form to Alex' button to see what happens.
➤ Edit the mailto … instruction to include your email address.
➤ Complete the form with your details and click 'Email the Form to Alex'.
➤ If you are using the correct email application you will be able to check your emails to see what format the data is submitted in once it is emailed.

Introducing JavaScript: Validating form contents

Learn

To help ensure the correct type of data is entered by the user developers will often program a number of **validation checks** into the form.

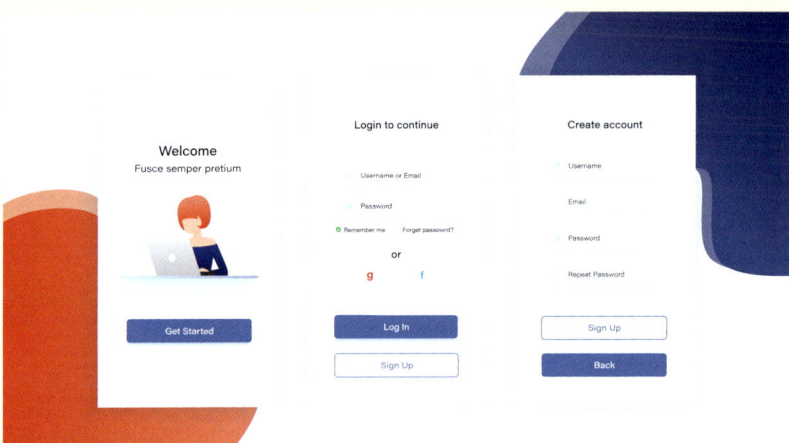

KEYWORDS

validation checks: checks carried out automatically during data input to help ensure only appropriate data is entered

client-side script: a small program which runs on the user's computer

server-side script: a program which runs on a web server in response to input from the web page user

Validation checks are normally carried out before the user submits the data in the form to the website owners. Most forms will have a button for the user to press when they have completed all of the details.

The code used to validate the data on the form is often run on the user's computer. Code which runs on the user's computer is an example of **client-side script**. Most developers will use JavaScript to do this.

When data is input and submitted to a web server it can sometimes lead to code being executed on the web server, rather than on the user's computer. The example used at the start of this chapter referred to checking a user's login details before allowing them access to a website, for example a gaming website. Another example could be checking a stock database on an online store to see if an item the user requested is in stock. Both are examples of **server-side script**. Once the code is executed on the webserver which hosts the website the results of processing, e.g. whether the item is in stock, will be sent back to the user. We will only look at client-side scripts in this chapter.

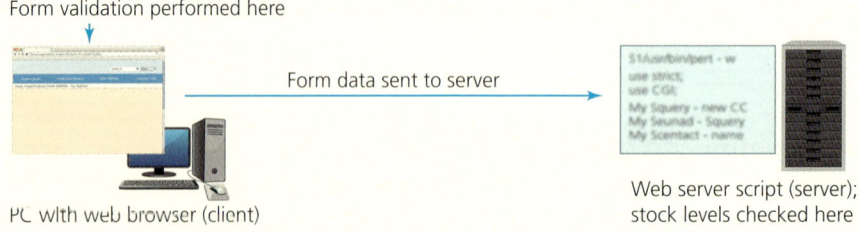

Form validation performed here

Form data sent to server

PC with web browser (client)

Web server script (server); stock levels checked here

Like CSS, JavaScript can be integrated into a web page in a variety of methods. It too can be included in-line, internally or as an external file which is accessed by an HTML document. The web browser knows it is using JavaScript rather than HTML or CSS as JavaScript instructions are enclosed inside the `<script> </script>` tags.

JavaScript can be used to validate user input before it is submitted by the user. To do this, a short JavaScript program or **function** can be added to the script tags to return a message to the user if the data they have entered into a form field is not valid. The JavaScript function need only be executed when a particular event occurs, for example when the user clicks a button on the screen. Programming used this way, which depends on input from the user, is called **event driven programming**.

The term 'function' is used to declare the start of each individual function or procedure, in this case the function is called **"validate _ form"**.

The data to be validated; for example, a value in the First name field in an application form, is read into the procedure as a parameter, indicated by **()** placed after the function name.

The script to be executed as part of the function **"validate _ form"** is written inside inside **{}**.

Script tags are added to the HTML document before the JavaScript function can be added.

```
 3  <head>
 4    <title> About Web-Pro Games </title> <!-- browser title -->
 5
 6    <link rel="stylesheet" href="https://www.w3schools.com/w3css/4/w3.css
 7
 8
 9  <script>
10
11    function validate_form()
12    {
13
14    }
15
16
17
18    </script>
19
20    </head>
21
22  <body>
23  <div class="w3-container w3-light-blue">
```

KEYWORDS

function: a sub-program designed to perform a particular task; a named unit of code that can be called in a program

event driven programming: when a portion of a program is only executed after an event occurs as the application is running; for example, the user clicks a button on screen

parameters: values or variables that are passed into a function from the main program; they are used in calculations and processing within the function

The script can now be edited to create a parameter which is linked to each data entry element in the HTML form.

Here the value in the **firstname** field in the form called **"apply"** is being read into the function called **validate_form** and it is being stored in a variable called **"x"**:

```
 9  <script>
10
11    function validate_form()
12    {
13
14    var x = document.forms["apply"]["firstname"].value;
15
16
17
18
19    }
20
21
22
23  </script>
```

Algorithmic thinking

Algorithmic thinking involves the use algorithms and combinations of coding constructs to help solve complex problems. We will look here at how we can combine HTML elements and attributes to develop a form which:

- ✪ could potentially be used to allow a user to submit the contents of a completed form by email
- ✪ can check each field is completed by the user before the form is submitted by email.

Practice

Now that the users are able to submit data we need to provide some client-side script to help validate the data they are entering in the form.

➤ Use the name attribute to give the form element the **name="apply"** in your competition.html file. See line 86 in the image below to help you understand how to edit the form element you have already added to competition.html.

> This means when the JavaScript is called to help validate the contents of the form it will only focus on this area of the HTML document.

```
79
80
81    <!-- add application form here -->
82
83    <div class="w3-container w3-pale-yellow">
84
85    <h3>Competition Application Form </h3>
86    <form name="apply" action="mailto:alex@webprogames.com" name="submit"
87
88    First name:    <input type="text" name="firstname"> <br>
89    Second name:   <input type="text" name="secondname"> <br>
90
```

We have given the form element the name **"apply"**.

Remember, on page 97, we applied the action attribute to the submit button added to the bottom of the form earlier. This means the user can now send the contents of form called **"apply"** by email to alex@webprogames when they click on the submit button at the bottom of the form.

➤ Add an opening and closing **<script> </script>** tag to the **<head> </head>** part of your **competition.html** document. The JavaScript you are going to use to help validate parts of the application form will be written inside **{}**. Remember, any parameters passed in and out of the function are represented using **()**.

> Functions are executed only when they are called so they are ideal for applications which use event driven processing.

Alex would like to make sure the user enters data into all of the text boxes on the competition entry form.

You will need to tell the browser which value you wish to check in the form fields in **competition.html**.

➤ Look at the code in **competition.html** where you created the text input box for the user to enter their name.

➤ You gave this text box the name **"firstname"**.

You want to tell the browser this is the value you want to validate.

You can use the following in your code to point to the value in the **"firstname"** text box.

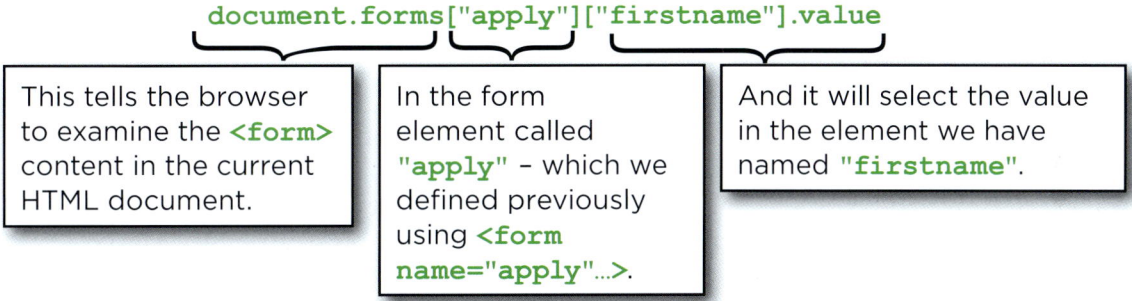

`document.forms["apply"]["firstname"].value`

| This tells the browser to examine the **<form>** content in the current HTML document. | In the form element called **"apply"** – which we defined previously using **<form name="apply"...>**. | And it will select the value in the element we have named **"firstname"**. |

This line of JavaScript will return the value that has been entered in the textbox **"firstname"** from the form called **"apply"**. Once we have that value, we can perform some validation on it just as we can in other programming languages.

Edit the **competition.html** to include JavaScript which can be used to validate the data being entered into the form by the user:

➤ Open Notepad++.

➤ Open **competition.html**.

➤ Edit the script tags to declare a new variable called **"x"**.

➤ Set **x** to be equal to **document.forms["apply"]["firstname"].value**.

> Don't forget the **;** at the end of the line of code.

```
competition.html ✕

 9   <script>
10
11     function validate_form()
12     {
13
14     var x = document.forms["apply"]["firstname"].value;
15
16
17
18
19     }
20
21
22
23   </script>
24
25   </head>
```

Use the following code to apply a **presence check** (a check to ensure this field is not left blank) to the input textbox you called `"firstname"`.

```
📁 competition.html ❌
 9   <script>
10
11   function validate_form()
12   {
13
14   var x = document.forms["apply"]["firstname"].value;
15
16
17       if (x =="")
18       {
19           alert("Please enter your First Name");
20           return false;
21       }
22
```

KEYWORD

presence check: a check to ensure a data entry field is not left blank

alert() in JavaScript is the same as print() in Python. It allows a program to display on screen messages for the user.

`==` is the 'equal to' symbol used in JavaScript.

Here we are checking If x is `""` (that is, has no value). If so, then this means that nothing has been entered into the `"firstname"` field in the form called `"apply"`.

If `x = ""` is TRUE, then the message 'Please enter your First Name' is displayed, and the 'return false' statement will stop the function from being executed until the user fixes the problem.

DID YOU KNOW?

In JavaScript the return false statement is used to prevent something from happening, so if you are trying to submit a form the return false will stop this from happening.

Now that we have added a validation check for the `firstname` text box in the `"apply"` form we need to provide an event so the function `validate_form` can be called and executed when the user tries to submit their application form.

➤ Edit the `<form>` tag to include a new attribute called `onsubmit`.

```
85   <div class="w3-container w3-pale-yellow">
86
87   <h3>Competition Application Form </h3>
88   <form name="apply" action="mailto:alex@webprogames.com" name="submit" onsubmit="return(validate_form());">
89
90   First name:  <input type="text" name="firstname"> <br>
91   Second name: <input type="text" name="secondname"> <br>
```

Now, when the user clicks the submit button on the HTML form:

➤ the user's browser will try to email the contents of the form to alex@ webprogames

➤ the `validate_form` function will be carried out.

Use this attribute to call the **validate_form** JavaScript function once the user clicks the 'Email the form....' button.

Using the return statement with the function name in this way allows the function to return messages back to the browser, such as error messages or an instruction to stop submitting the form.

When the `validate_form` function is executed it should take each field on the form (in turn) and:

1 Check to ensure it has not been left blank.

2 Display a message to the user to tell them what the problem is with the form.

3 Prevent the form from being submitted until the errors are corrected.

➤ Save **competition.html**.

➤ Run the page in the browser window.

➤ Click on the submit button without entering any data for First Name on the competition application form. The following message should now appear:

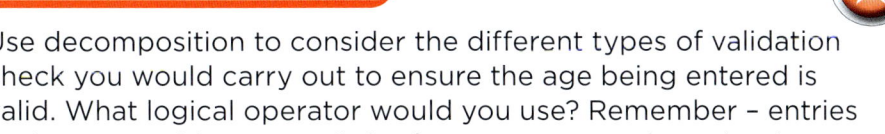

Young Game Developer Competition

- Do you think you have what it takes to be a game developer wi Pro Games?
- Let us see if you have what it takes. Enter our competition by fi the form b̶ nation pack.
- This compe ple aged between 11
- You must ter!

Competitio

First name: [   ]
Second name: [   ]
Gender: ○ Male ○ Female ○ Other
Age: [   ]
Adults Telephone: [   ]

Enter the telephone number of an adult who has given you permissic

Email Form To Alex

> Remember to create a variable for each value first, then create a link between the variable and the text box before adding the if statement to carry out the presence check.

➤ Repeat this process to create a suitable variable for the other text box fields in the competition application form.

Computational Thinking

Use decomposition to consider the different types of validation check you would carry out to ensure the age being entered is valid. What logical operator would you use? Remember – entries to the competition can only be from young people under the age of 15.

Go further

The competition is only open to children under the age of 15. Alex would like to include a validation check which first of all ensures users can only enter a numeric value for their age.

◆ Look at the code in **competition.html** where you created the text input box for the user to enter their age. We gave this text box the name **"age"**.

We want to tell the browser this is the value we want to validate. We can use the following to do so:

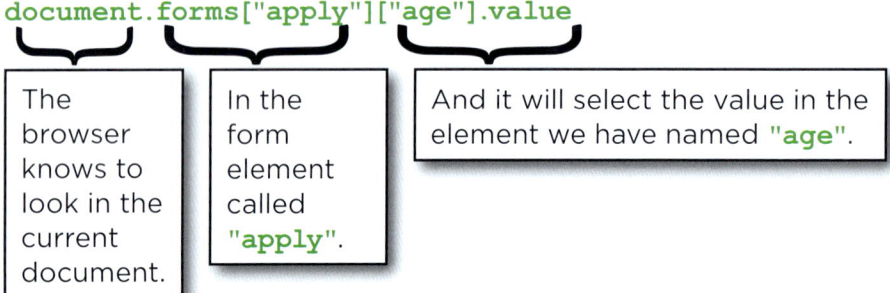

```
document.forms["apply"]["age"].value
```

| The browser knows to look in the current document. | In the form element called **"apply"**. | And it will select the value in the element we have named **"age"**. |

◆ We will need to assign this value to a variable and then carry out additional processing on the contents of that variable.
◆ We can use a special predefined JavaScript function **isNaN()** along with an IF statement to check if the age value entered into the form called **"apply"** is Not a Number (**isNaN**)

💾 competition.html ❎

```
1    <!\DOCTYPE html>
2    <html>
3    <head>
4     <title> About Web-Pro Games </title> <!-- browser title -->
5
6     <link rel="stylesheet" href="https://www.w3schools.com/w3css/4/w3.css"> <
7
8
9    <script>
10
11    function validate_form()
12    {
13
14        var y = document.forms["apply"]["age"].value;
15
16        if (isNaN(y))
17        {
18            alert("You must enter a number for your age")
19            return false;
20        }
```

◆ Save **competition.html**.
◆ Run the form in the browser.
◆ Try entering a text value as age.
◆ Click on the 'Email the form ...' button, the following message should appear:

the form below. We will send you an informa

- This competition is only open to young peopl
- You must have and adults permission to ente

Message from webpage ✕

⚠ You must enter a number for your age

OK

Gender: ○ Male ○ Female ○ Other

Age: t

Adults Telephone:

Challenge yourself

Alex has decided that he will limit the competition entry to young people between the ages of 10 and 15.

He has asked you to include this as a final validation check on the application form.

We have already assigned the input age to the variable y on page 104. We can use this variable to perform another validation check on the age value This is time we will create a range check which only allows inputs between a certain range of values.

The pseudocode for this validation check is:

```
if (age is < 10 OR age is >15)

    display an alert("Sorry you are not the correct age for this
    competition");

    stop executing this event (submitting this form)
```

You may remember that OR is a Boolean operator. Instead of using words for Boolean operators, JavaScript uses symbols. The symbol for the OR operator is **||**.

With a friend discuss how you would complete the following JavaScript code to ensure only young people between the ages of 10 and 15 could participate in the competition.

```
if (y _____ || y _____)

{

    _____ ("Sorry you are not the correct
    age for this competition");

    _____;

}
```

➤ Edit the code in **validate_form()** so that the age range is now limited to between 10 and 15 years of age.

➤ Save **competition.html**.

➤ Test your validation check by entering an age outside the allowed age range.

You will notice that we now have two separate If statements used to validate age on **"apply"** form.

With a friend discuss how you could make this more efficient. The following pseudocode might help you:

```
If (Is Not a Number (y) OR y <10 OR y >15)

        display an alert ("Please enter a value between 10 and 15");

        stop executing this event (submitting this form)
```

Use this pseudocode to help you edit the code in **validate_form()** so that the validation check to ensure a number is entered and the age range on age (between 10 and 15) are carried out using only one IF statement

➤ Save **competition.html**.

➤ Test your validation check by entering an age outside the allowed age range and by typing in a letter instead of a number.

Final project

Alex has decided to change the third page on his website. Instead of providing users with a sample game plan and tutorials he has decided to provide a local coding training camp for young people who would like additional experience in programming.

Alex has asked you to design and create the third page for him.

It should contain

➤ some details about the date, time and location of the training camp which will be held in your school (your school can decide on the date and time for the camp)

➤ details of the age group the training camp is open to (under 15s only)

➤ a map of the area so potential visitors can find the school

➤ a hyperlink to the Google maps website so they can get directions to your school (www.google.com/maps)

➤ an application form which collects the name, address and age of anyone who is interested; the application should be validated.

The web page should have the same look and feel as the other pages in the website so should include the same CSS classes and styles and hyperlinks in the same location.

> Change the name of the file **sample.html** to **course.html** and don't forget to update your hyperlinks on the other web pages (**index.html** and **competition. html**) so all navigation links work correctly.

Evaluation

Now that the website is complete it is important that you test all parts of the site to make sure they work correctly before Alex takes ownership of it.

✪ Open **index.html** and test all of the hyperlinks in the navigation section.

✪ Browse to the Courses page you created.

o Ensure that your map image opens and displays correctly.

o Ensure that your hyperlink to Google maps works correctly.

o Click on your submit button for the course application form.

o Test each text box in the form to make sure the user cannot leave it blank.

o Test the age text entry box to make sure that anyone over the age of 15 cannot apply.

✪ Ask a friend to test and evaluate your web page. Ask them if they think the layout, font, text style and general look of the page matches the look and feel of the rest of the website.

o Make a note of their comments and if you have time make changes to improve your website.

o Make a note of any changes you made and why.

Why network computers?

In 1837, Charles Babbage created one of the first computer designs. It was called the 'Analytical Engine'. Charles Babbage and Ada Lovelace, a nineteenth century writer and mathematician, worked on the design together. Ada Lovelace has been called the world's first computer programmer.

Lovelace wrote an algorithm that was meant to be processed by Babbage's computer. The computer was never built but Ada's contribution was considered to be very important. She realised that computers could be used for much more than just calculations.

▲ Ada Lovelace, a nineteenth century writer and mathematician.

Early computers were standalone and could not easily share data. Today, the world's computer networks exchange massive amounts of data every second. Cyber security specialists work to ensure the data is kept safe as it travels around the world. They use techniques such as encryption to protect data from hackers and cyber security threats.

In this unit you will learn about:

→ the different types of networks and their advantages and disadvantages
→ the hardware required to connect networks
→ the different wireless technologies used in networks
→ how data travels on a network
→ the role of encryption in protecting data
→ legal issues relating to the use of computers.

KEYWORDS

encryption: a process which scrambles data making it unreadable; the data can only be read by someone who has the key to decode it

hacker: a person who has gained unauthorised access to a network or computer with intent to damage or destroy it

cyber security: protecting systems, data and software from digital attacks

Why is cyber security important?

SCENARIO

GreatEng is a new engineering company. The company has three small offices in different major cities. The director of the company has asked you to come into its offices and review its use of computing technology. The company has a large number of computers and printing devices. Employees send designs and client data between the different offices every day. Your task is to provide GreatEng with advice on its current set-up and methods of improving its technology layout. You will be expected to offer advice to the company based on the content of a report template your teacher will download for you.

But before you can do that, you need to understand the main concepts behind networks and the effects of using them.

Do you remember?

Before starting this unit you should know:

✔ how businesses make use of VoIP and video conferencing and social media

✔ the importance of digital communication systems to businesses and how they rely on LANs and WANs

✔ how businesses ensure that they use technology safely and the threats to cyber security

✔ how to create and edit a simple movie

✔ how to create and edit a simple sound recording

✔ how to use the internet to research information.

Making networks work

Learn

Remember that a LAN is a local area network and a WAN is a wide area network. A LAN which is connected using wireless technology is called a wireless local area network (WLAN).

Modern businesses rely on networks – they are an essential part of their day-to-day business. A network is used to share information both inside and outside of the organisation.

This table lists some of the advantages and disadvantages of networks.

Advantages of networks	Disadvantages of networks
Sharing hardware devices like laser printers. Installing software once on the file server, which gives all computers on the network access. When files are stored on a file server they can be shared across the organisation. Communication can be done via email and instant messaging. Users can log on at any computer and access their files. Backup of data on the file server is carried out to ensure that there is no loss of important information. Security on the network can be managed centrally by a network manager who can give users different levels of access.	If a large number of users are logged on using large data files or complex software applications, then the network performance can be slowed down. If a virus enters the system it can spread quickly to all computers and data on the network. So, it is important that a network has up-to-date virus software installed to protect it. Setting up and managing a network can be expensive as hardware such as file servers and routers needs to be purchased. Some networks require a dedicated network manager to manage the network and ensure good day-to-day performance.

> Backing up data means safely storing a copy of the data in case the original data is damaged or lost.

> Different levels of access might mean that some users cannot install software on their computers.

How a network is put together

A LAN links computers in buildings together using different types of network cables or through wireless connections (WLAN). Data is transmitted from one computer to another along these cables or wireless connections. Computer networks are constructed using a combination of the following components:

File server

A **file server** is the main computer on the network. It is more powerful than all of the other computers with a large amount of memory and hard disk space. A network file server will hold:

➤ network operating system software

➤ application software such as LibreOffice

➤ user data files created by the users on the system

➤ system software which will manage the network resources and security

➤ utility software such as a virus checker.

The file server manages files and network security across the network and makes sure that only authorised users log on to the system. The log on process makes use of usernames and passwords.

Network interface card

The network cable is inserted into the port shown. This connects the network.

Each computer must have a network interface card (NIC) so that it can communicate with the file server and all other computers on the network. The network card provides a port for the network cable. You can see an example of an NIC that can connect to a wired network in the picture above.

Most computers, laptops and devices are wireless enabled. This means that they have a wireless network interface card (WNIC) already installed, which allows them to connect to a wireless network.

Network cables

Computers can be connected to a network using network cables. The cables plug directly into the network card contained inside each computer and data travels along the cables to and from the file server. Network cables are often made of copper but parts of the network may also use fibre optic cables.

DID YOU KNOW?
Fibre optic cables transmit data carrying pulses of light and data can travel at high speeds.

KEYWORDS

backup: a copy of data stored safely in case the original data is destroyed or damaged

security: the protection of data and hardware on the network

file server: the main computer on the network; it holds data and software and manages security and backup

username: a unique name given to a user on a network which can be used to log on

password: a set of characters known only to the user which is used with the username to log on

network interface card: an internal hardware device which enables a computer to connect to a network using a cable

wireless enabled: the capability to connect to a Wi-Fi network

Wi-Fi: the technology that allows a device to connect to the internet at high speed without the use of wires; the technology uses radio signals to transmit data

wireless network interface card (WNIC): an internal hardware device that allows the computer to connect wirelessly to the network

network cables: generally copper cables used to link each computer in the network to the file server

Switches

A **switch** is a single connection point for a group of computers. The switch is connected to the file server and organises communication between the file server and the computers connected to it. Switches route data to specific computers on the network.

Hub

A network **hub** is computer hardware used to connect a number of computers together. Hubs are used for small local area networks (LANs). Hubs are very similar to switches except that they send data to all computers connected to them, rather than specific computers. This makes them less efficient but they are a cheap and easy way to connect computers so that they can share resources like internet connections.

Router

A **router** is hardware which connects networks together. A router is most commonly used to connect a LAN to the internet. A router can be wired or wireless.

A **wireless router** has a **wireless access point (WAP)** built in to it – this allows a computer to connect to a LAN.

This equipment is important as it allows employees within a company to move desks and take their laptop with them while remaining connected to the network.

Home broadband 'routers' are often a combination of a switch and a router.

A router may have a security feature, such as a **firewall**, integrated into it.

> A firewall monitors and filters data entering and leaving the network. It uses security settings or rules which block data which does not comply with the organisation's security policy.

Bridges

A network **bridge** joins two separate computer networks.
The network bridge enables communication between the two networks and provides a way for them to work as a single network. Bridges can extend local area networks to cover a larger physical area than the LAN can reach.

KEYWORDS

switch: a device which is a connection point for a group of computers on a network; the device is then connected to the server; switches can send data to the correct computer on the network as each computer is connected to a switch

hub: computer hardware used to connect a number of computers together; they are similar to switches except they send all data to all connected computers; there are also USB hubs which are used to connect a number of devices to a computer

router: a hardware device which connects networks together; for instance, a LAN and the internet

wireless router: combines the functions of a router and a wireless access point

wireless access point (WAP): a hardware device that allows other Wi-Fi devices to connect to a wired network

firewall: hardware or software designed to prevent or allow access to a private network; it can prevent unauthorised internet users from accessing the network

bridge: a network bridge†joins two separate computer networks and enables communication between them

Decomposition

A network is a complex structure made up of many different devices and other components such as cables. You are going to use decomposition to break the network into individual components and show them on a diagram or map.

✪ Look at this diagram of a network. Use the words in the list below to label the different parts of the network, 1–10.

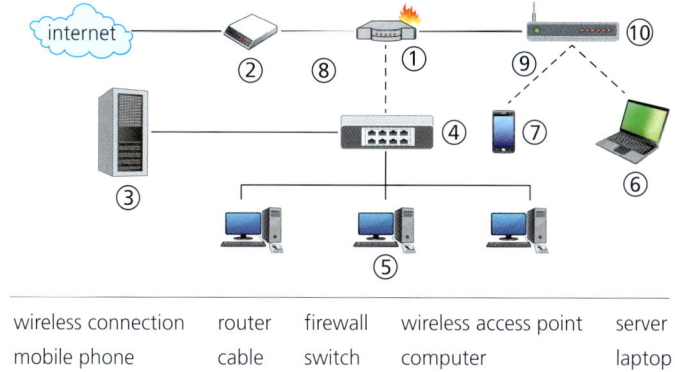

wireless connection	router	firewall	wireless access point	server
mobile phone	cable	switch	computer	laptop

✪ When you have completed the diagram, make a list of the 10†items in the diagram and add a brief explanation of what each one does on the network. You can do this using a word processor or pen and paper.

✪ Using the diagram above and your list of items, research a network at school or at home and see if you can identify each of the items on the list.

Practice

➤ GreatEng uses standalone computers in some sections of the company. You have been asked by the owner to complete a report on the problems with using standalone computers and why the company should connect all computers to the network. Your report should contain the following sections:
  o the problems with using stand-alone computers
  o the advantages of using a network.
➤ Your report should also contain a list of the equipment required to make the network work.
➤ You can use a word processor to complete the report.

Wireless working

Learn

Bring your own device: Using Wi-Fi and Bluetooth on a network

A personal area network (PAN) is a computer network which is used to transmit data between different personal devices and for connecting to the main network. The network covers a small range close to the individual user.

A wireless personal area network (WPAN) makes use of Wi-Fi and **Bluetooth** to connect devices.

Wi-Fi and Bluetooth are communication technologies which allow devices to connect to a network wirelessly.

Access to Wi-Fi, through wireless access points (WAPs), can be found in many public locations, providing free wireless internet access, for example, in schools, businesses, hotels and airports. In these situations passwords may not be required or the password is publicly displayed in the location. Secured Wi-Fi networks require the user to provide a password in order to log on and passwords are only made available to authorised users.

How does Wi-Fi work?

A Wi-Fi network makes use of radio waves to send data across a network. It works in the following way:

1 When uploading files, digital data is translated into a radio signal by the computer's **wireless adapter**.

2 This radio signal is then sent, via an antenna, to the router.

3 The router (which contains a switch) will decode the signal, convert it back to digital data and send it to the internet through a wired connection.

4 When data is received back from the internet, it passes through the router and is converted to a radio signal that can be received by the computer's wireless adapter.

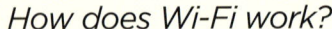

internet

Webcam
HDD
Cable modem
Printer
Mp3 player
Wireless router
Media PC
Desktop PC
Wireless media player
IP camera
Digital camera
Smartphone
Laptop
Entertainment system

This table outlines the advantages and disadvantages of Wi-Fi for a business.

Advantages of Wi-Fi for a business	Disadvantages of Wi-Fi for a business
• Wi-Fi capability is integrated into a wide range of mobile computing devices such as computers, laptops, printers, smartphones. • It is simple to connect a device to the network therefore it is easy to expand the network. • Provides mobility within an organisation as users can log on in any location using a wide range of devices. • Networks can be set up without wires. • Wi-Fi networks can be protected to ensure only authorised users can log on.	• Wi-Fi networks are limited by their range – devices will lose connection if they move away from the WAP after a certain distance. • Signal strength can vary according to how close you are to the wireless router. • The data transfer rate to individual computers may decrease when the number of devices connected to the Wi-Fi network increases. • The connection may not be secure. Some Wi-Fi networks may not be properly secured and may allow others to 'snoop' on devices using the network. This is usually because encryption methods have not been correctly implemented.

A Wi-Fi network is created by placing WAPs in many locations around a building. The signal from the WAPs should overlap so that there are no **black spots** and users can walk freely from one room to another with a continuous signal.

Data transmission speeds are measured in **megabits per second (Mbps) or gigabits per second (Gbps)**, where 1 bit is a 0 or 1. (1 Gbps = 1000 Mbps.)

Speed: Newer Wi-Fi 6 connections can transmit at a maximum of 9.6 Gbps. But most Wi-Fi is slower than this.

Range: Wi-Fi can be accessed up to 45 metres from a router or WAP.

How does Bluetooth work?

Bluetooth is radio wave technology designed to communicate over short distances of less than 10 metres. This means that the devices communicating must be relatively close together. It is used to download photos from digital cameras, to link hands-free headsets to mobile phones, to connect a mouse to a laptop and for many other purposes. Bluetooth uses less power than other wireless technologies and is much cheaper to use. Bluetooth enabled devices

can connect directly together at no cost, without the need for a router or a provider. This technology is targeted at voice and data transfer applications.

Bluetooth devices automatically detect and connect to each another.

1 Each pair of devices randomly pick a **channel** from those available; if that channel is taken they pick another one.

> Bluetooth uses a different frequency of radio waves than Wi-Fi.

2 During communication the pair of devices shift frequency. This helps prevents interference from other electrical appliances and improves security.

3 Up to eight Bluetooth devices can link at one time and they form a network called a **piconet**. Each device can join or leave the piconet at any time. Bluetooth devices have to be synchronised or paired when joining a piconet. Each device may have to enter a code to ensure that it has permission to join the network.

This table outlines some of the advantages and disadvantages of Bluetooth.

Advantages of Bluetooth	Disadvantages of Bluetooth
<ul><li>Can penetrate solid objects</li><li>Does not need line of sight</li><li>Low cost</li><li>Less power used</li><li>Easily connects to other Bluetooth enabled devices</li></ul>	<ul><li>Lower level of security</li><li>Data transmission rate is lower than other wireless technologies</li><li>Short range</li></ul>

The range of a Bluetooth device depends on the class of Bluetooth being used.

Class of Bluetooth device	Intended range
Class 3	<10 metres
Class 2	10 metres
Class 1	100 metres

Class 1 devices use more power than class 2, which use more power than class 3.

Speed: Bluetooth can transmit at speeds of up to 5 Mbps.

Supporting the WAN: Satellite transmission

Much of the Earth is covered in water and so using cables for data transmission is not always possible nor cost effective. Satellites orbit the earth and have many uses, for example in navigation and GPS, to monitor weather and to support digital communication. Communication satellites are connected together to create a global network, covering vast and remote areas where it is not practical to use cables.

Communications satellites can be used to send and receive radio signals for all types of communications including television, telephone and internet. Each different type of communication signal is converted to radio waves and then sent from a transmitting **satellite dish** to a receiving satellite.

DID YOU KNOW?

The majority of satellite dishes have been designed to receive data – only some satellite dishes can transmit and receive data.

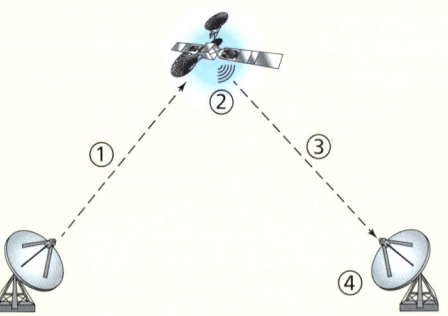

Communication is completed in stages:

1 A satellite dish somewhere on Earth transmits a signal to a satellite.
2 The satellite receives the signal, increases the strength of the signal (amplifies it) and then changes the frequency of the signal so that there is no confusion between incoming and outgoing signals.
3 The signal is transmitted back to a different location on Earth.
4 The signal arrives at the receiving satellite dish somewhere on Earth.

DID YOU KNOW?

Companies can connect to cloud-based services using a WAN. These services are available via the internet and include software applications, data storage facilities and communication tools like email. iCloud is an example of a cloud based service.

KEYWORDS

Bluetooth: a short-range technology used to connect devices together; it uses radio waves to communicate
wireless adapter: the general term used for a device that can connect a laptop or computer to a wireless network
black spot: an area which is not covered by Wi-Fi
megabits per second (Mbps) and gigabits per second (Gbps): the speed of data transfer; 1Mbps means one million (1000000) bits are transmitted each second; 1Gbps means one billion (1000000000) bits are transmitted each second
channel: a particular frequency at which data is transmitted on a particular network
piconet: a temporary network formed when two or more Bluetooth devices connect together
satellite dish: a dish-shaped aerial used to transmit and receive data

Practice

Wireless technology is used in many places in our everyday lives. In your school and home you will see many examples of this.

This is Dara. He plays games online and makes use of a games console to connect to the internet.

Dara uses the following devices:
➤ wireless controller
➤ wireless headphones
➤ games console
➤ mobile phone.

Dara needs both Bluetooth and Wi-Fi to play the games online. His family also has a satellite dish for connection to a WAN. Dara does not know what each is used for when he is playing so he has come into school to ask his friends about the different technologies.

You are going to create a movie to help Dara understand the technology.
➤ First, copy and complete the following tables:

Devices which use Bluetooth to connect together	Devices which use Wi-Fi to connect together

	Bluetooth	Wi-Fi	Satellite
Range			
Speed/performance			
How it works			
Advantages			
Disadvantages			
How does Dara use this technology?			

➤ With a friend, use the information in the tables to create a script for your movie. The script should explain to Dara:
  o the basics about Bluetooth, Wi-Fi and satellite
  o which wireless technology, if any, each of his devices uses
  o what a PAN is and which of his devices might create a PAN.

➤ Edit the movie using MovieMaker or another simple video editing tool so that it runs smoothly. The movie should:
  o last no more than two to three minutes
  o have an introductory screen naming the people who produced it
  o have music overlaid in at least one section
  o contain a voiceover in at least one section
  o have final credits thanking those students who took part.

➤ Review your movie and discuss the use of wireless technology in your school.
  o Are there any black spots? Why do you think this is?
  o What are students using Wi-Fi and Bluetooth for?
  o Are there any improvements that could be made?

➤ GreatEng will be using both Bluetooth and Wi-Fi technology in their offices. Recommend an appropriate technology for each of the following tasks, and explain why.

Task	Wi-Fi or Bluetooth	Why?
The receptionist uses a headset to connect to the telephone system		
The engineers log on to GreatEng's computer system to access designs stored in the office		
The engineers transfer files from their mobile phone to their laptop		
The secretary uses a wireless keyboard and mouse to operate a computer		
The employees save data to a cloud-based server		
The manager sends an email to all customers to inform them about costs for services		

Getting technical: Routing data

Learn

Think about the amount of information moving around the internet. Have you ever wondered how each piece of information gets to the correct destination?

Imagine you want to stream a song from a music provider such as *Spotify*. The song must be streamed from the internet to your device. When the song plays it seems as though your computer is connected directly to the provider. But this is not the case. If the internet was made up of direct connections it could not cope with all of the people using it.

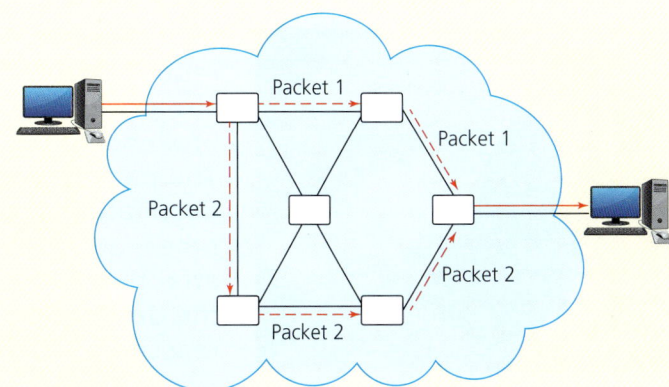

When information is transmitted across the internet it does not need to follow a direct path to the destination computer and nor does it need to be sent in one chunk. Instead, in the example of streaming a song, the data is sent from a *Spotify* web server via lots of different routers across the internet until it finally reaches your computer. The data that makes up the song being streamed is broken down into a number of **packets**.

Each packet of data contains details of the **internet protocol (IP) addresses** of its destination and where it came from, and a packet number relating to its order in the overall data (in other words, which part of the song it represents).

Imagine this scenario ...

A customer orders a large sofa from a furniture manufacturer. The sofa is too large to send in one piece, so it is delivered in parts. The manufacturer sends five packages, labelled 1 to 5 to the customer address, containing all the parts of the sofa. The packages are sent out on different trucks and each truck takes a different route to the customer's house. The truck with package 2 has been held up due to heavy motorway traffic. The customer receives the packages one at a time in the following order 4, 3, 1, 5, 2. When all of the packages have arrived, the customer can put the parts together to create the sofa. Packets of data are managed in a similar way.

Routers manage the movement of packets from the source to the destination computer, based on the destination internet protocol (IP) address.

The router selects the best route for each packet to travel to reach its destination. Each packet may travel a different route, as network traffic changes constantly. The objective is to get the packet to the destination using the most efficient route.

Packets may arrive at different times and in any order.

When all packets have arrived, the data that makes up the song is reassembled and checked for any errors at the destination computer.

All types of digital data can be transmitted using this approach.

> Having options for data packets to take different routes makes the network **fault tolerant**. That is, if parts of the network are damaged it can still transmit packets of data simply by selecting an alternative route. This feature makes the internet reliable for transmitting data.

So, when you request the song from a streaming service, the song is broken into packets before being transmitted. The packets are sent along various routes to their destination IP address and arrive at different times, out of order. In order for the song to play effectively, all packets must be present and the destination computer must know how to reassemble the packets correctly.

The computer knows how to do this because as well as the song data, each data packet contains some other information called protocols. Different protocols do different things:

TCP/IP is a communications protocol used on networks which helps to ensure reliable transfer of data on a fault tolerant network based on IP addresses.

Transmission control protocol (TCP) is one part of the TCP/IP protocol which checks the data packets to ensure they are present before sending an acknowledgement for each packet received. If any packets are missing, TCP will request that the missing packets are re-sent. Once all of the packets arrive, the song can then be played. This process happens every time an email is sent or an image is downloaded.

IP addresses

An IP address is a number which uniquely identifies a hardware device on a network and makes it easy to send information to that device using the TCP/IP protocol.

There are two types of IP address: IPv4 and IPv6.

An IPv4 address looks like this

191.103.72.101 (this is IPv4, an older standard that is scheduled to 'run out' of unique addresses).

An IPv6 address looks like this:

2001 : adb8: 3333 : 4444 : 5555 : 6666 : 7777 : 8888 (this is the new standard for IP addresses, which uses a hexadecimal numbering system and which will allow trillions of devices to have unique addresses).

No two computers on the internet have the same IP address.

It is important that a unique IP address is assigned to your computer. If two devices on a network have†the same IP address, there will be a problem. The internet will not work on one or both of them, depending on the router.

Small networks have a dynamic host configuration protocol (DHCP) server, usually the router, which assigns IP addresses to devices on a network every time they connect to it. It is also possible to manually assign an IP address to your computer, but first you must check what format the address should take.

If a device is connected to a network you can view its IP address in the control panel. The connection details (right) show an IP address for a computer on a network.

An IP address along with a **subnet mask** is used to determine the network that a computer is on.

A subnet mask defines the range of IP addresses that can be used on a network.

The subnet mask 255.255.255.0 tells us that the IP†addresses of computers within the subnet (or sub network) must have the same value in the first three sections. The last section of the IP address can have any value between 0 and 255.

For example the IP addresses 10.0.2.198 and 10.0.2.199 would be in the same subnet. But 10.0.1.198 would not.

> You can access your public IP address by going to the Settings section of your computer. This is an example of what you might see:
>
> **Properties**
>
> | | |
> |---|---|
> | IPv4 address: | 10.154.135.8 |
> | IPv4 DNS servers: | 10.181.128.7 |
> | Primary DNS suffix: | CE3.EN.Net |
> | Manufacturer: | Realtek |
> | Description: | Realtek PCIe GBE Family Controller |
> | Physical address (MAC): | D8-9E-F3-87-86-AA |

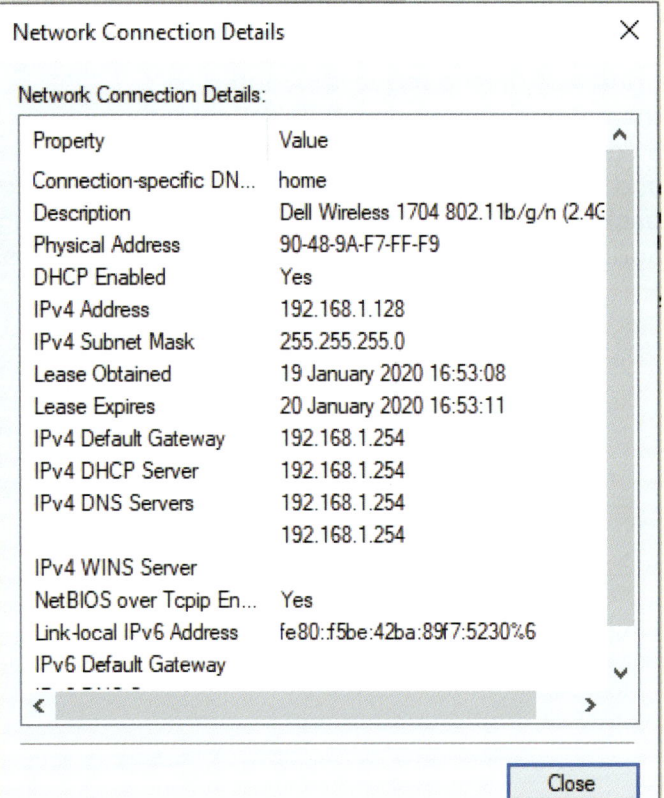

The subnet mask 255.255.255.0 tells us that 256 devices can connect to the sub network and each device will have a unique IP address.

Devices on the same subnet can talk to each other without going through the router.

Larger networks with several thousand computers may use a subnet mask of 255.255.0.0. This tells us that there could be 256 devices on each of 256 sub networks.

Private IP addresses are used inside a local area network. They are used by computers, smartphones, gaming consoles and wireless printers. These IP addresses allow the devices to communicate with the router and all other devices on the network. They are private because they are internal to the network and cannot be accessed across the internet.

Public IP addresses can be accessed over the internet. They are assigned by the internet service provider. This is the main address that the local network uses to communicate with the internet. Usually this address is assigned to the router. The public†IP address allows all devices on the network to communicate with computers around the globe.

IP addresses and web pages

When you type a URL into the browser, using TCP/IP the request is routed to the correct web server. TCP/IP creates a connection between your computer and the web server. The required web page is then broken into packets and the process of data transmission begins. Web addresses are user-friendly forms of IP addresses.

Imagine trying to remember an IP address instead of a web address.

KEYWORDS

packet: unit of data which travels along a network as a single package

internet protocol (IP) address: a unique address which identifies an individual device on the internet

fault tolerant: the capability of a computer network to continue operating if a problem occurs

TCP/IP: a combination of communications protocols which allows devices on the internet to connect and send and receive data, using IP addresses

transmission control protocol (TCP): a network communications protocol for ensuring that data packets are sent error-free over the internet

subnet mask: divides an IP address into the network address and the host address and allows networks to be divided up for better performance

private IP address: an IP address that is allocated to a networked device and is internal to the network

public IP address: an IP address that is allocated to a device on the internet by the internet service provider; it is the main gateway through which data will enter a LAN from the internet

Practice

You are going to check an IP address for your own computer.

➤ Access the Control Panel on your PC.
➤ Click 'Network and internet', then 'Network and Sharing Center'.
➤ Click the Wi-Fi connection.
➤ When the Wi-Fi Status box appears, click on the 'Details...' button.

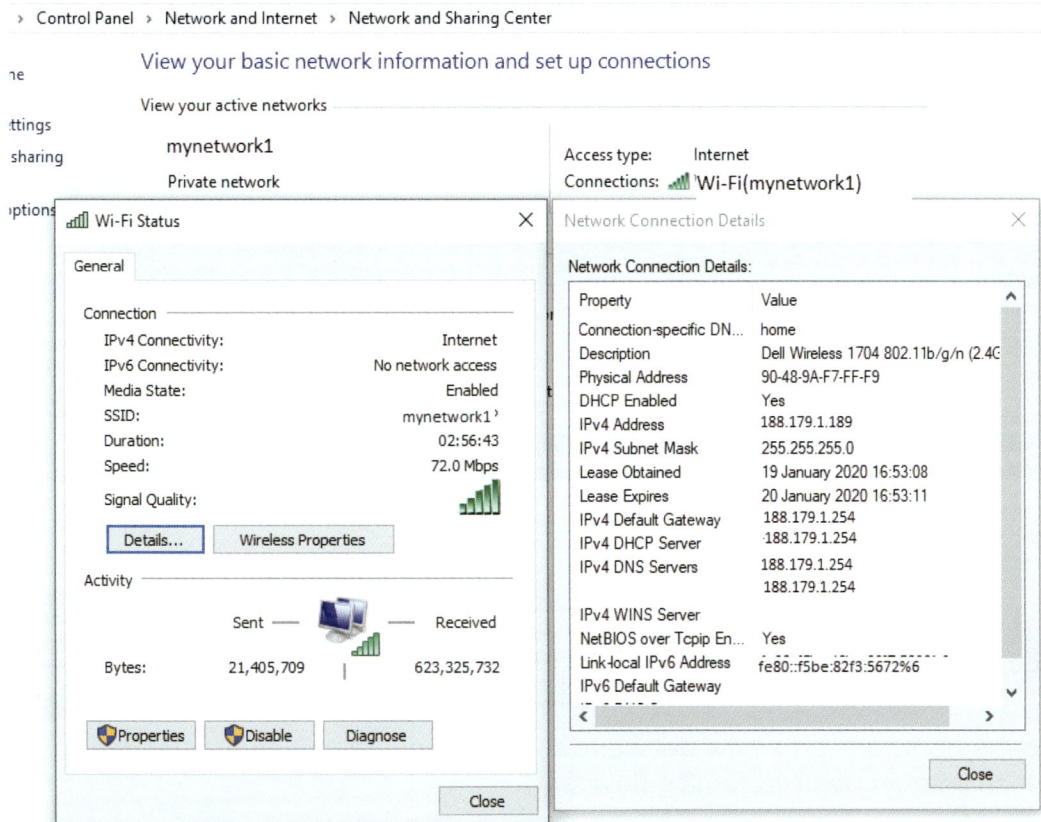

You can also go to the Command Prompt by typing 'cmd' in the search bar and pressing enter. Then type ipconfig into the Command Prompt box and press enter.

Command Prompt

```
C:\>ipconfig
```

This is the sort of information you will see.

```
Link-local IPv6 Address. .. : fe80::f5be:82f3:5672%6
IPv4 Address . . . . . . . : 180.193.1.128
Subnet Mask . . . . . . . : 255.255.255.0
Default Gateway . . . . .. : 180.193.1.254
```

➤ Write down the IP address and the subnet mask.

➤ Look at the IP information above. Explain how the format of the IPv4 address is correct if the computer is using the subnet mask 255.255.255.0. (Look at the section above on subnet masks to remind yourself about how the subnet mask determines what IP addresses can be used.)

GreatEng is opening a new office and needs to implement a network. You have been asked to interview candidates for the post of Network Technician. The Network Technician is expected to understand all aspects of routing data, IP addresses, subnet masks, TCP/IP and public and private IP addresses.

Here are some of the interview questions:

Interview questions

You will need to refer to these sets of data:

Data set 1: Data from a computer on the company's network
Link-local IPv6 Address. . . . . : fe80::f5be:82f3:5672%6
IPv4 Address . . . . : 180.193.1.128
Subnet Mask . . . . :255.255.255.0
Default Gateway . . . . : 180.193.1.254

Data set 2: Data from an employee's mobile phone using the network	
IP Address	180.193.1.124
Subnet Mask	255.255.255.0
Router	180.193.1.254

1. What is the function of an IP address?

2. Explain the difference between the two IP addresses in Data set 1.

3. How can you tell that the computer and the mobile phone are on the same network?

4. The company wants to add a new device to the network. Write down a suitable IP†address that could be used for the device.

5. What is the difference between a public and private IP address?

6. Explain how packet switching and IP addresses are used to transmit data on a network.

➤ Write a set of model answers to these six questions.

➤ With a partner, carry out the interview with you as the interviewer asking your questions and then swap around. You should record each interview.

➤ When you have both completed the interviews play back the recordings to review your knowledge and understanding. Discuss between the two of you whether you think each candidate would get the job and why?

➤ Make a list of your reasons why the job was or was not given to each person. This can be provided to GreatEng to help them select the Technician.

Data on the move

Learn

The manager of the new office at GreatEng has to buy the equipment and devices for the new network. There are many devices that could help improve the business but here are some he can buy.

Device	Advantages	Disadvantages
Laptop with WNIC, Wi-Fi and Bluetooth	When connected to a wireless LAN, laptops can access the server and all peripherals available to network users The laptop can connect to Bluetooth enabled devices such as printers, other laptops, cameras More portable than desktop PCs; employees can move around the office and log in to the LAN from any location	Expensive Smaller screens than desktop monitors Usually slower than desktop PCs
Tablets with Wi-Fi and Bluetooth	Smaller and lighter than laptops Portable Larger screens and keyboards than mobile phones, making online reading and typing easier for users	Smaller screens than laptops and desktop monitors On screen keyboards can be difficult to use compared to keyboards used for desktops
Mobile phone with 5G, Wi-Fi and Bluetooth	Can be used to connect to other mobile phones and the network for file transfer Can connect directly to the internet using 5G or via Wi-Fi Portable People are more likely to have a smartphone Much easier to access the internet whilst on the move as the device is hand held	Small screens and keyboards can limit the user in what they can do A website which does not have a version for smartphones will not display properly

KEYWORD

5G: fifth generation mobile networks providing high speed data transfer

Practice

GreatEng is going to purchase some mobile devices for the new office. The new office will be involved in creating engineering designs for clients. This involves using a complex software package to create the design, printing the designs and emailing designs to clients. They have a budget of $20 000 and they want to buy laptops, tablets and mobile phones for staff. There are 20 members of staff. Each member of staff must have a laptop and either a tablet OR a mobile phone. At least three members of staff require a high-performance laptop.

➤ Prepare a one-page electronic catalogue, suitable for emailing, which will show the possible devices that could be used.

➤ You can use the internet to research the devices that may be useful to the staff at GreatEng.

➤ Your catalogue should include:
   o a picture of each device
   o the possible uses for the devices in the company
   o the advantages and disadvantages of using each device
   o the current price of the device and the number of devices you would buy for the office
   o the overall cost of buying a number of the devices for the office.
   You can use a graphics package or a word processor to produce the catalogue page.

➤ The company needs to buy two wireless access points. The manager has suggested two devices:

	Device 1	Device 2
Connectivity technology	Wireless	Wireless (Wi-Fi 6)
Data transfer rate	1300 MBps	up to 6 Gbit/s
Frequency band	2.4 GHz	5 GHz

Wi-Fi 6 is the next generation Wi-Fi; it is almost 10 times faster than standard Wi-Fi

➤ Create a document which explains:
   o why a WAP is required for the network
   o the difference between the connectivity technology and the data transfer rates for the two WAP devices above
   o the differences between the 2.4 GHz and 5 GHz frequency bands (you will need to conduct some research for this).

➤ Discuss the WAP devices with a friend and together recommend one of the WAP points for use in the office.

Keeping it all secure

Learn

Data which travels on a network or on the internet needs to be protected. Think about the amount of data which travels every day on the internet. This data contains personal details about people, bank details and important information relating to business and commerce. What if the data is intercepted by a hacker (someone who wants to steal or destroy information that does not belong to them) or is accidentally received by the wrong person?

Data must be secure when it is moving on a network. One way of ensuring that the data is safe is to use encryption. Encryption has been around for a long time – long before computers were invented. An early form of encryption was in the form of ciphers.

Ciphers are examples of symmetrical encryption. A cipher uses a 'secret' key to change the original message. The sender and receiver need to know the key in order to encrypt and decrypt the message. One disadvantage of this method is that all of the people involved need to know the key and so it may be easy for hackers to get the key and decode the message.

> **DID YOU KNOW?**
> Honey encryption creates encoded text used to trick hackers. The hacker guesses an encryption password, but honey encryption always outputs realistic-looking data, even for incorrect passwords. This means a hacker does not know when they have guessed the right password. This type of encryption is constantly growing and it prevents hackers from getting access to important, encrypted information.

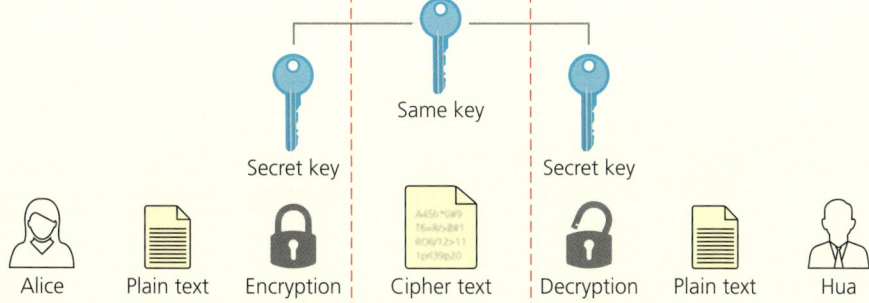

Alice — Plain text — Encryption — Cipher text — Decryption — Plain text — Hua

Let's look at three methods of symmetrical encryption: Caesar's cipher, tic-tac-toe cipher and atbash cipher.

Julius Caesar was an ancient Roman emperor who used a cipher to send messages that no one could read other than the intended recipient. Caesar's cipher works by using a key. The key was used to shift all of the letters of the alphabet a number of letters. For example, using a shift of 3, A becomes D, B becomes E etc. The encrypted message is called ciphertext.

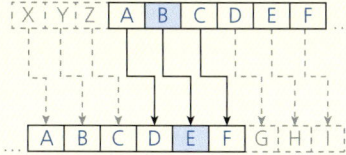

The person receiving the message only needed to know the shift value and it could be decoded. However this approach was not very secure as there are only 25 possible different shifts in the Roman alphabet. It would not take too long to figure out the message.

The tic-tac-toe cipher is another example of a cipher. This time, letters are replaced by symbols.

Letters are placed into grids, as shown below.

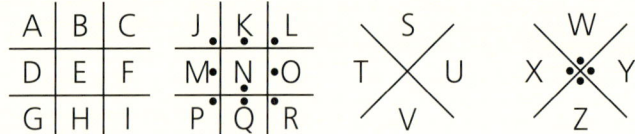

Symbols are then determined by the grids – each letter is represented by the lines or images in its grid location. For example:

A = ⌋   Q = ⊡   T = >   Z = ⋀

The atbash cipher is one of the earliest used. It is another example of symmetrical encryption. It is a simple substitution cipher. It reverses the normal (plain text) alphabet to create a cipher text alphabet. This cipher is easy to break as you only need the alphabet that is being used. The encryption algorithm is well known. For example, using the Roman alphabet:

Plaintext alphabet	A	B	C	D	E	F	G	H	I	J	K	L	M	N	O	P	Q	R	S	T	U	V	W	X	Y	Z
Ciphertext alphabet	Z	Y	X	W	V	U	T	S	R	Q	P	O	N	M	L	K	J	I	H	G	F	E	D	C	B	A

The cipher text 'SVOOL' is decrypted as 'Hello'.

Computers use the same principles behind ciphers to encrypt communication between sender and receiver, making them unreadable if they are intercepted. Encryption is a process which 'scrambles' data using an **encryption key**, making it appear meaningless to those without the key. This provides security for data when it is being stored and during transmission. The encryption keys that computers use are far more complex and difficult to break than the simple ciphers we have looked at.

Public key encryption

A disadvantage of the symmetric encryption method is that anyone with the secret key can decrypt the message. However **public key** encryption is an example of **asymmetrical encryption** which uses two different keys, a public key and a private key. The keys are exchanged over the internet or a network.

When Alice wants to send Hua an important message, she uses his public key to encrypt the message. The public key is known and available to anybody who wants to send Hua a message. She then sends the encrypted message to Hua. When it arrives, Hua uses his private key to decrypt the message. The private key is known only to Hua and is needed to open the file. This means that, if the message is intercepted by a hacker, it cannot be decrypted because the hacker does not have Hua's private key.

This will ensure that the data remains confidential. Only the intended recipient can decrypt and view the content of a message.

You may be wondering how a public key is accessed. One way of doing this is by using digital certificates. This is an electronic document which contains the public key and information about the person or network who owns the public key. Businesses use digital certificates to ensure secure communication between their website and a customer's web browser. The customer can access their public key through a digital certificate. There are certificate authorities which issue these certificates, for example Verisign.

HTTPS is an example of a secure encryption protocol that is used on the internet. Web pages using this protocol generally have a digital certificate to prove they are authentic. Customer details are protected whilst they are sent to the website using public key encryption.

Data can also be encrypted whilst it is being stored. Sensitive data on a file server could be stored in encrypted form to ensure that it is not viewed by the wrong person on the network, and if it was stolen it could not be read.

KEYWORDS

cipher: a method of encrypting text by replacing each letter with other symbols or letters

symmetric encryption: a form of encryption that uses the same key for encrypting and decrypting data

decrypt: decode or unscramble data using the required key

Caeser's cipher: a substitution cipher where a letter is 'shifted' a certain number of places along the alphabet

tic-tac-toe cipher: a replacement cipher which uses grids and symbols to replace letters

atbash cipher: a very old method of encrypting which reverses the alphabet to create cipher text

encryption key: information used by software to encrypt or decrypt data

public key: a key which is known that is used to encode or encrypt data

asymmetric encryption: a form of encryption that uses two keys, one for encrypting the data and another for decrypting the data

Practice

➤ Decrypt these two messages below that have been encrypted with the tic-tac-toe cipher.

1. ⸠□□⸸⸢‹⸞‹⸢⸣⸥›⸤∨□⸦‹⸢□

2. ⸦⸢‹⸸›⸞⸸⸢⸥⸸⸫‹

➤ Decrypt this person's name; it has been encrypted with Caeser's cipher with a shift value of 3.
DGD ORYHODFH

➤ Write a short message of your own using tic-tac-toe cipher. Ask a friend to decode it.

When walking through the GreatEng offices you have noticed staff making purchases on behalf of the company using credit cards. The manager often sends emails about staff and their performance using his personal email address. Employee records are accessible by everybody in the company if they know the password to the secretary's computer. You are going to carry out a training session for employees which involves them understanding encryption and ciphers.

Algorithmic thinking and pattern recognition

✪ In pairs create a cipher of your own. You can create a paper-based cipher or use a spreadsheet to create it.

✪ Write a set of guidelines which will describe how the cipher works. You can use a word processor for this.

✪ Create a number of encoded messages containing key facts about encryption using your cipher.

✪ Pass your messages to another group and ask them to try and crack the cipher.

✪ After 10 minutes, pass the guidelines to the group and ask them to decipher the message.

Ask the group to evaluate your cipher and the guidelines. They should discuss:

➤ how easy the cipher was to crack

➤ how effective the guidelines are to help use the cipher

➤ suggest two possible improvements to the cipher.

You want employees to be careful about data and to ensure that any sensitive data is encrypted at GreatEng. Write a set of short notes on the use of public key encryption and how this could help GreatEng keep customers' data safe.

Staying within the law

> ### Learn
>
> When organisations use computer systems there are laws that they must abide by.
>
> For example, all of the software on a network needs to have a licence. The company must purchase the correct number of licences for the number of computers that are going to use the software. Most countries around the world have laws that are designed to protect the intellectual property rights of those who create material based on their own ideas. This applies to books, music, art, software and all other creative work. You need to make sure that all of the software downloaded and used in GreatEng is legal and licensed. **Software licencing** and **copyright** laws protect code and software from being copied or distributed illegally.
>
> **Plagiarism** is also prohibited under these laws. This is where people use something that another person has written and pretend that they have written it.
>
> Computers can be hacked and hackers can damage and steal data. Two of the problems associated with computer misuse are hacking and **computer viruses**.
>
> ➤ Hacking is unauthorised access to computers or data, unauthorised changing of data.
>
> ➤ Computer viruses cause damage to computer systems.
>
> Most countries have laws to protect people against computer misuse with penalties depending on the seriousness of the crime. For example, hacking into a computer and changing data may carry a more severe penalty than simply hacking into the computer and viewing the data.
>
> Dealing with people's data is a serious matter. Personal data must be protected and this is enforced legally around the world. For example, your medical records and school data would be protected under this type of law. Any data which is personal is protected and generally cannot be shared without consent.
>
> For instance, in Europe the law protecting personal data is called **General Data Protection Regulation (GDPR)** and the people about which the data is held are known as **data subjects**. Data subjects in Europe have the right to:
>
> ➤ know their data is being collected
>
> ➤ get copies of their data
>
> ➤ have their data corrected if it is wrong
>
> ➤ have their data deleted
>
> ➤ limit how an organisation uses their data
>
> ➤ get their data from an organisation
>
> ➤ object to the use of their data
>
> ➤ understand how decisions are being made using their data
>
> ➤ raise concerns about the way in which an organisation is using their data.
>
> Countries around the world have their own legislation that sets out the rights of individuals and the responsibilities of organisations who process their data. Organisations must comply

with all of these laws in each country or risk being prosecuted. It is good practice for organisations to:

➤ have procedures in place to ensure that data is held securely and kept up-to-date

➤ train staff regularly and ensure that they are aware of the laws and the consequences of breaking the laws in the countries in which they operate

➤ ensure they use only legally purchased software

➤ have procedures to secure data and prevent **data breaches** and **data theft**.

One common problem is that our personal data is collected in many different places; for example:

➤ when we are online using a website

➤ when we use a customer loyalty card in a supermarket

➤ our location details are obtained from our mobile phone GPS signals

➤ CCTV images can also track our location.

This data could be misused by companies, passed onto other companies or analysed and used for marketing purposes. In some countries it is illegal for organisations to share data they have with other organisations without the permission of the data subject.

Data theft is an issue facing all organisations which collect data. For example usernames and passwords or credit card details are regularly stolen from online companies. These can be used to make fraudulent purchases.

> Can you remember the terms: phishing, pharming and spyware? If not, do some quick internet research to remind yourself what each of these are.

An organisation must ensure that their employees use the computer system in an ethical way. At GreatEng, after interviewing staff, you realise that there has been very little training on this topic and the computers regularly need to be restored after a virus attack.

KEYWORDS

software licencing: an agreement which gives permission to use a software program

copyright: protects software and other things like books from being copied or misused

plagiarism: taking someone else's work or ideas and passing them off as one's own

How can plagiarism be avoided?

computer viruses: software designed to damage a computer

General Data Protection Regulation (GDPR): a European law, which protects people's personal data and ensures that companies protect the data and use it appropriately

data subjects: the people about which data is held; for example, an employee (or you!)

data breaches: the illegal viewing, accessing or modification of data perhaps by a hacker

data theft: when data has been acquired illegally without the permission of the company or individual to which it belongs

Practice

Now that GreatEng is making use of a wide range of technologies to do business, following the law is very important.

➤ Create a set of guidelines for the company to help them ensure they remain compliant with any data protection or copyright or misuse laws that apply in your country.
➤ Your guidelines should include:
  o the name of the law
  o a simple explanation of the law and how it can be broken
  o a list of possible penalties if the company break the law
  o a list of things the company must do to be compliant with the law.

Go further

An organisation can take a number of measures to protect data. At present GreatEng make use of usernames and passwords. However, the building doors are kept open during the day and most employees leave the building for lunch.

You have visited another local company and have discovered that they use **physical security** methods. Physical security is the protection of the hardware, software, data and personnel from physical events that could result in the loss of **business critical data**. This includes vandalism, theft, and malicious damage as well as natural disasters like flooding or fire.

These physical security methods include fences and security cameras to control access to the office. There is also a central security camera area which monitors all areas of the building.

Each employee wears a security ID card and uses this to gain access to different parts of the building. Each employee only has access to the areas that they work in and to general areas, such as the canteen. The security card controls their access to each area.

Heat and smoke sensors linked to the Internet of Things control fire safety.

Rooms that contain highly important information have doors that automatically lock and a biometric scanning system which monitors who enters and leaves the room. Biometrics is the study of measurable biological characteristics. This includes the use of fingerprint and facial recognition. The company also has a strict policy regarding passwords.

KEYWORDS

physical security: the protection of hardware, software, networks and data from the effects of a physical attack or event such as a flood

business critical data: data that is vital to the operation of the business

◆ All passwords must be reset every 60 days using a password that has not been used before. Users are prompted to change their passwords before they expire.

◆ All passwords must be at least 10 characters long and must contain a mix of numbers, letters and special characters.

◆ Passwords must be kept confidential and never written down.

◆ Selecting a good password is important so that the data is well protected. A good password should not be easy to guess. A good password should be:

  ❏ made up of numbers and letters. You should use a mix of upper and lower case letters.

  ❏ at least eight characters long

  ❏ changed regularly.

GreatEng is based in an old building in the outskirts of the city. There is a company car park and four doors through which employees can gain entrance to the building.

The company have taken your advice on installing a network, and now have valuable computers, engineering equipment, network equipment and hold data for more than 2000 customers.

Decomposition

As their technical adviser you have been asked to prepare a physical security plan to help protect the equipment and data. You will use decomposition to break down two of the main parts of a security plan:

✪ secure areas and access control

✪ reporting issues and weaknesses.

Here are some of the subsections that the security plan should include.

Secure areas and access control

✪ Security devices to be used on the outside of the building and an explanation of why each device is needed.

✪ A list of users who are authorised to use the building. (You can use five of your classmates for this.)

✪ A list of things that the five users will be able to do on the system.

✪ An explanation of how you will control access to the system. For example, biometrics, staff ID passes, and usernames and passwords.

Reporting issues and weaknesses

✪ An explanation of how employees can report weaknesses in the system that could cause loss of data.

Using the plan above, add details in each of the subsections and review the plan with a partner. Is the plan strong enough to protect your system and data from physical attack?

Challenge yourself

You have already seen how messages are broken down into packets and sent across the network. It is important that the data within the packet arrives undamaged and correct. Remember the trucks used to deliver the different packages for the sofa? What if one of the packages became damaged or a cushion for the sofa was lost? It is important to check the contents of each package to ensure it is complete and correct.

A data packet also needs to be checked to ensure that it has arrived complete and correct. If it is incomplete or incorrect we say that the data is corrupt.

When data is being transmitted along cables or wirelessly it can become corrupted. Computers must be able to check for, detect and correct errors in the data when it arrives.

Let's assume that data is transmitted in the binary format of 1s and 0s and that data is transmitted 8 bits at a time.

> Do you remember that bits are binary digits (1s and 0s) and that all digital data is transmitted as a series of bits?

Parity

Parity checking is one method of detecting errors in data when it arrives at a destination computer. There are two types of parity checking – odd parity and even parity.

Odd parity: a parity bit is added to the bit pattern to ensure that the number of 1s in the bit pattern is odd.

Even parity: a parity bit is added to the bit pattern to ensure that the number of 1s in the bit pattern is even.

For example, we wish to send the following data which is represented by a 7-bit number: 1100101.

Adding an odd parity, the new number would be **1**1100101. The parity bit shown in red is a 1 because there were four 1s in the original number; we need to add an extra 1 to make the number of 1s odd.

Adding an even parity, the new number would be **0**1100101. In this case the parity bit is 0 because there were four 1s in the original number and so we didn't need to add any more to make the number of 1s even.

The receiving computer will check the parity of the bit pattern to ensure it is correct. If it is not then this implies that there has been an error in sending the data, and so the receiving computer will request that the data is sent again.

Parity checking has one weakness. If the original data is:

0011001

and this is sent and checked using even parity, then adding the parity bit changes the data to:

10011001.

Imagine that a power surge caused the data to be corrupted and when the bit pattern arrives at its destination one bit in the pattern has been changed, marked in blue. The corrupted bit pattern is now:

1001**0**001.

Even parity checking will detect an error as there are now an odd number of 1s in the bit pattern. This data will have to be re-transmitted.

But what if the power surge caused two bits to change value as shown?

1001**0**101

The data received is incorrect, but an even parity check will not detect the error as there are still an even number of 1s in the pattern. (An odd parity check would have the same problem.)

Therefore, the weakness of parity is that it cannot detect errors when two changes occur.

Also, if two bits are transposed (change places), parity cannot detect an error because the parity remains correct.

Checksum

Checksum is another method of detecting errors in data transmission. Using the block of data to be sent, and a pre-defined algorithm, the sending computer calculates a checksum. The checksum is sent along with the block of data to the receiving computer. The receiving computer uses the block of data and the same mathematical algorithm to calculate the checksum. The two checksums are compared. If they do not match, an error in the data is assumed and the receiving computer will request that the data is resent.

Check digits

Check digits are used to check for errors in values entered onto a computer system. The check digit is calculated from all the other digits in the code. These are found on barcodes and ISBN numbers.

Let's say the barcode on an item in a supermarket is damaged and the scanner cannot read it. The shop assistant must type the code instead. When the barcode is typed at the checkout, the check digit is calculated. If the calculated check digit does not match the one typed in, an error is assumed and the code will have to be re-entered. The check digit will identify transposition errors and omitted digits. A check digit might be calculated differently for different products or in different applications.

Calculating a check digit

ISBN is the abbreviation for the International Standard Book Number. All books that are published in the world have an ISBN number – including this one! ISBN numbers are 13 digits in length.

978-1-5104-1496-**9**

(9 is the check digit)

To calculate the check digit for an ISBN:
➤ Take the ISBN number and weight each digit starting at the left hand side using 1 and 3 repeatedly.

➤ Multiply the digit by the weighting:

Weighting	1	3	1	3	1	3	1	3	1	3	1	3
Digit	9	7	8	1	5	1	0	4	1	4	9	6
Result	9	21	8	3	5	3	0	12	1	12	9	18

Add each result together:

9 + 21 + 8 + 3 + 5 + 3 + 0 + 12 + 1 + 12 + 9 + 18 = 101

➤ divide 101 by 10:

$101 \div 10 = 10$ remainder 1

➤ take the remainder from 10:

$10 - 1 = 9$

9 is the check digit used to ensure that the rest of the ISBN has been read or entered correctly. If the calculations are carried out and the result obtained is not equal to the check digit, then the code will be rejected.

These methods of validation and verification ensure that data entered is as correct and reliable as possible. However, the fact that data entry is carried out by a human operator means that it could be entered erroneously, even if it is valid.

➤ How would the following bit patterns be sent?

Bit Pattern	Using ODD parity	Using EVEN parity
0110101		
1101101		

➤ Describe how an error is detected using parity checking.
➤ Prove that this ISBN number is correct:

ISBN 978-1-78017-326-9

➤ GreatEng has decided to sell specialist equipment to engineers. They want to use a check digit system for the product numbers of the equipment. Product numbers are four digits long and the fifth digit represents the check digit. Here are some sample product numbers not including check digits:

3415 – Protective head gear

3416 – Toolbox

3417 – Pliers

3418 – Flash light

➤ Using the sample product numbers, create your own check digit system that will validate the product number when it is entered into the system.
➤ Using your check digit system, calculate the check digit for each of the products above.
➤ Ask a friend to use your method to verify that one of the product numbers above and its check digit are correct.

Final project

FineDining Ltd is a family-run restaurant business used by many people in the city. The company have 5 restaurants and they also have a takeaway located at each of the restaurants. In order to be competitive the family have decided to use technology to improve their business. Currently each restaurant has computers and tills that are not connected to any networks. They have come to you and are asking that you provide advice in the form of a proposal document. You can use a word processor to create the document. Your document should have the following headings:

➤ How could the company use a local area network?
➤ What advantages could using a WAN bring to the company?
➤ What type of equipment would the company need to buy to make the LAN work? Explain why each piece of equipment is needed.
➤ What devices would be suitable to use on a LAN which is connected to the internet?
➤ Should Wi-Fi and Bluetooth be available in the restaurants? If so, why?
➤ How can encryption help keep data secure during transmission?
➤ The company will hold details about customers and transactions. What are the problems associated with collecting data and transmitting data?
➤ Why should the company apply to a Certification Authority for a Digital Certificate?
➤ What areas of training should be provided for staff?
➤ Will members of staff need to take on new roles or responsibilities?

Evaluation

➤ Swap your proposal with another student and discuss the similarities and differences in your reports.
➤ Create a list of areas that must be included to help the business succeed.
➤ Review your original proposal and see how it compares to your agreed list.

Unit 9.5

Designing, coding and documenting solutions

Bringing it all together with coded solutions

You have learned about creating solutions to problems using computational thinking. You have created solutions using algorithms and pseudocode. In this chapter, you will bring together many of the skills you have already learned to create a working software application.

Many software applications are written to process large amounts of data collected from a source.

For example: when training, Olympic swimmers wear small body sensors called accelerometers which record data about the way in which they swim. The data they collect includes how fast they turn in the pool, the frequency of their kicks while swimming, or the acceleration of their body through the water. All of this data is recorded and analysed to help their coach identify areas for improvement for individual swimmers. The coach can develop an individual training plan for each swimmer based on the data. As swimmers improve, so does their chance of winning a medal at the Olympics. The software required to analyse the data is written and designed by a programmer. This is a process which involves a number of stages and you are going to learn about these in this section.

In this unit you will:

→ be introduced to the key members associated with the development of a large project
→ learn how Gantt charts are used to support project management
→ create wireframes to show how output screens will appear

KEYWORDS

Gantt chart: a bar chart that shows a project schedule

Draw a simple Gantt chart for a project you are working on.

wireframe: a layout diagram of a screen or web page

→ use pseudocode or flowchart **algorithms** to create a design which incorporates different data types

→ create a program which collects and processes data for a local swimming club; the program will contain **reusable code** and functions with **parameters**

→ develop a **test plan** to ensure that the program only accepts valid data and outputs the correct information

→ record the results of tests and any **corrective measures** taken

→ evaluate the program's performance in terms of the **user requirements** which have been provided by the local swimming club.

KEYWORDS

algorithm: a step by step representation of a solution written in pseudocode or using a flowchart

reusable code: code written so that it can be called and reused in different parts of the program

parameters: values or variables that are passed into a function from the main program; they are used in calculations and processing within the function

test plan: a tabular layout which enables a programmer to plan the testing of a program

corrective measures: the actions taken by the programmer after testing to correct errors in the programs

user requirements: a list of tasks that the program should perform agreed between the user and the analyst

SCENARIO

As a member of a software development team, you have been asked by Riverside Swimming Club to develop a software package for them.

People applying to join Riverside Swimming Club usually try out in the pool first. The applicant's fastest 6 times for swimming a length of the 25 metre pool are recorded.

Then they must log on to a computer, enter the 6 length times and take a short test about water safety.

If they pass the test with a score of 40 or more and their average length time is less than 28 seconds, they can become a member.

At the end of the test a message will be displayed on the screen telling them their score, average length time and whether they can become a member or if they need additional training.

You are part of a team of people who are going to help develop this software. The team roles in a normal software development team are outlined together with their responsibilities below.

Role	Responsibilities
Analyst	The systems analyst will consult with clients to identify their requirements for the new system. He or she will analyse the costs and benefits of introducing the new system.
Project Manager	The project manager will plan the project, and set timescales and deadlines for when tasks should be completed. They will assign people to tasks and ensure the team have the necessary hardware and software to do the job.
Designer	The designer creates a detailed document which specifies exactly what the software needs to do. This can be used by the programmer to create the code.
Programmer	The programmer uses the design document to create code which will carry out the functions listed in the user requirements. The programmer will test the program to ensure it works as expected.
User	The user is the person who will use the new program. They specify what the program should do and will be involved in some of the testing.

In this scenario we will focus on the roles of the Designer, Programmer and Project Manager.

Decomposition – breaking the problem down

The software should provide facilities for applicants to:

✪ log in to the system

✪ enter the six length times

✪ take the short quiz to measure their knowledge about water safety

✪ output their score and average length time with a message about whether they can join the club or need more training.

Before starting this unit you should know how to:

➔ use the Python programming language to create, run and save a program

❯ use sequence, selection and repetition in Python

➔ use validation to ensure that user input is correct

➔ test and evaluate a Python program

➔ process a list structure in Python

➔ sort items in a list.

You should also have completed the other Stage 9 units, in particular 9.2, which will provide you with the skills mentioned above.

Wireframes

Learn

As a designer, you are appointed to the design team. You will need to help the team to design a solution for the Riverside Swimming Club.

Using decomposition we have already identified how the overall brief can be broken down into four sub-problems. The design should ensure that:

➤ all inputs are validated

➤ screen designs are considered – for example the positioning of messages to the user and presentation of information on the screen.

Designing a solution involves creating:

➤ wireframes: these show the layout of the screen as it may appear to the user

➤ algorithms written in pseudocode or as flowcharts: detailing the step by step logic behind your solution

➤ a **data dictionary**: a table listing all of the data items to be used in the solution. The data dictionary will list the name, data type and a description of the data together with a sample value.

Separate design solutions can be applied to each of the four sub-problems.

Decomposition

Here is a structure diagram which shows a breakdown of the main problem into sub-problems for the Riverside Swimming Club System.

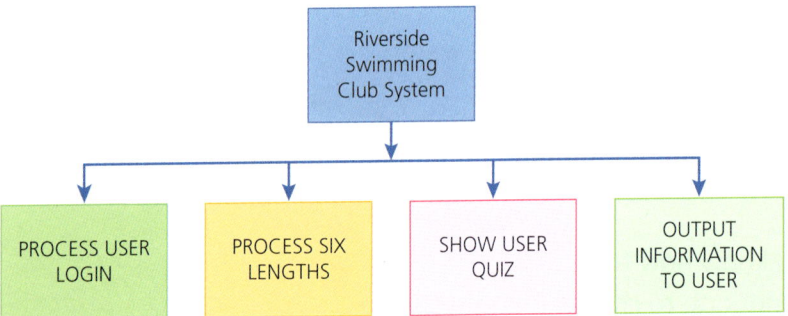

Looking at the structure diagram we can see that the four main processes are :

PROCESS USER LOGIN

PROCESS SIX LENGTHS

SHOW USER QUIZ

OUTPUT INFORMATION TO USER

KEYWORD

data dictionary: information about the data used in the program; usually presented in a table structure

Learn

To move the design process forward first we will create a wireframe for the sub-problem PROCESS USER LOGIN.

A wireframe is a visual outline of how the screen will look. It contains the main parts of the screen but may not include all of the details. It can be drafted using pen and paper or on a whiteboard and then created using a word processor. You can show the user the wireframe and make changes to it to suit their requirements.

Wireframing is important because it allows you (the designer) to plan the layout and interaction for a screen without being distracted by colour. When you are creating a wireframe you need to have a clear picture in your mind about how the screen should look. Here are some pointers to help you.

➤ If possible, do some research; look at other examples of a login screen.

➤ Decide on what you want to include.

➤ Carry out the following tasks and questions:
   • What is the purpose of the screen?
   • List the information that needs to be shown on the screen.
   • Draft a layout for your screen and ensure that all the information required has been included.
   • Look at where you have positioned the text. Is it easy to read and in the correct order?
   • Have you created a title which helps the user understand what is required?
   • Is there any help text required on the screen?
   • Is there space in the correct position to input data?
   • Do you need to include any more information?

➤ Check the layout.
   • Think about the purpose of the screen and how best to organise the information.
   • A login screen will ask the user to enter a username and password, so these will need to be included on the screen.
   • You may decide to have the username entered on one page and the password entered on another.
   • You will also have to decide if there is any other information to be included on this screen, such as instructions to the user.
   • When you have decided on the layout, make a pen and paper draft or a whiteboard draft of your ideal screen layout.

➤ Show the draft to the user or a member of the team and change it if necessary.

➤ Create an electronic copy of the final wireframe using a word processor.

One possible solution to the requirements of the PROCESS USER LOGIN is a wireframe such as this:

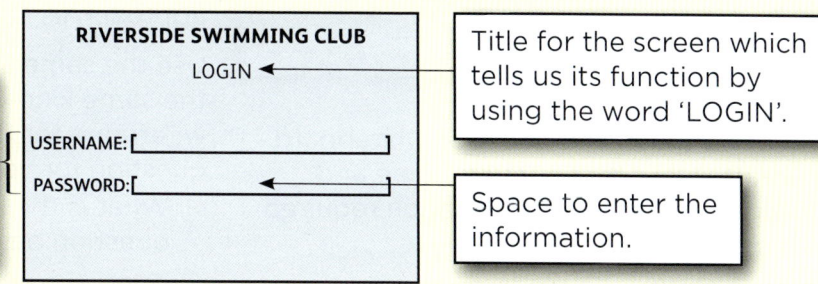

Prompts 'USERNAME' and 'PASSWORD' which tell the user where to enter the username and passwords.

RIVERSIDE SWIMMING CLUB
LOGIN ◄
USERNAME: [   ]
PASSWORD: [   ]

Title for the screen which tells us its function by using the word 'LOGIN'.

Space to enter the information.

This can be used as a map for the programmer to create the screen.

Practice

Now you need to design a wireframe for the sub-problem PROCESS SIX LENGTHS.

Remember that the wireframe design must meet the requirements of the club, which are that the user must enter the times it took them to complete each of six lengths. The club would like these entries to be on the same page where the username and password was entered.

Now you should ask yourself the following questions.

➤ What is the purpose of this section of the program? Write a few sentences on what PROCESS SIX LENGTHS must do.
➤ Want do I want to include on the wireframe for this section of the program? List the information that needs to be shown on the screen.

You will need to have:
o a prompt or message to the user for entering the time for each length
o a space for entering the time for each length.

For example, you can make a list like this.

○ What do I want to include?
○ A title to tell the user what is going
○ to happen
○ some blank lines
○ Prompt to enter time for length 1
○ Space to enter time for length 1
○ and so on...

➤ Create a pen and paper or whiteboard draft layout for your wireframe and ensure that all the information required has been included.

➤ Check the layout. Show your wireframe draft to a friend and discuss it using the following questions.
o Is the purpose of the wireframe clear to the user?
o Is the organisation of the prompts and spaces correct and logical?

> You don't want length 6 being entered before length 1.

o Is the screen complete; for example, are all six lengths asked for?
o Do you need to add anything else such as a help instruction to the user?
➤ Make any changes to the draft wireframe following your discussion.
➤ Create an electronic copy of the final wireframe using a word processor.

Once you are happy with this wireframe, create a wireframe for the third sub-problem SHOW USER QUIZ.

The user quiz will present the user with six multiple choice questions. Each question will have three possible answers **a**, **b** or **c**.

The first question is as follows:
1 How can cold water affect your swimming capability?
   a It does not
   b It is harder to swim as you can get cramp
   c It is easier to swim as it cools you down

All other questions follow the same approach as Question 1.

Use the same approach as before, asking the same kind of questions, to design your wireframe for this sub-problem. A key question for you to consider is:
➤ What is the best way to put each question on the screen?

Design algorithms using flowcharts and pseudocode

Learn

We have looked at a possible wireframe for PROCESS USER LOGIN so now we will design the algorithm for this sub-problem.

First we need to carefully consider exactly what the swimming club want their login page to do. They have said that:

➤ the user login requires them to enter their username and password

➤ the username and password must match that set by the club for applicants

➤ the stored username set by the club is **Applicant1**

➤ the stored password set by the club is **Sw1mm1ng@**

➤ they do not want the program to end if a user enters the wrong username and password – they should be able to keep trying.

We can map these user requirements to elements of code that we will need. Look at the table below.

User requirement	Code element
The user login requires them to enter their username and password.	Print statements to print a title on to the screen. Input statements to capture the values for username and password.
The username and password must match that set by the club for applicants.	An IF statement with a condition which • checks to see if the username entered matches that stored AND checks to see if the password entered matches that stored • outputs a message if invalid details are entered.
The user must be able to keep trying until a valid username and password is entered.	A conditional loop with a condition that will check a Boolean variable; the Boolean variable will be set to FALSE at the beginning of the loop. It will be changed to TRUE inside the IF statement if the user enters valid username and password details. If the user enters invalid details, an error message will be output.

Here is a flowchart to show the process.

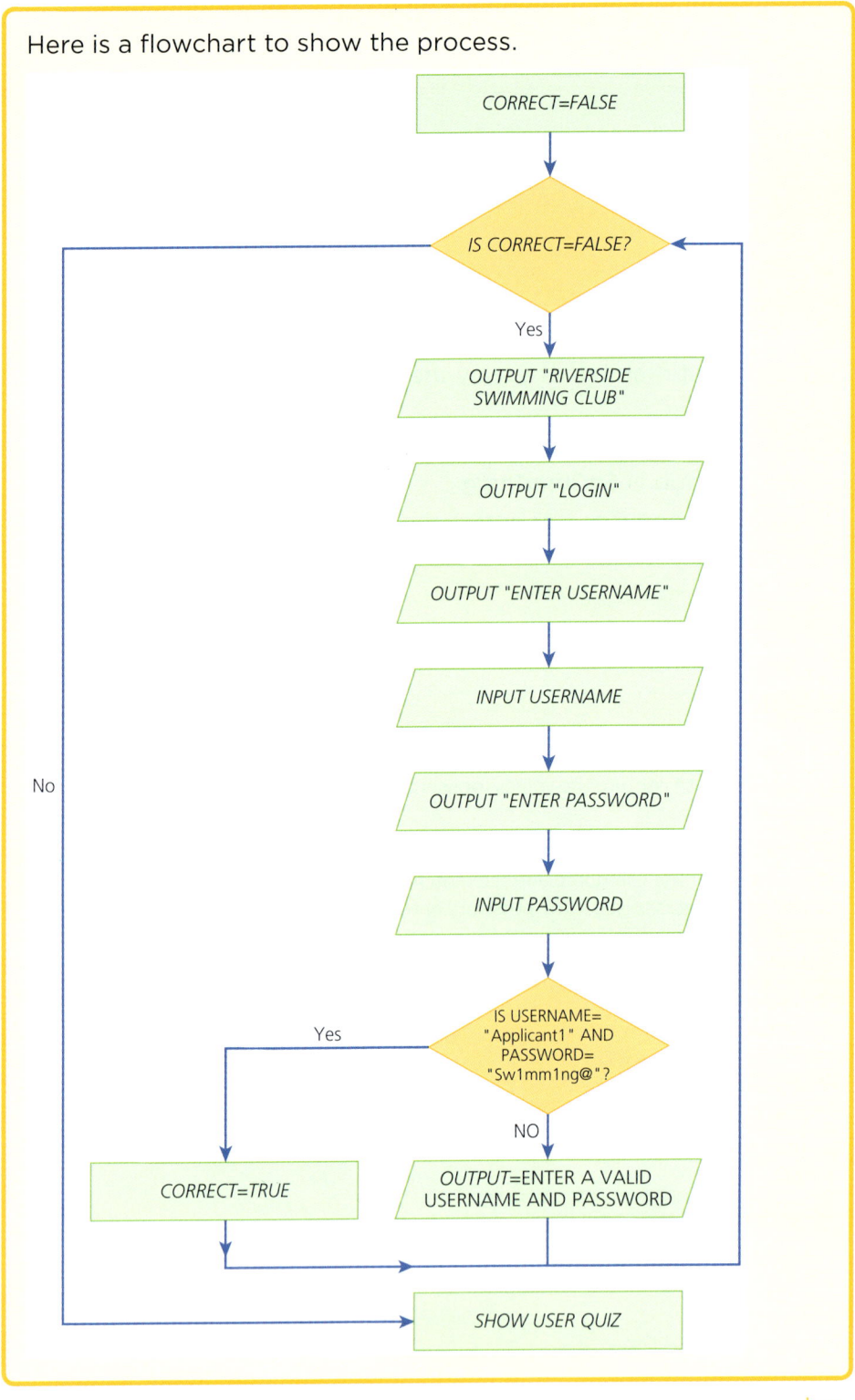

We can write this flowchart as an algorithm:

```
CORRECT = FALSE

WHILE CORRECT = FALSE

        OUTPUT "RIVERSIDE SWIMMING CLUB"

        OUTPUT "LOGIN"

        OUTPUT "USERNAME:"

        INPUT USERNAME

        OUTPUT "PASSWORD:"

        INPUT PASSWORD

        IF USERNAME="Applicant1" and PASSWORD= "Sw1mm1ng@"

            CORRECT=TRUE

        ELSE

            OUTPUT "ENTER A VALID USERNAME AND PASSWORD"

        END IF

END WHILE
```

Practice

Now you will design an algorithm for SHOW USER QUIZ. First you need to consider what the requirements are for this sub-problem. The swimming club has told you the following:

➤ The user quiz will present the user with six multiple choice questions.
➤ Each question will have three possible answers **a**, **b** or **c**.
➤ If the user enters the correct answer they will get 10 points.

Consider how the algorithm can do this for one question first. Think about how you would ask someone the question. For example: ask your friend:

'How can cold water affect your swimming capability?'

a It does not.

b It is harder to swim as you can get cramp.

c It is easier to swim as it cools you down.

The correct answer is **b**.

This will help you to create a flowchart.

	Map to flowchart
Ask the question: 'How can cold water affect your swimming capability?'	OUTPUT QUESTION 1 TEXT
State answer a '**a** It does not'	OUTPUT QUESTION 1 OPTION a
State answer b '**b** It is harder to swim as you can get cramp'	OUTPUT QUESTION 1 OPTION b
State answer c '**c** It is easier to swim as it cools you down'	OUTPUT QUESTION 1 OPTION c
Listen to your friend's answer	INPUT USERANSWER
Check to see if the answer is correct If it is correct, give them 10 points	IF USERANSWER = CORRECT ANSWER QUESTION 1 ADD 10 TO POINTS (POINTS=POINT+10)

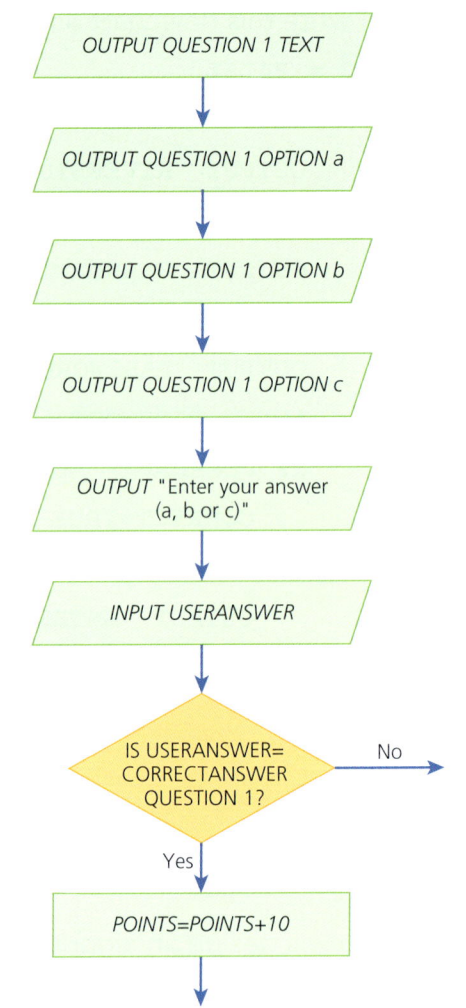

To create the flowchart use the statements above. Here is part of the flowchart (right).

To amend the flowchart so that it works for all six questions, we need to add a loop that will ask six questions.

We can use a FOR loop to count the questions. Let's say the FOR loop runs from 0 to 5 (this is because we are going to store the questions in a list structure later). You will need to check back to Unit 9.2 to remind yourself how we use lists in Python. Remember, the first element in the list is element 0, the second is element 1, and so on.

Here is part of the flowchart containing the loop for SHOW USER QUIZ, to ask the six questions. Note: the flowchart is not complete – can you see what is missing?

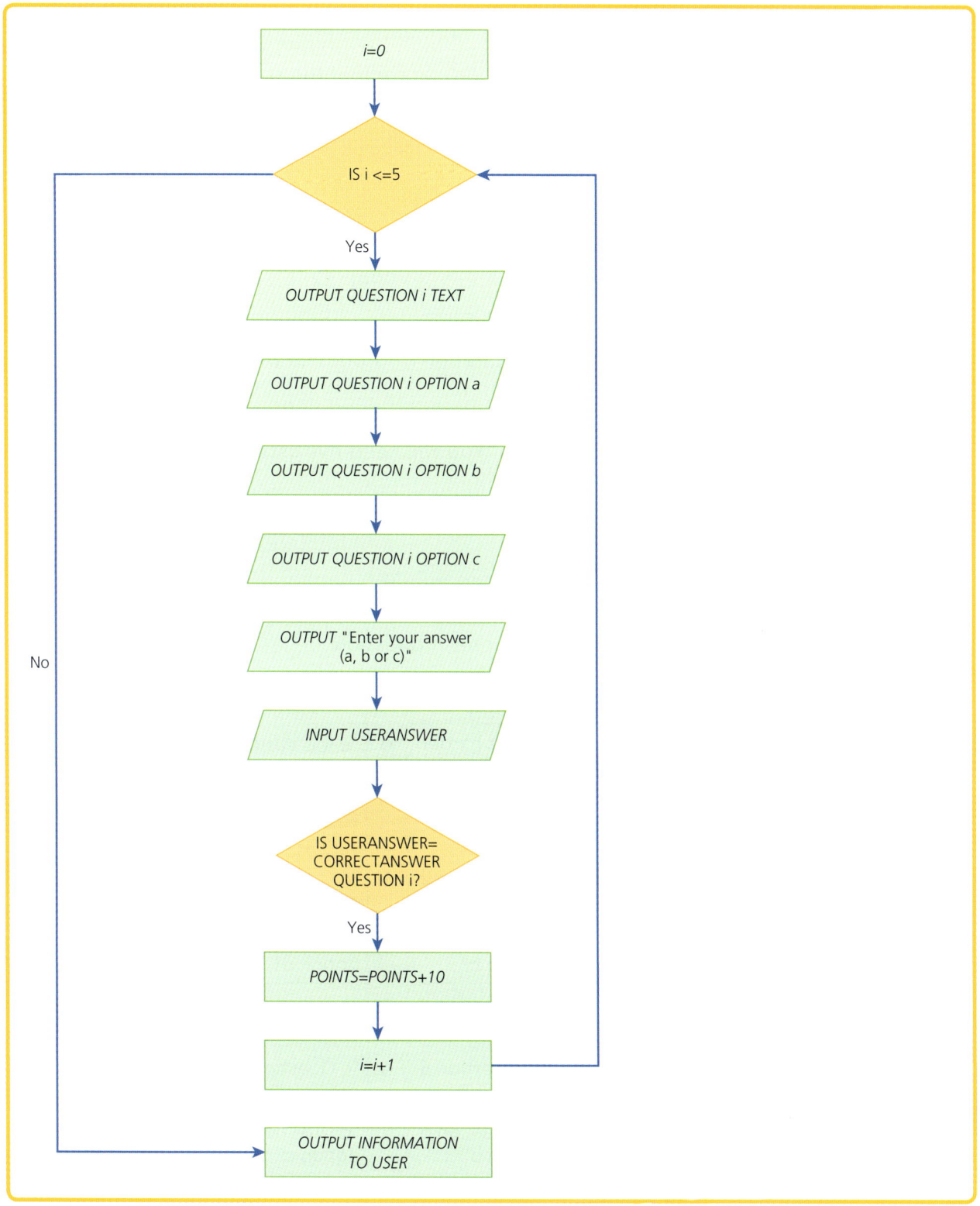

Translating a flowchart to pseudocode

To create pseudocode from a flowchart you can use each of the statements in the boxes.

To create the for loop, use a FOR loop of the appropriate length, and enclose the statements using END FOR. Note that the FOR statement checks to see if the value of i is less than or equal to 5.

```
FOR i = 0 to 5

[enter statements here]

END FOR
```

Now create the pseudocode for SHOW USER QUIZ.

You will need to think about how the questions can be stored so that they can be well-presented on the screen.

One way is to store the questions, answers and correct answers in separate lists. These multiple lists can store data as shown below. You will need five lists as follows:

QUESTIONS – will hold the six questions

ALIST – will hold the six option a answers

BLIST – will hold the six option b answers

CLIST – will hold the six option c answers

CORRECTANS – will hold correct answers for each question

> Review Unit 9.2 where you learned how to use lists in Python.

	QUESTIONS		ALIST		BLIST		CLIST		CORRECTANS
0	"How can cold water affect your swimming capability?"	0	"a It does not."	0	"b It is harder to swim as you can get cramp."	0	"c It is easier to swim as it cools you down."	0	"b"
1	"Question 2 text"	1	"a Question 2 option a"	1	"b Question 2 option b"	1	"c Question 2 option c"	1	Question 2 correct answer
2	"Question 3 text"	2	"a Question 3 option a"	2	"b Question 3 option b"	2	"c Question 3 option c"	2	Question 3 correct answer
3	"Question 4 text"	3	"a Question 4 option a"	3	"b Question 4 option b"	3	"c Question 4 option c"	3	Question 4 correct answer
4	"Question 5 text"	4	"a Question 5 option a"	4	"b Question 5 option b"	4	"c Question 5 option c"	4	Question 5 correct answer
5	"Question 6 text"	5	"a Question 6 option a"	5	"b Question 6 option b"	5	"c Question 6 option c"	5	Question 6 correct answer

The pseudocode to create two of these lists has been created for you:

```
ALGORITHM

QUESTIONS=["How can cold water affect your swimming capability?",
"Question 2 text", "Question 3 text", "Question 4 text", "Question 5
text", "Question 6 text"]

ALIST=["a It does not", "a Question 2 option a", "a Question 3 option a",
"a Question 4 option a", "a Question 5 option a", "a Question 6 option a"]
```

Use the information you have to think about how the remaining lists can be set up. You will need to create three more lists called BLIST, CLIST and CORRECTANS, as shown on page 150. Copy and complete the lists on page 150 so that they contain five more questions and answers, of your choice, about water safety. Keep these safely as you will use these questions and answers in your code on page 160.

Generalisation

Once you have created pseudocode for SHOW USER QUIZ you can use the methods described above to try and create pseudocode for the sub-problem PROCESS SIX LENGTHS.

You will need to consider the following.

❂ Six length times need to be entered, so a loop will be required.

❂ The length time must be between 20 and 30 seconds, therefore each length must be validated to ensure it is in this range.

❂ The length times entered must be stored in a list.

❂ The average of the length times must be calculated.

As this is a more complex example, here is a flowchart for one potential solution to the problem:

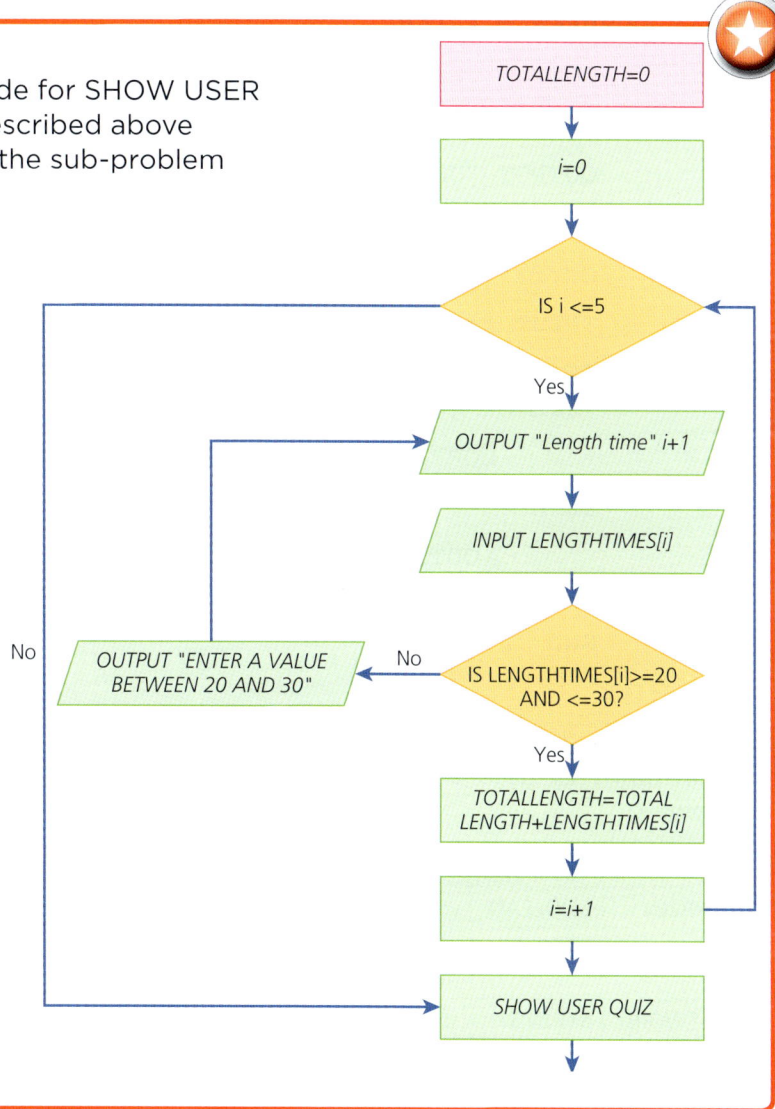

Data dictionaries

Learn

The final thing that a designer needs to do is create a data dictionary. This is a table listing all of the data items to be used in the solution. The data dictionary will list the name, data type and a description of the data together with a sample value.

We will consider how to create a data dictionary for PROCESS USER LOGIN

We need to consider what the **data requirements** are for the sub-problem PROCESS USER LOGIN.

Look at the algorithm that we previously wrote:

```
CORRECT = FALSE

WHILE CORRECT = FALSE
        OUTPUT "RIVERSIDE SWIMMING CLUB"
        OUTPUT "LOGIN"
        OUTPUT "USERNAME:"
        INPUT USERNAME
        OUTPUT "PASSWORD:"
        INPUT PASSWORD
        IF USERNAME="Applicant1" and PASSWORD=
        "Sw1mm1ng@"
                CORRECT=TRUE
        ELSE
                OUTPUT "ENTER A VALID USERNAME AND
                PASSWORD"
        END IF
END WHILE
```

KEYWORD

data requirements: the data items required for the program

We need to identify any data that is being used within the algorithm. That data is highlighted in blue and consists of the following:

Data	Data type	Descriptions	Sample valid data
CORRECT	BOOLEAN	variable controls the loop	TRUE
USERNAME	STRING	stores the username entered by the user	Applicant1
PASSWORD	STRING	stores the password entered by the user	Sw1mm1ng@

Practice

Now you need to create data dictionaries for sub-problems PROCESS SIX LENGTHS and SHOW USER QUIZ.

Start with PROCESS SIX LENGTHS.

➤ Look at your pseudocode and identify any data that is being used. It might help to highlight it.
➤ For each example, create a table like the one below and give:
  o the name of the data
  o the data type (for example, string, real, integer, Boolean)
  o a description of what the data is used for in the algorithm
  o an example of valid data.

Data	Data type	Descriptions	Sample valid data

> Remember that each of the lists are examples of data that will need to be captured in the data dictionary.

Repeat this process for SHOW USER QUIZ.

Solving sub-problems using functions and procedures

Learn

You will now take on the role of a Programmer. A design document has been handed to the programming team. It is not necessarily the same as the design document that you yourself created! However, as a programmer you must become used to implementing other people's design solutions.

You must use the design document to create a Python program that will perform the tasks requested by the Riverside Swimming Club.

To do this you will need to create a procedure that implements the pseudocode for PROCESS USER LOGIN, which has been given to you below.

```
CORRECT = FALSE

WHILE CORRECT = FALSE

        OUTPUT "RIVERSIDE SWIMMING CLUB"

        OUTPUT "LOGIN"

        OUTPUT "USERNAME:"

        INPUT USERNAME

        OUTPUT "PASSWORD:"

        INPUT PASSWORD

        IF USERNAME="Applicant1" and PASSWORD="Sw1mm1ng@"

            CORRECT=TRUE

        ELSE

            OUTPUT "ENTER A VALID USERNAME AND PASSWORD"

            CORRECT =FALSE

        END IF

END WHILE
```

Before you can do this you need to revisit the Going Further task (page 70) in Unit 9.2 to remind yourself about functions and procedures. Here is a brief recap:

A user-defined function or procedure is made up of:
➤ keyword "def" which is at the start of the function/procedure header
➤ a function/procedure name
➤ parameters which are used to pass values to the function/procedure; these are optional
➤ a colon (:) at the end of the function/procedure header
➤ a set of indented Python statements which make up the function/procedure body.

In addition, a function also includes:

➤ a return statement which returns a value to the main program.

Remember, a procedure is just the name for a function that does not return any values.

So, to define a procedure called **processuserlogin** you would use the following code:

```
# A function to process user login


def processuserlogin():
    correct=False
    while (correct==False):
        print("        RIVERSIDE SWIMMING CLUB")
        print
        print
        username=input("Username: ")
        print
        password=input("Password: ")
        if (username=="Applicant1" and password=="Swlmmlng@"):
            correct=True
        else:
            print("Enter a valid username and password")
            correct=False


#call the processuserlogin function
processuserlogin()
```

Procedure heading.

Code for PROCESS USER LOGIN which was designed above. It corresponds to the flowchart and pseudocode.

Call from the main program to run the **processuserlogin** procedure.

Here is a simple example of a procedure. Can you identify these six parts in the screenshot below?

1	keyword def	Yes
2	procedure name	printgreeting
3	parameters	name
4	:	Yes
5	indented Python statements which make up the procedure body	Yes
6	return statement	No

```
def printgreeting(name):
        #This function outputs a greeting to
        # the person whose name is passed in as parameter
        print("Hello, " + name + ". Good morning!")


printgreeting("John")
```

Heading with a parameter called **name**.

Call to the parameter **printgreeting** which passes the argument **"John"** into the function.

Indented Python statements making up the body of the procedure.

There is no return statement so this is a procedure with a parameter.

The call to the procedure is by its name followed by the parameter; for example:

printgreeting("John")

Look at the screen shot below. This function is called **findlargest**.

```
#a user defined function which has
# two parameters num1 and num2
def findlargest(num1,num2):
        # This function returns the largest of two numbers
        # to the main program
        if (num1>num2):
            largest =num1
        else:
            largest=num2
        # the return statement returns the largest number
        return largest


#the main program starts here


# this is the first call to the function findlargest
# 7 and 9 are passed as parameters into the function
# num1 will be 7 and num2 will be 9 inside the function
biggest=findlargest(7,9)
print ("The largest number is ", biggest)
# biggest will hold the value returned from the function

# this is the second call to the function findlargest
# 9 and 7 are passed as parameters into the function
# num1 will be 9 and num2 will be 7 inside the function
biggest=findlargest(9,7)
print ("The largest number is ", biggest)
# biggest will hold the value returned from the function


first=int(input("Enter first number  "))
second=int(input("Enter second number"))

# this is the third call to the function fundlargest
# this time values input by the user are passed to the function
#num1 will have the value of first and num2 will have the value of second inside the function
biggest=findlargest(first,second)
print ("The largest number is ", biggest)
|
```

There are two parameters in the heading and a **return** statement. The **return** statement is used to return the largest of the two numbers.

Look at an example of the call statement for **findlargest**.

biggest = findlargest(7, 9)

The **call** statement is part of an assignment statement because the value returned from the function must be stored in a variable in the main part of the program. The variable called **biggest** will hold the value of the largest number.

The function is called three times using different values.

Can you identify the six parts of the function, as outlined in the table on page 155?

Now let's look at how to create a user-defined function for PROCESS SIX LENGTHS. The function will have one parameter, the list of length times, and it will return the **averagelength** to the main program

1	keyword def	Yes
2	function name	processsixlengths
3	parameters	lengthtimes
4	:	Yes
5	indented Python statements which make up the function body	Yes
6	optional return statement	Yes – return averagelength

Review the flowchart for PROCESS SIX LENGTHS on page 151 and look at the pseudocode you produced as part of the Practice task on page 151.

`OUTPUT "RIVERSIDE SWIMMING CLUB"` `OUTPUT "Enter swim times for six lengths"`	Output a heading onto the screen
`TOTALLENGTH=0`	Set the value of TOTALLENGTH equal to zero. This will be used to hold the total of all the lengths entered before calculating the average
`FOR i = 0 TO 5`	Use a for loop to move through and fill up each element in the list
`OUTPUT "Enter length time", i+1`	Prompt the user to enter a time for each length. i+1 is used so that the number following "Length time" is understandable by the user. For example the code will output Enter length time 3 – when entering element 2 into the list
`INPUT LENGTHTIMES[i]`	Write the value entered to the list

`WHILE LENGTHTIMES[i] < 20 OR`
`LENGTHTIMES[i] >30`
`        OUTPUT "ENTER A VALUE BETWEEN`
`        20 AND 30"`
`        INPUT LENGTHTIMES[i]`
`END WHILE`
	While loop to validate the value entered so that it is between 20 and 30

`TOTALLENGTH=TOTALLENGTH+LENGTHTIMES[i]`	Add the value entered to the TOTALLENGTH
`END FOR`	The end of the for loop
`AVERAGE= TOTALLENGTH/6`	Calculate the average of the lengths entered and store it in a variable AVERAGE

The function **processixlengths** will have one parameter – the list which will hold the length times. The list is called **lengthtimes** and this list has been created outside of the function, in the main program. New values are being added to the list within the function, which will return the average length through a return statement to the main program.

To see how this function works, and how the parameter **lengthtimes** is passed into the function, look at the code below.

```
# A function to process the six length times

def processsixlengths(lengthtimes):
        print("         RIVERSIDE SWIMMING CLUB")
        print("Enter swim times for six lengths")
        totallength=0

        for i in range(0,6):

# add a new loop to validate the length
            valid=False
            while (valid==False):
                user_input=input("Length time "+str(i+1))

                if len(user_input)==0:
                    print("Enter a value please")
                else:
                    lengthtimes[i]=int(user_input)
                    if (lengthtimes[i]<20 or lengthtimes[i]>30):
                        print("Enter a value between 20 and 30")
                    else:
                        valid=True



                totallength=totallength+lengthtimes[i]
        average=totallength/6

        return average

#call the processuserlogin function
processuserlogin()

#call the processsixlengths function
average=processsixlengths(lengthtimes)
```

> The average is calculated inside the function, so it must be returned to the main program.
>
> A function can return one single value using the return statement.

> The call to the function includes "lengthtimes" as an argument. An argument is the value that you pass to a procedure parameter when you call it. The variable "average" will hold the average value returned from the function.[†]

158

Practice

In this exercise you will create a function for SHOW USER QUIZ. You need to look at the following pseudocode you have been given:

```
QUESTIONS=[" How can cold water affect your swimming
capability?", "Question 2 text", "Question 3 text",
"Question 4 text", "Question 5 text", "Question 6
text"]

ALIST=["a It does not", "Question 2 option a",
"Question 3 option a", "Question 4 option a",
"Question 5 option a", "Question 6 option a"]

BLIST=["b It is harder to swim as you can get
cramp", "Question 2 option b", "Question 3 option
b", "Question 4 option b", "Question 5 option b",
"Question 6 option b"]

CLIST=["c It is easier to swim as it cools you
down", "Question 2 option c", "Question 3 option
c", "Question 4 option c", "Question 5 option c",
"Question 6 option c"]

CORRECTANS=["b", "question 2 correct answer",
"question 3 correct answer", "question 4 correct
answer", "question 5 correct answer", "question 6
correct answer"]

POINTS=0

OUTPUT "RIVERSIDE SWIMMING CLUB"

OUTPUT "WATER SAFETY QUIZ"

FOR i = 0 TO 5

        OUTPUT "QUESTION",i

        OUTPUT QUESTIONS[i]

        OUTPUT ALIST[i]

        OUTPUT BLIST[i]

        OUTPUT CLIST[i]

        OUTPUT "Enter your answer (a, b or c)"

        INPUT USERANSWER

        IF (USERANSWER=CORRECTANS[i])

        POINTS=POINTS+10

        END IF

END FOR
```

➤ Open the file called **questions.py** provided by your teacher.

➤ You are going to create a function to complete SHOW USER QUIZ.

➤ First write the heading for the function **showuserquiz**. Here is some information to help you: This function will have no parameters but it does return the value for TOTALPOINTS to the main program.

➤ Review the pseudocode you have created and flowchart on page 149 for the SHOW USER QUIZ process.

➤ Now add the code which will create the lists for the quiz. When writing the code for this, you must create the lists that will hold the questions, answers and correct answers within the function. Review Unit 9.2 where you have used lists for data and the section of algorithm on page 151.

You are going to complete the code for creating the questions using the questions you were asked to design on page 151.

The first question and **alist** list has been to the program for you. Review this code before undertaking the tasks.

➤ Complete the questions list using the questions you created in in the task on page 151.

➤ Complete the **alist** list using the answers you created in the task on page 151.

➤ Now you must add the **blist** list by adding the option b answers for your questions.

➤ Complete the **clist** list by adding the option c answers for your questions.

➤ Complete the **correctans** list by adding the letter which represents the correct answer for each of your questions.

➤ Now use the algorithm on page 159 to write the rest of the code for SHOW USER QUIZ.

➤ The function does not have any parameters but it will return the points gained by the user. So, you will need to put a return statement at the bottom of the function.

➤ Add a call to the function in the main program.

➤ Review the function called PROCESSSIXLENGTHS to remind you of how this is done.

Remember that the call to the function must be part of an assignment statement as it returns a value. You must have a variable which will hold points when it is returned from the function **showuserquiz**.

Project management

Learn

The **project manager** has to plan the work that needs to be done. The work may be broken down into small sections. He or she needs to ask how long each task will take or how many people will be required to complete the task.

Time – all tasks should be allocated an amount of time to complete and a **deadline** for completion.

Cost – all projects have a budget. That is, the amount of money available to spend on the project. The project manager must ensure that the project is completed without overspending so each stage of the project is allocated a budget.

The project manager will monitor and record the work done at each stage and create a schedule.

Gantt charts

A Gantt chart is a horizontal bar chart. The tasks are written along the *y*-axis and the duration is written along the *x*-axis.

First, the project manager must allocate estimated durations for each task. An example for a simple project is shown below.

Stage	Duration (days)
Analysis	1
Design	2
Coding	3
Testing	2
Evaluation	2

KEYWORDS

project manager: the person who is responsible for managing the scheduling, costing and timing of a project

deadline: a date by which a particular task must be completed

What deadline do you have for a project you are working on now?

DID YOU KNOW?
Henry Gantt developed Gantt charts to help him schedule work in factories.

Abstraction

When planning a project there are some general characteristics that all projects have. For example all projects have distinct tasks; we need to know what each task is but we do not need to know exactly what is involved in each task. Abstraction is used to create a simple Gantt chart showing the general characteristics of the project plan. The Gantt chart shows:

- the tasks to be carried out
- the order in which the tasks should be completed
- an approximate timescale for each of the tasks
- what should be achieved at any point during the project.

	1	2	3	4	5	6	7	8	9	10
Analysis	■									
Design		■	■							
Coding				■	■	■				
Testing							■	■		
Evaluation									■	■
Duration (Days)	1	2	3	4	5	6	7	8	9	10

The project manager can use this chart to help keep track of how the project is going. From this chart you can see when each task should be completed.

Practice

➤ As project manager for the Riverside Swimming Club you have created the following table showing the estimated duration for each of the tasks from analysis to evaluation.

Stage	Duration (days)	Comments
Analysis	2	This stage involves meeting with the staff at Riverside Swimming Club to find out what they need. We can then list the user requirements. 1 day for meeting the staff to find out what they need. 1 day for creating the user requirements and then getting the manager at Riverside Swimming Club to check and agree them.
Design	2.5	We have to design four sections of code: |	Wireframe	Algorithm	Data dictionary
PROCESS USER LOGIN		0.5 days	
PROCESS SIX LENGTHS		0.5 days	
SHOW USER QUIZ		1.0 day	
OUTPUT INFORMATION TO USER		0.5 days		 Three of the design sections require half a day as shown above. However, the SHOW USER QUIZ section is more complex as it uses lists, therefore more time will be needed.
Coding	4	1 day for each section of code. We must translate the algorithms into code.
Testing	2	Half a day to test each section of code.
Evaluation	2	1 day to evaluate the outcome of the testing. 1 day to let the staff of Riverside Swimming Club evaluate the software and give feedback.

➤ From the table, create a Gantt chart showing how long each task will take. Download and modify RSC1.docx to create your Gantt chart. Use a word processor to create your Gantt Chart and call it **RSC1.docx**.

Go further

Testing is the process of checking a system or parts of the system to ensure that it is free of bugs and defects and that it meets the user requirements. This is done by executing the program and entering test data. The outcome of the testing is documented (written down). Any errors or bugs are highlighted and then they can be fixed by the programmer.

The aim of testing is to ensure that the program:
◆ is error-free
◆ meets the user requirements
◆ operates efficiently.

Testing must be planned before being executed and results recorded.

Programmers cannot test for every eventuality but they use a number of techniques to test for as many as possible.

White box testing identifies errors in syntax, logic and dataflow within the code. Black box testing focuses on inputs and outputs. (See the Did you know box on page 72.)

Python IDLE helps programmers by identifying errors. Syntax errors are identified immediately and the program will not run.

For instance, this next section of code has a syntax error. A message box is displayed and there is a red highlight which appears where the error has occurred. Once the error has been corrected, the program will run.

The red highlight identifies the line with the error. Can you identify this syntax error?

```
File   Edit   Format   Run   Options   Window   Help

# A function to process user login


def processuserlogin()
    correct=False
    while (correct==False):
        print("          RIVERSIDE SWIMMING CLUB")
        print
        print
        username=input("Username: ")
        print
        password=input("Password: ")
        if (username=="Applicant1" and password=="Swimming@"):
            correct=True
        else:
            print("Enter a valid username and password")
            correct=False


#call the processuserlogin function
processuserlogin()
```

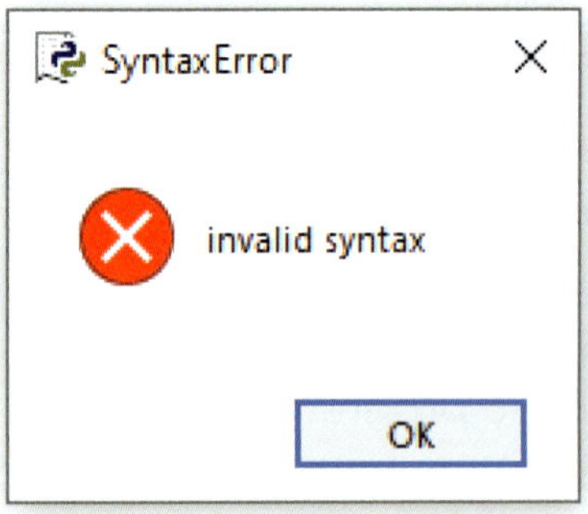

SyntaxError ✕

❌ invalid syntax

OK

Sometimes errors are not so easy to detect. When a program contains logic errors, it will run but it may produce unexpected or incorrect results.

```
            RIVERSIDE SWIMMING CLUB
Username: Applicantl
Password: Swlmmlng@
Enter a valid username and password
            RIVERSIDE SWIMMING CLUB
Username: |
```

We know that the correct username and password for Riverside Swimming Club are

Username = **Applicant1**

Password = **Sw1mm1ng@**

This user has typed the correct username and password, but is told that the values are invalid. Can you identify the logic error?

Answer: The IF statement contains an incorrect value for the username:

```
password=input("Password: ")
if (username=="Applicant" and password=="Swlmmlng@"):
    correct=True
else:
    print("Enter a valid username and password")
    correct=False
```

Test data must be selected for each type of testing. Generally, a thorough test plan includes a combination of:

Test data	
Extreme data	This helps to test that the system can deal with the highest and lowest data values that are acceptable. This can also include data on the boundary. For example in the lengthtimes list the value has to be between 20 and 30. In this case the test data would normally include the numbers 20 and 30 as extreme values.
Valid data	Used to test that the system operates as expected with normal data.
Erroneous data	Data that should not be accepted or is the wrong data type. Used to test that the system can process invalid data and does not crash when invalid data is entered.

Creating a test plan

A test plan for any solution should be presented in tabular format. It should incorporate black box and white box testing, list the test data and expected output.

Let's say we want to test the **processsixlengths** function.

Remember the user requirements:

1 Log in to the system.
2 Enter the six length times.
3 Take the short quiz to measure their knowledge about water safety.
4 Output their score and average length time with a message about whether they can join the club or need more training.

Create a test plan table which will test the validation code for the input of the six length times. The test table created here does not test for the average value or the rest of the code in PROCESS SIX LENGTHS.

◆ Open the file Lengths.py provided by your teacher. Run the program using the values in the test table below. Carry out the testing and complete the two remaining columns using screenshots to show the outcome.

Test Number	Reason for test	Test data	Expected output	Observed output	Match/ corrective measures	User requirement
1	Valid data	25	Accepted			2
2	Invalid data	35	Rejected			2
3	Extreme data	20	Accepted			2
4	Extreme data	30	accepted			2

◆ Compare your results with the screenshot below. Did you get the same results as those shown?

Test number	Reason for test	Test data	Expected output	Observed output	Match/ corrective measures	User requirement
1	Valid data	25	Accepted	RIVERSIDE SWIMMING CLUB Enter swim times for six lengths Length time 125 Length time 2	Match – no corrective action	2
2	Invalid data	35	Rejected	RIVERSIDE SWIMMING CLUB Enter swim times for six lengths Length time 125 Length time 235 Enter a value between 20 and 30	Match – no corrective action	2
3	Extreme data	20	Accepted	RIVERSIDE SWIMMING CLUB Enter swim times for six lengths Length time 120 Length time 2	Match – no corrective action	2
4	Extreme data	30	Accepted	RIVERSIDE SWIMMING CLUB Enter swim times for six lengths Length time 130 Length time 2	Match – no corrective action	2

◆ Now run the program and try pressing the enter key instead of a value? What happens? You should find that the program crashes and gives you a message like this:

```
        RIVERSIDE SWIMMING CLUB
Enter swim times for six lengths
Length time 1
Traceback (most recent call last):
  File "N:\hodder2019\9.5Mon7Oct\9.5 PROGRAMS\Lengths.py", line 42, in <module>
    average=processsixlengths(lengthtimes)
  File "N:\hodder2019\9.5Mon7Oct\9.5 PROGRAMS\Lengths.py", line 29, in processsi
xlengths
    lengthtimes[i]=int(input("Length time "+ str(i+1)))
ValueError: invalid literal for int() with base 10: ''
```

The program cannot handle null data.

Write out a new line for test plan by completing the table below.

Test number	Reason for test	Test data	Expected output	Observed output	Match/corrective measures	User requirement
5	Null Data					

◆ Now open the file called **Lengths2.py** provided by your teacher. This program contains a new version of the function **processsixlengths** which checks to make sure that the user does not enter null data.

◆ Test the new version of the function using the line you have created for the test plan above.

◆ Open the document called **RSC3.docx** and complete the line for test number 5 using a new screen shot which shows that the program now works.

◆ Add three further tests to the test plan in **RSC3.docx**. You could include tests for valid, invalid and extreme data.

◆ Make a list of any further corrective measures which are required as a result of the testing. Add these at the bottom of the test plan.

◆ Add a new test plan for **processuserlogin** to **RSC3.docx**.

◆ Open the file called **Lengths2.py** provided by your teacher.

◆ Test the **processuserlogin** function using your test data and include screenshots to show the observed output.

◆ Save **RSC3.docx**.

Challenge yourself

The Riverside Swimming Club has informed you that they want the data in the lengthtimes list sorted. As a team of programmers you have been asked to create the code for a new process called SORTLENGTHS. The pseudocode for this process is shown below:

```
SORTLENGTHS

FOR i= 0 to 5

   FOR j=0 to (5 - i)

      IF lengthtimes[j] > lengthtimes [j+1]

         temp = lengthtimes [j]

         lengthtimes [j] = lengthtimes [j+1]

         lengthtimes [j+1] = temp

      END IF

   END FOR

END FOR
```

SORTLENGTHS(LENGTHTIMES) will be a procedure that takes the LENGTHTIMES list and sorts it smallest first. You have already learned how to sort a list of values in Unit 9.2. Review this section to remind you how to do this.

> Review the work completed on sorting in Unit 9.2 to remind yourself of how the SORTLENGTHS function should work.

Once you are happy you are going to write the code for this procedure.
➤ Open the program called **CY.py** provided by your teacher.
➤ Working on SORTLENGTHS:
  • The procedure will have one parameter, **lengthtimes**.
  • Write the procedure heading on paper.
  • The code you write inside the procedure will need to sort the list smallest first.
  • You will need to use the bubble sort.
➤ Enter the code for SORTLENGTHS into the program **CY.py**.
➤ Open the document called **RSC2.docx**.
➤ Add the pseudocode for the **sortlengths** procedure.
➤ Add a test plan for SORTLENGTHS to ensure that it works appropriately. Remember†to:
  • include black box and white box tests
  • think about valid, erroneous and extreme data.
➤ Carry out the test plan to ensure the code in **sortlengths** is working. Remember to add the relevant screenshots.
➤ Note any corrective measures that you had to take to improve the program.

Final project

As you undertake the final exercise in this chapter you should have noticed that different students' solutions will look different. That is to be expected as no two people will solve a problem in exactly the same way.

➤ The final function that the program needs is OUTPUT INFORMATION TO USER.

➤ This is a very important function and must give the user the correct information.

➤ You are going to create the wireframe, pseudocode, data dictionary and code for this process.

➤ Create a wireframe for the screen which will output the information to the user. You need to include the following on the screen:
  ● six length times sorted
  ● the average length time
  ● the number of points the user has achieved
  ● a message stating whether or not they can become a member of the club.

➤ Create the pseudocode for OUTPUT INFORMATION TO USER. This pseudocode will represent the body of the function you will write later.

➤ The code inside the function must check to see if the user can become a member. To do this you need to check if they have scored 40 or more points AND if their average swim time is less than 28. You will need to use an IF statement to do this.

➤ Create the data dictionary for the process OUTPUT INFORMATION TO USER. Use the headings that you have used previously for this. The data used in this section is the `lengthtimes` list, `average` and `points`.

➤ Open the program called **SC.py** provided by your teacher.

➤ Note the following whilst working on OUTPUT INFORMATION TO USER:
  ● It will have three parameters, `lengthtimes`, `average`, `points`. Type the function heading now.
  ● The code must output the contents of the list `lengthtimes` in order of smallest first.
  ● It must also output the average length time.
  ● It must also output the points achieved in the quiz by the user.
  ● It must display a message telling the user if they can become a member of the club.
  ● The IF statement inside the function must check to see if the user can become a member.

➤ Your completed program should have five functions:
  ● `processuserlogin`
  ● `processsixlengths`
  ● `sortlengths`
  ● `showuserquiz`
  ● `outputinformationtouser`

➤ Open your document called **RSC3.docx**.

➤ Add a test plan for **outputinformationtouser** to ensure that it works appropriately. Remember to:
  - include black box and white box tests
  - think about valid, erroneous and extreme data.
➤ Carry out the test plans to ensure the program is working.
➤ Note any corrective measures that you had to take to improve the program.
➤ Save **RSC3.docx**.

Evaluation

➤ You now have files called **RSC1.docx** (from page 163 where you created a Gantt Chart) and **RSC2.docx** (which contains the design section of the project).
➤ Create a folder called 'Riverside Swimming Club' on your computer and place the documents into the folder.
➤ Open a new blank document and save it as **RSCPROJECT. docx**.
➤ Add the contents of **RSC1.docx**, **RSC2.docx** and **RSC3.docx** to the document called **RSCPROJECT.docx**.
➤ Add a title page to the document with a relevant graphic.
➤ Place page numbers onto the document.
➤ Go to the bottom of the document and add a new section called Evaluation.
➤ Copy the tasks that the software should perform, from page 141, into the document. Comment on how your programme has achieved each one of these.
➤ Analyse your testing and the data used. You can do this by carrying out the following.
  o Your test data includes some failed tests. Refer to these and comment on how the test failure helped improve the program.
  o Refer to the breadth of the test data in terms of Valid, Invalid, Null and Extreme tests and state how you have used this type of test data for each section of the program.
  o Mention any changes that you had to make to the program after it was tested.
➤ Discuss any limitations you have found in the program. You can do this by listing any problems you discovered after testing the program.
➤ Save **RSCPROJECT.docx**.
➤ Save the document as a **.pdf** and allow others to review it.

Unit 9.6

Choosing and using: Databases and spreadsheets

Business data management: Spreadsheets or databases?

Data management is key to the operation of successful businesses. Many large organisations analyse massive quantities of continually changing data in an attempt to increase productivity and profit. Data analysis on such a large scale is known as **big data**.

The concept of big data can be described using **3Vs**:

→ Volume: the massive quantities of data collected and analysed by companies on an ongoing basis.

→ Velocity: the speed at which data is processed and turned into useful information.

→ Variety: the various formats data can now be presented in, for example, audio, video, image, text.

Here are some examples.

Company	Type	Example of big data use
UPS	International delivery	UPS analyses **vehicle telematics** from cars and trucks along with advanced algorithms to help calculate the best routes, automatically control engine idle time, and predict when maintenance is needed.
T-Mobile	Mobile phones	Combines data from a number of its customer management, billing and social media applications to help predict when a customer might want to leave the organisation and go to another mobile phone company.
Google	Technology company	Google works closely with the U.S. Centers for Disease Control to track when users are inputting search terms related to e.g. flu topics. Working together, the two organisations can help predict which regions may experience outbreaks.
Next Big Sound	Online music analytics provider	Next Big Sound uses **data analytics** to help musicians and bands evaluate online activity such as Facebook likes, YouTube views and Twitter mentions so bands can understand their audience.
Netflix	Media streaming service	Netflix analyses international viewing habits before it creates and buys programs that will appeal to their audience.

KEYWORDS

big data: refers to the large quantities of data that can be mined (analysed) for information by large organisations; big data can be described using 3Vs

3Vs: term used to explain the concept of big data (volume, velocity and variety)

vehicle telematics: information telecommunications from vehicles – this includes monitoring and broadcasting of vehicle location using GPS, engine status, and so on

data analytics: the process of extracting meaningful information from raw data using automated processes and algorithms

DID YOU KNOW?

Big Data is big business these days. Every two days, digital users create as much data as humans did from the beginning of time until 2003!

The amount of data businesses need to collect, process and analyse has increased dramatically in recent years. Businesses collect data from social media, email, online forms and even from other organisations. They use a range of computer applications to help them cope with such large amounts of data. Two of the most popular applications used by businesses to help with this task are databases and spreadsheets. The difficulty faced by many organisations is deciding which one to use, and when.

In this unit you will learn about:
→ the key differences between databases and spreadsheets
→ the key points to consider when deciding which application best suits your organisation's needs.

DID YOU KNOW?
Google processes more than 63 000 search queries every second.

SCENARIO

Gig-Well is a new local concert promoter and event production company. It organises and promotes gigs and events with artists from all over the world. This year, Gig-Well is organising Par-T in the Park in your home town.

The owners of Gig-Well need some advice on selecting software to allow them to keep track of ticket sales, ticket production and profit from the sales of tickets and merchandise at the Par-T event.

They have asked you to help them decide between the use of a spreadsheet or a database application to help them with these tasks.

Do you remember?

Before starting this unit, you should be able to:
✔ identify at least one database and one spreadsheet application
✔ identify potential uses for spreadsheet and database applications in a business-related scenario.

You should also know that:
✔ database and spreadsheet applications are both used to store data in a structured format, under headings
✔ databases can be used to provide increased data integrity; data integrity refers to the correctness and accuracy of data stored in a database application
✔ spreadsheets can be used to help organisations analyse data by using formulas and graphical presentations to present data in a useful format
✔ users assign different data types to individual data items stored in databases and spreadsheet applications. For example, data stored as a numerical data type can be analysed differently from data stored as a text data type or a date/time data type.

Databases or spreadsheets: Making the decision

Learn

For organisations that analyse and process a lot of data, it can be difficult to decide which application best suits their needs. In some cases, organisations may need to use both applications for different types of processing.

Both databases and spreadsheets can store large quantities of data and both can be used to analyse data in different ways. When deciding which best suits their needs a business should look at what they want to do with their data. If a company wants to carry out detailed analysis they should use a spreadsheet application. If, however, they want to be able to produce outputs for other people, such as professional reports, and maintain a high level of data integrity, then they would be better using a database application.

Data integrity can be compromised in large databases if data redundancy occurs. Data redundancy refers to the unnecessary repetition of data in a large database. When more than one copy of the same data item is held in a database, errors can be made when data is being entered or updated and this can lead to incorrect results from data processing. Carefully-designed databases reduce data redundancy and help maintain data integrity.

Databases and spreadsheets can be used for a variety of uses.

Databases	**Spreadsheets**
• Allow data types and field names to be assigned to data items • Use automated methods to help validate data entered into a database • Can employ range of query methods to extract useful data from a database and support data analysis using calculation in formulas • Reduce data redundancy through the creation of databases with more than one data table • Allow the creation of forms to support data input and navigation around a complex database • Allow the creation of reports to present data in an appropriate format for the end user	• Can be used for entering and storing numerical data • Allow users to format stored numerical data for presentation • Allow users to create formulas to help analyse stored data • Can be used to create charts to produce visual presentations of stored data • Use data and linked formulas to help users make predictions about the future if input data changes • Can be used to sort and filter options to extract useful data

For example, a company storing a lot of customer order and sales data to produce invoices and receipts might also want to be able to carry out analysis of sales and profits, and be able to make predictions about how changes in price might affect overall profits.

A company might decide to create a database to store details about customers, products and orders, so they can use forms for data input and create a user-friendly interface for customers.

They might also then decide to create a spreadsheet, to quickly analyse sales and profits and identify trends in sales.

Some of the points listed in the table below can help organisations decide which application to use and when.

Use a database when …	Use a spreadsheet when …
• you need a user-friendly interface with menus for users • you want to maintain data integrity • you need to be able to produce professional reports for output • data needs to be updated frequently • you need to provide a data source for programmed applications or web-based applications	• you need to analyse numerical data • you need to make predictions using **what-if questioning** • you need to be able to quickly produce charts to help analyse data

KEYWORD

what-if questioning: the process of making predictions about outcomes in a scenario by changing input values to see how they impact on related output

Practice

The owners of Gig-Well have explained to you how they would like to analyse and use the data collected when organising the Par-T in the Park event.

Tickets are divided into three categories: Gold, Silver and Bronze. Each colour represents a different price level and a different zone in the park where the event will he held. They need to be able to limit sales to each zone.

They also intend to sell other branded merchandise, such as T-shirts and sweatshirts.

In summary, they would like you to:

➤ carry out a detailed analysis of the costs required to organise and run the event, and use this data to help them decide on ticket and merchandise prices, and to work out how many tickets they need to sell to make a profit

➤ collect details from customers purchasing tickets and other merchandise, and use these details to produce personalised invoices for each customer with their name and address

➤ produce a detailed report telling them how many tickets they have sold for each zone, along with the total number of tickets sold overall

Database applications: User requirements

Software developers normally develop solutions for clients. Before they can even start to produce the design documents for a database application it is important that they are very clear about the user requirements for the application. They will start by working out, with the client, what questions the database is expected to answer and what output the database is expected to produce.

In this part of the unit you will learn:

→ to extract the user requirements for a database solution from a user's description of the problem

→ how to interpret the contents of a data dictionary and an entity relationship diagram (ERD) and to produce a working database

→ to produce simple and complex queries and reports

→ to create customised forms for data input

→ to combine forms and macro structures to support navigation around a user database.

Entities are the people or things represented in a database application. Each type of entity will be stored in its own separate table. For example, a dentist's database storing details about patients and their appointments will contain a table which stores all of the details about all of the patients. It will also have a separate table storing details about all of the appointments they have made.

KEYWORDS

client: the person for whom an application is being developed

user requirements: a document which specifies what the user expects the software to do

entity relationship diagram (ERD): a diagram used to show how entities such as people, objects, and so on relate to each other within a database

entities: the people or things represented in a database application

macro: a small program written to complete a repetitive task automatically

SCENARIO

The Gig-Well owners have discussed their data processing needs with you. You have decided that a database solution would be best to help them manage their ticket purchases. Following some detailed discussions you have helped them produce the following list of user requirements.

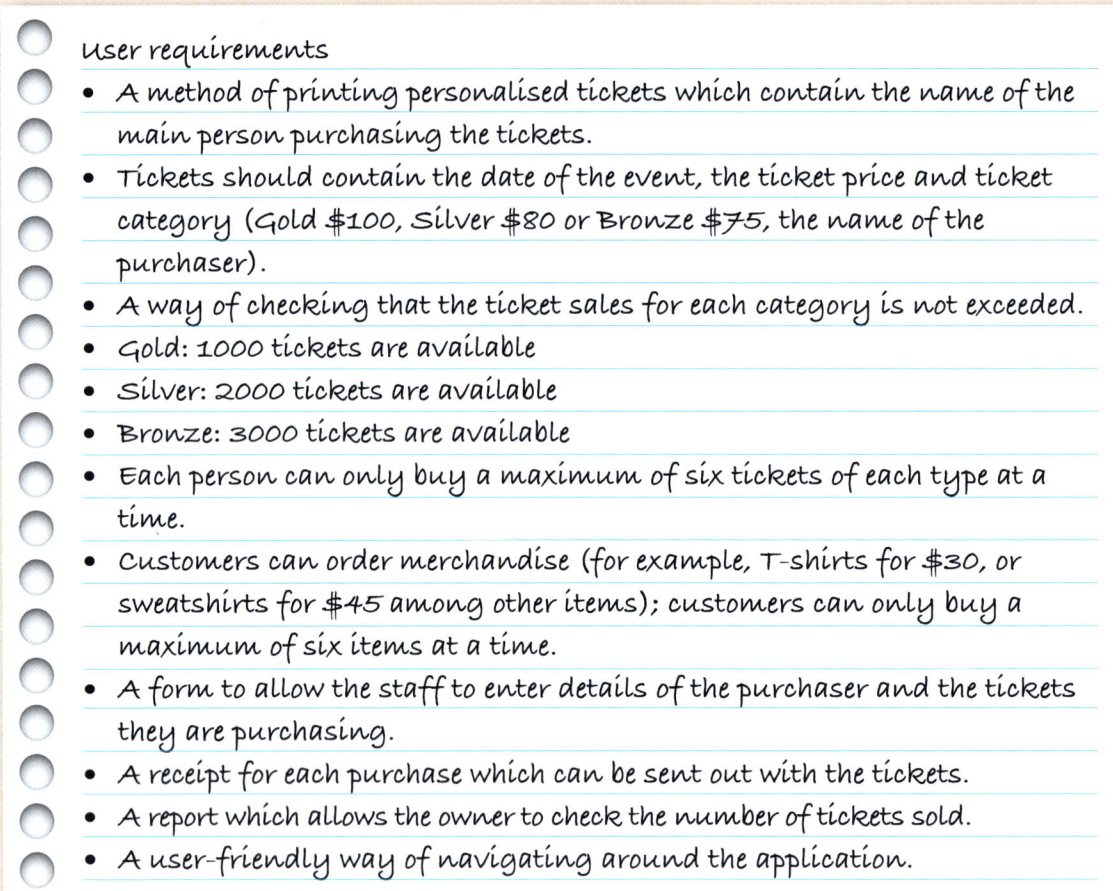

User requirements
- A method of printing personalised tickets which contain the name of the main person purchasing the tickets.
- Tickets should contain the date of the event, the ticket price and ticket category (Gold $100, Silver $80 or Bronze $75, the name of the purchaser).
- A way of checking that the ticket sales for each category is not exceeded.
- Gold: 1000 tickets are available
- Silver: 2000 tickets are available
- Bronze: 3000 tickets are available
- Each person can only buy a maximum of six tickets of each type at a time.
- Customers can order merchandise (for example, T-shirts for $30, or sweatshirts for $45 among other items); customers can only buy a maximum of six items at a time.
- A form to allow the staff to enter details of the purchaser and the tickets they are purchasing.
- A receipt for each purchase which can be sent out with the tickets.
- A report which allows the owner to check the number of tickets sold.
- A user-friendly way of navigating around the application.

Your task is to work with your development team to help them produce the final application.

Do you remember?

Before starting this unit, you should be able to:
- ✔ create data tables in a database
- ✔ create relationships between tables to form a relational database
- ✔ create forms for data input to a database
- ✔ assign appropriate datatypes to data items in a database
- ✔ apply some validation rules to fields in database tables
- ✔ create simple queries to extract data from a database
- ✔ access the SQL version of a *Microsoft Access* query in a database structure.

Database solutions: Designing solutions

Learn

When developing a database to solve a problem, developers will spend a lot of time planning their solution. You should understand how a relational database will involve the production of a **data dictionary** and an entity relationship diagram (ERD).

KEYWORD

data dictionary: a document used to describe the tables used in a database

Computational Thinking

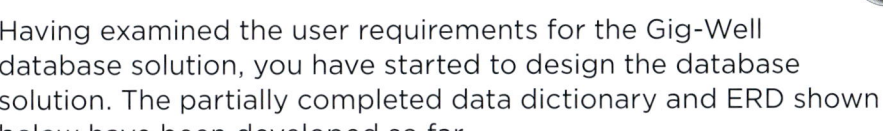

Having examined the user requirements for the Gig-Well database solution, you have started to design the database solution. The partially completed data dictionary and ERD shown below have been developed so far.

custTBL

Attribute name	Data type	Field length	Validation	Example/description
CustID	autonumber			Key field
Title	text	5	Presence check and can only be Mr, Miss or Mrs	Lookup list containing Mr, Miss, Mrs only
Surname	text	30	Presence check and input mask	To ensure starts with capital letter
Firstname	text	30	Presence check and input mask	To ensure starts with capital letter
HouseNum	text	5	Presence check	
Address1	text	30	Presence check and input mask	To ensure starts with capital letter
Address2	text	30	Presence check and input mask	To ensure starts with capital letter
Country	text	30	Presence check	

productTBL

Attribute name	Data type	Field length	Validation	Example/description
ProductID	autonumber			Key field
Description				Can only be Gold, Silver, Bronze, SS or TS (for Sweat shirt or T-shirt) Cannot be left blank
Size				Can only be XS, S, M, L or XL Does not need to be entered if Description is Gold, Silver or Bronze
SellingPrice				Cannot be left blank and price must be between $10 and $100

orderTBL

Attribute name	Data type	Field length	Validation	Example/description
	autonumber			Key field
CustID				Cannot be left blank. Foreign Key field. Creates link with custTBL
ProductID				Cannot be left blank. Foreign Key field. Creates link with productTBL
Quantity				Cannot be left blank Must be between 0 and 6
Paid				A True/ False data type

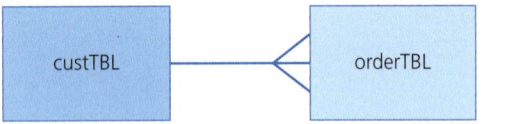 

custTBL — orderTBL — productTBL

Your task is to complete the data dictionary for the database.

- ✪ Use the process of abstraction to help you determine the most appropriate data types, field lengths and validation checks in the tables called productTBL and orderTBL.

- ✪ Generalise your experience of database applications to decide on the most appropriate primary key fields for the table called orderTBL.

- ✪ The process of generalisation should allow you to understand that each database table should only contain one copy of the data related to each product and customer and that in most ordering systems a customer can order more than one product at a time. Use the process of abstraction to complete the ER diagram shown above by drawing a line between orderTBL and productTBL to illustrate the type of relationship that should exist between the two tables.

Do this by thinking about an example data item for each field heading. Then think about: the most appropriate data type you could select to store that data item, the largest number of characters needed to store that data item and whether there are any limits (validation checks) you would like to place on the user when they are entering data into each field.

Your teacher will give you a copy of a word-processed document called **Gig-Well Database Design.docx** to help you complete this task.

Practice

Once you have completed your database design you should:

➤ Open *Microsoft Access*.
➤ Create each of the three tables.
➤ Create the appropriate relationships between the three tables.

We can see from the data dictionary that the attribute ProductID in orderTBL is being used to create a link between orderTBL and productTBL.

The relationships to be created between the tables can be illustrated using this completed ERD:

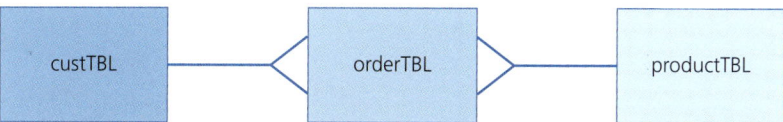

To help with data input we can use the lookup wizard to help create this link.

➤ Open orderTBL.
➤ Click on the data type for ProductID and select Lookup Wizard.

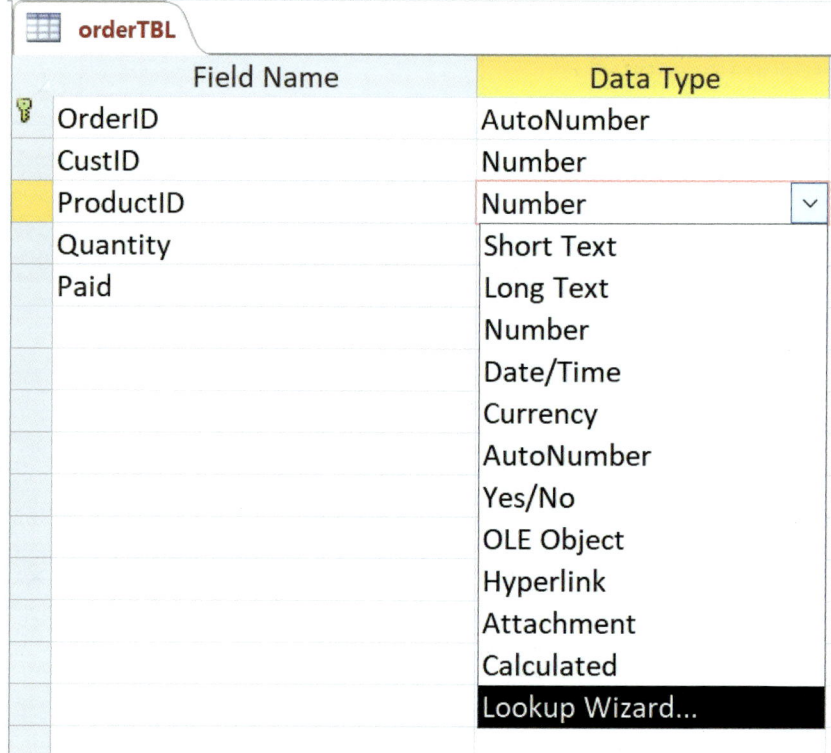

➤ Select 'I want the lookup field to get the values from another table or query' and click Next. This allows us to create a link to the existing productTBL. This means the user cannot place an order for a product which does not already exist in the productTBL. This helps maintain data integrity.

➤ Select Table: productTBL and click Next.

Lookup Wizard

Which table or query should provide the values for your lookup field?

Table: custTBL
Table: orderTBL
Table: productTBL

View

⦿ Tables   ○ Queries   ○ Both

Cancel   < Back   Next >   Finish

➤ Click on the double chevron to move all available fields across to the right hand panel of the dialogue box.

> This will allow the user to see all of the data associated with any ProductID when they try to add a new item to a customer's order. Doing this means the user can add an item without having to know the ProductID.

Lookup Wizard

Which fields of productTBL contain the values you want included in your lookup field? The fields you select become columns in your lookup field.

Available Fields:

Selected Fields:

>
>>
<
<<

ProductID
Description
Size
SellingPrice

Cancel   < Back   Next >   Finish

➤ Click on Next and then display the records in ascending order by ProductID and click on Next again.
➤ Click on Finish.
➤ The following message will be displayed. Click Yes.

Lookup Wizard   ✕

⚠ The table must be saved before relationships can be created. Save now?

Yes   No

Using ProductID in this way has created a relationship or a link between orderTBL and productTBL. Later, when the user needs to create an order for a new product this relationship will allow them to view the list of all possible products contained in the table called productTBL. They will select an item from that list and add it to their customer order.

➤ Click Database Tools and then Relationships to check the two tables have been linked.

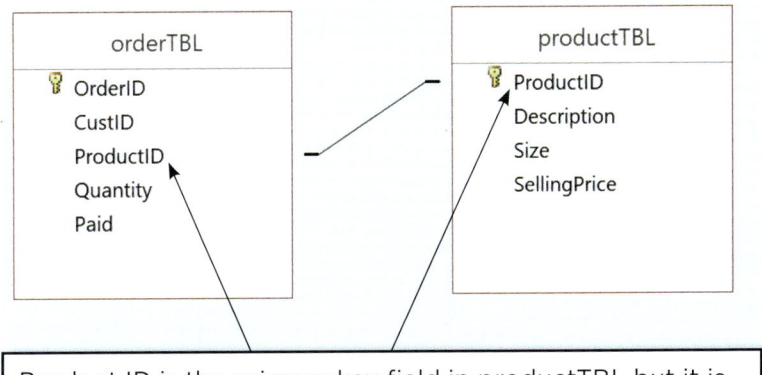

Product ID is the primary key field in productTBL but it is a foreign key in orderTBL and used to create a relationship between the two tables.

It is important that the user is able to add more than one product to each order. To do that a one-to-many relationship must be created (in other words, there can only ever be one record associated with each product in the productTBL but that product can appear many times in orderTBL).

When linking two tables in a database the primary key field from one table must exist in the second table before the relationship can be created. When this happens the field is known as a foreign key in the second table.

➤ Double click on the link line between the two tables and select '**Enforce Referential Integrity**' and '**Cascade Delete**'. This will edit the relationship to make sure that:
  o an order cannot be placed for a product that does not exist in productTBL (Enforce Referential Integrity)
  o if a product is deleted from productTBL, all related orders will be deleted from orderTBL (Cascade Delete).

➤ With a friend, discuss what fields are used to create a similar link between custTBL and orderTBL.

➤ Create a similar relationship between these two tables by:
  o creating a lookup value in orderTBL first
  o editing the relationship to Enforce Referential Integrity and Cascade Delete.

The final relationship view should look like this:

KEYWORDS

Enforce Referential Integrity: an entry for an item with a foreign key field cannot be placed in a table if that item does not already exist in the linked lookup table

Cascade Delete: if an item is deleted from a linked lookup table, all related entries will be deleted from the table which uses the lookup table as a data source

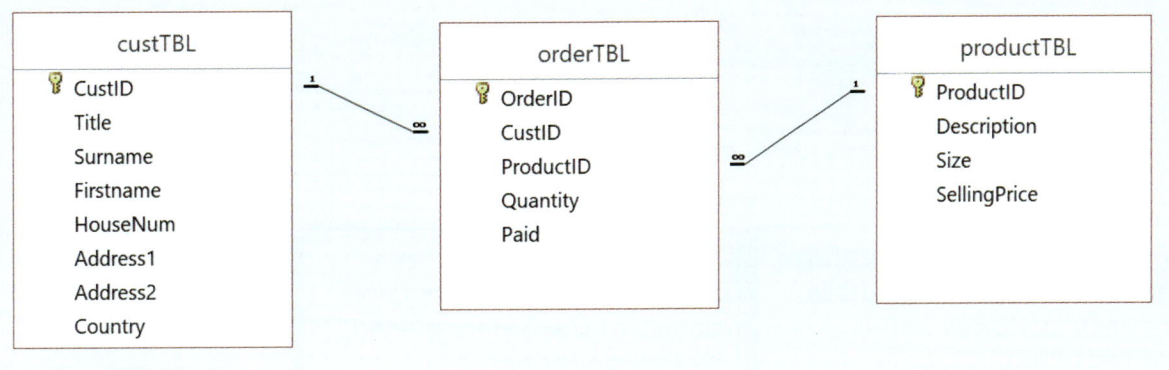

Entering data: Bound and unbound forms

Learn

You should already know that **forms** in database applications are **objects** that can be used to create a **user interface** for the database application. When creating database forms, developers can create a form and link it to one or more database tables. This form can then be used to input, display or edit data directly from a table. A form used this way is called a **bound form**.

Database developers can also create forms which are not linked to a data table. These forms are called **unbound forms**. Unbound forms can be used to create navigation menus to help the end user move through the system.

In relational databases, forms can be bound to more than one table. Data from the second table can be shown in a **subform**.

For example, the form shown below is being used to enter customer details and order details into the Gig-Well database. This one form is bound to a table containing customer information and a second table containing details of orders placed by that customer.

> We will look at unbounded forms later in this unit.

> Remember that foreign key fields are used to create links between database tables.

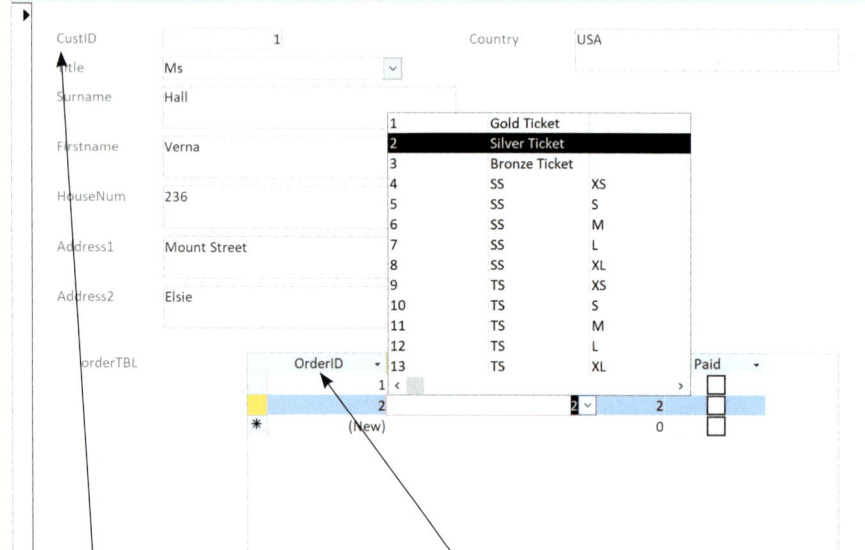

First table bound to this form is a table containing details of each customer in this organisation.

Subform; the second table bound to this form contains details of the orders placed by this customer.

KEYWORDS

form: a database object containing labels, text boxes and buttons to help users input, view or edit data in a database

object: the group of items which can be produced when creating a *Microsoft Access* database, including tables, forms, queries and reports

user interface: the means used to allow a user to communicate with a computer system

bound form: a form which is linked to a data source such as a table and which is then used to input, display or edit data directly into a table

unbound form: a form which is not linked to any data sources but can be used to help users operate the database

subform: a form which has been inserted into another form

Abstraction

When creating a form for data entry it is important to remember that the form presented to the user must be user friendly and easy for them to follow. The way a form is presented to the end user might not exactly reflect the way the data is stored in a database table. For example, field headings may differ slightly, the data may be presented in a slightly different order on the form. Use abstraction to consider how the layout of a data entry form can be amended to make it easier for the user to understand.

Practice

> The owner of Gig-Well wants the database to include forms to allow them to view or edit the contents of each individual table.

Use the file called **Gig-WellDB** provided by your teacher for the rest of the database related tasks in this unit.

Use your existing knowledge to create a data entry form for:

1 custTBL
2 productTBL.

Remember to edit the forms in design view. Make sure that all field and attribute names are clearly displayed on the form and that they are easy for the user to understand. You may also want to:

> edit the background colour, font, text size or text colour on the forms
> edit the layout of the fields on the forms
> edit the attribute names to ensure the user understands what data needs to be added
> include a title which explains what the form is used for
> include the Gig-Well name on each form or a logo for the company which you could create yourself.

> Remember to keep all forms consistent in presentation.

Your two forms should look similar to the one shown:

> Test the new forms by adding your own details as a new customer to custTBL.
> Gig-Well has introduced baseball caps as a new product for sale for $10.00. Add this information to productTBL.

The owners of Gig-Well would also like a single form which can be used to enter both customer details and order details at the same time. This form will be bound/linked to both custTBL and productTBL.

> Open *Microsoft Access* and then open **Gig-WellDB**.

Customer Details Form

CustID	1	(This value will be automatically assigned)
Title	Ms ⌄	(Please select from list provided)
Surname	Hall	Firstname Verna
House Number	236	
Address1	Mount Street	
Address2	Elsie	
Country	USA	

> ➤ Click Create and then Form Wizard.
> ➤ Select custTBL and then click the double chevron to add all fields to the form.
> ➤ Select orderTBL.
> ➤ Use the single chevron to add the necessary fields from orderTBL.

orderTBL will now be added to the form as a subform.

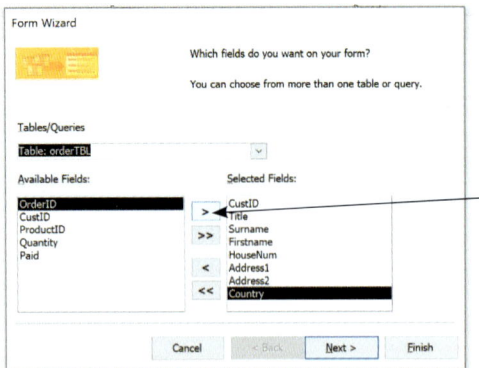

Click on each field in turn and then click on the single chevron to add the field to the form.

One field does not have to be added to the form. It has already been included using custTBL, so adding it again would confuse the user. Decide which field you do not have to add to the form to help make the form more user friendly.

> ➤ Select view by custTBL and then click Next.

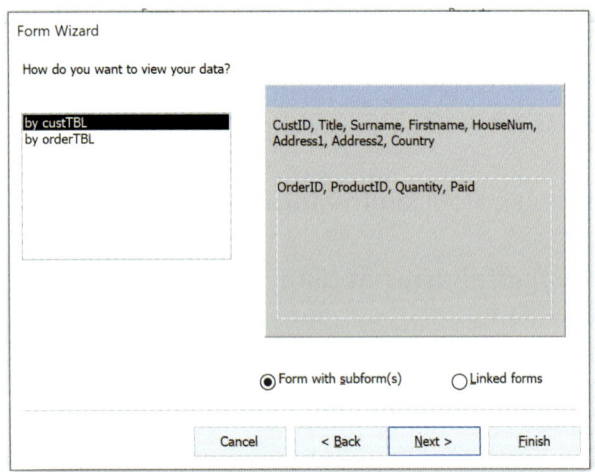

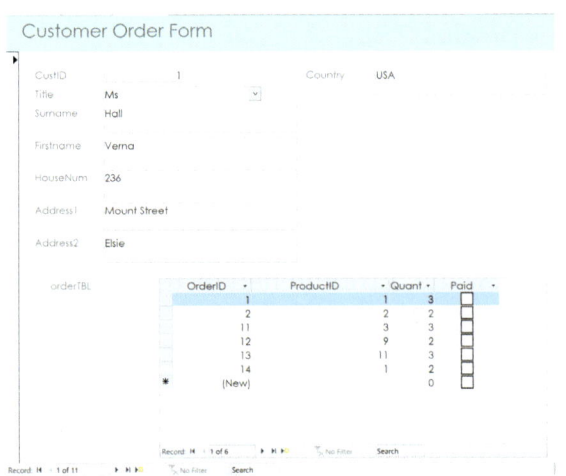

> ➤ Click Datasheet as the layout for your subform and click Next again.
> ➤ Name your form CustomerOrderFRM.
> ➤ Click Finish to create a form similar to the one shown above.
> ➤ Close *Microsoft Access*.

Computational Thinking

Use the process of generalisation to adapt the design for this last form to look like the other forms in your database.

Use the process of abstraction to edit the form labels to make sure they clearly explain what each field is being used to collect from the user.

Presenting data: Queries, reports and calculations

Learn

The way the data is presented will depend on the user requirements for the application. It is important that the output from the database can be used to answer the questions identified as part of the user requirements.

The output from a database may be:

➤ an onscreen list, for example the results of a simple query

➤ results of more **complex queries** which can be shown in a report.

But the output can be more complex still, for example:

➤ data from more than one **data source** can be combined and shown in one report

➤ data in a report can be analysed further, with additional calculations and formatting applied to it.

> Most databases will show these in a report so they are presented professionally.

KEYWORDS

complex queries: queries which extract data using more than one criteria on, from more than one data source, and may also include calculations

data source: a table or query used to provide data for display or further processing

In the example shown here we see data presented using a database report. Here, the report feature has been used to create a bill for a customer. It shows all of their purchases, in addition to final calculation used to work out overall total for the invoice.

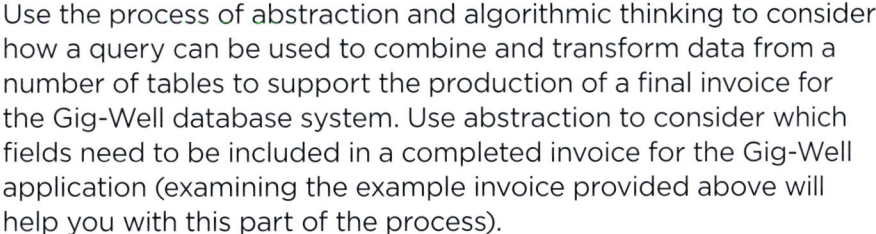

calculated field

⭐ Algorithmic thinking and abstraction

Use the process of abstraction and algorithmic thinking to consider how a query can be used to combine and transform data from a number of tables to support the production of a final invoice for the Gig-Well database system. Use abstraction to consider which fields need to be included in a completed invoice for the Gig-Well application (examining the example invoice provided above will help you with this part of the process).

As you consider the fields to be included, think also about the tables the fields are currently recorded in. Use algorithmic thinking as you work through the query wizard to add appropriate fields and criteria to the query being created for the customer invoice report.

Practice

The owners of Gig-Well want to use the new database to create an invoice for users when they buy tickets or other products from them. The report feature in *Microsoft Access* can be used to create a suitable invoice.

Before we can make our report we must create a query which will include data from all three tables. The query must also include new calculated data items.

You will need to create a new query to bring together all the fields you want to include in your invoice. You will then need to create a new report based on that query.

> A copy of this file with the completed relationships and forms can be provided by your teacher if you need it at this stage.

➤ Open *Microsoft Access* and open **Gig-WellDB**.

➤ Click on the Query Wizard.

➤ Using the process of abstraction and algorithmic thinking previously outlined, add the fields on the right to your query wizard. The fields on the right must be included in the order shown.

➤ When asked for a title for your query, name the report custinvoiceQRY.

➤ Click Finish and test your query by clicking on the Run icon.

➤ Examine the output from the query when it is run at this stage. The query at this stage will display the details for any orders placed by every customer in the database.

➤ Additional processing is needed to turn this into a query which can be used to provide customers with an invoice for their orders.

   o The query must also allow the user of the database to enter the custID for the customer currently placing the order.

   o It should also automatically calculate the total cost for each individual item purchased by that customer; for example, if a customer has ordered 2 Gold Tickets it should calculate this for the user.

➤ Let us edit the query design further to ensure it allows the end user to complete the two tasks outlined above.

   o Open the query in design view.

   o With a friend discuss the query design and consider how you might edit the query design to ensure it now allows the user to enter the custID for an individual customer as well as calculating the total cost for each individual item purchased by that customer. Some additional hints have been provided below.

Fields
CustID
Title
Firstname
Surname
HouseNum
Address1
Address2
Country
OrderID
ProductID
Description
Size
SellingPrice
Quantity
Paid

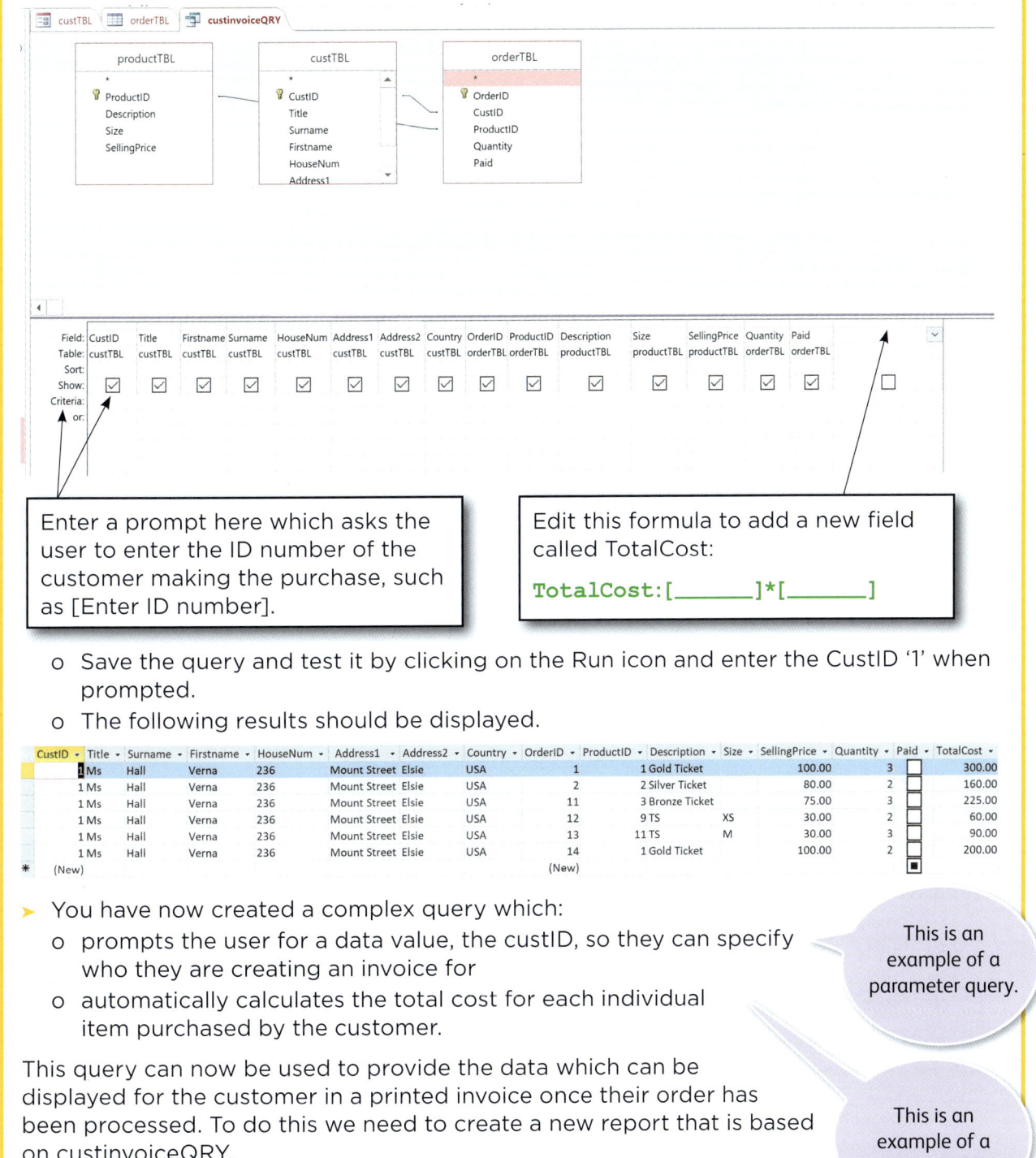

Enter a prompt here which asks the user to enter the ID number of the customer making the purchase, such as [Enter ID number].

Edit this formula to add a new field called TotalCost:

`TotalCost:[_____]*[_____]`

- o Save the query and test it by clicking on the Run icon and enter the CustID '1' when prompted.
- o The following results should be displayed.

- ➤ You have now created a complex query which:
  - o prompts the user for a data value, the custID, so they can specify who they are creating an invoice for
  - o automatically calculates the total cost for each individual item purchased by the customer

This query can now be used to provide the data which can be displayed for the customer in a printed invoice once their order has been processed. To do this we need to create a new report that is based on custinvoiceQRY.

This is an example of a parameter query.

This is an example of a calculated field.

➤ Open the Report Wizard.

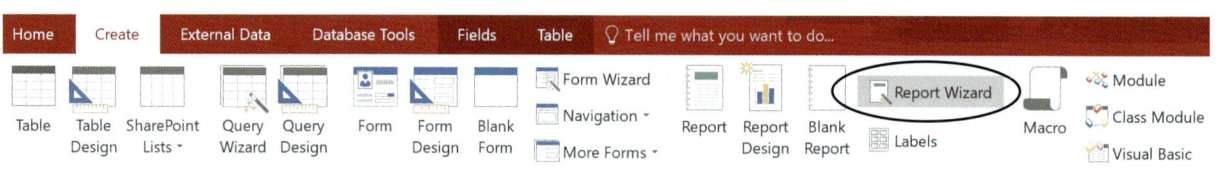

➤ Select custinvoiceQRY under Tables/Queries.

➤ Click on the double chevron to add all fields from custinvoiceQRY and click on Next.

This is the complex query you have just created which combines data from each of the three tables in the database.

➤ We do not want to group the data by ProductID so click on the single, backwards chevron (<) to remove the ProductID grouping; then click Next. Grouping the data would present the records with a sub-heading for e.g. TS and then list the different types of T-shirts underneath this sub-heading. This not the way we will display the data in our invoice.

➤ Order the records by Description and click Next, this will allow us to place the items ordered in alphabetic order according to the description field heading.

➤ Display with Landscape orientation and click Next. By selecting Landscape orientation we are ensuring the page is wide enough to fit all of the fields into one page.

➤ Name the report **custinvoiceRPT** and click Finish.

➤ The final report should look something like this:

We could use groupings if we had different categories of products that we wanted to display together in their groups; for example if we ordered lots of different T-shirts we could group them by size. By removing the grouping we are displaying the data in a standard list format.

custinvoiceRPT

custinvoiceRPT

ıstID	Title	Surname	Firstname	HouseNum	Address1	Address2	Country	lerID	Productl	Description	Size	lingPrice	ity Paid	TotalCost
1	Ms	Hall	Verna	236	Mount Street	Elsie	USA	1	1	Gold Ticket		100.00	3 ☐	300.00
1	Ms	Hall	Verna	236	Mount Street	Elsie	USA	2	2	Silver Ticket		80.00	2 ☐	160.00
1	Ms	Hall	Verna	236	Mount Street	Elsie	USA	11	3	Bronze Ticket		75.00	3 ☐	225.00
1	Ms	Hall	Verna	236	Mount Street	Elsie	USA	12	9	TS	XS	30.00	2 ☐	60.00
1	Ms	Hall	Verna	236	Mount Street	Elsie	USA	13	11	TS	M	30.00	3 ☐	90.00
1	Ms	Hall	Verna	236	Mount Street	Elsie	USA	14	1	Gold Ticket		100.00	2 ☐	200.00

➤ Save the report and close *Microsoft Access*.

Presenting data: Meeting users' needs

Learn

It is important that any new software solution is carefully designed to meet the needs of the client. The layout of reports must be tailored to look professional, especially if that report is being sent to customers. Unprofessional documents can present the wrong impression for customers.

KEYWORD

layout: the way data is presented or laid out on a screen or printed copy of a document

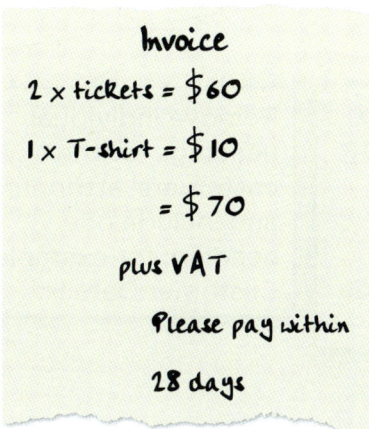

▲ This template is much more professional than the scribbled invoice on a scrap of paper.

Professional documents will:

➤ include data that is well spaced out and easy to read

➤ display all of the data necessary

➤ not repeat data unnecessarily

➤ include a company name or logo

➤ be easy to understand.

Practice

The report called **custinvoiceRPT** does not meet the needs of Gig-Well because it does not look very professional. The owners of Gig-well have said they want to be able to produce a professional invoice for their customers when they place an order.

Generalisation

With a friend carry out some research on the internet to decide what information an invoice should contain and how it should be displayed.

From your research, use generalisation to identify what aspects of your research could be incorporated into the layout of the invoice.

➤ Open **custinvoiceRPT** in design view.

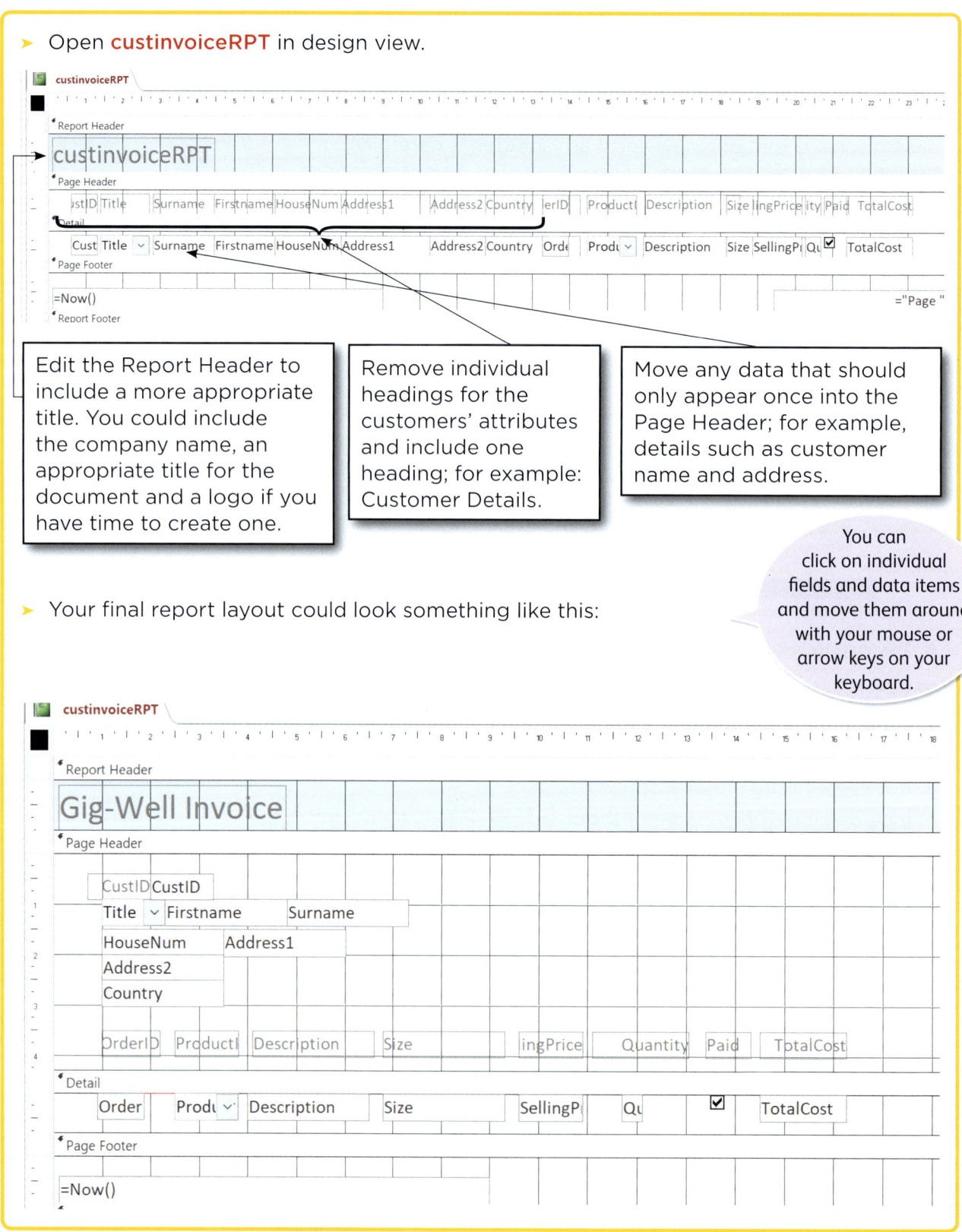

Edit the Report Header to include a more appropriate title. You could include the company name, an appropriate title for the document and a logo if you have time to create one.

Remove individual headings for the customers' attributes and include one heading; for example: Customer Details.

Move any data that should only appear once into the Page Header; for example, details such as customer name and address.

You can click on individual fields and data items and move them around with your mouse or arrow keys on your keyboard.

➤ Your final report layout could look something like this:

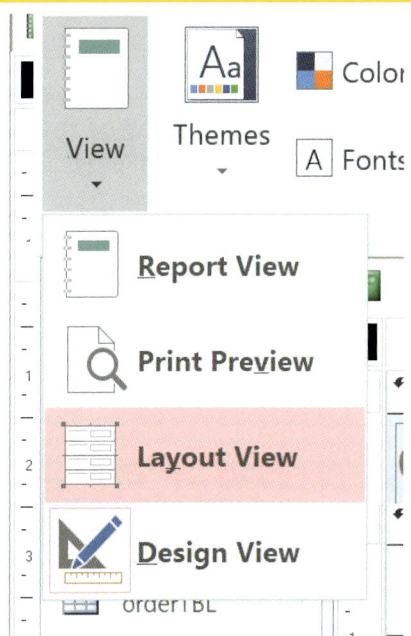

> ➤ Preview your report by swapping to layout view.
> ➤ Edit the layout of your report to make sure you can see all data on the report and all field headings.

The owners of Gig-Well have looked at the invoice you have produced and said they would like to make the following changes to the layout.

1 The items should be sorted by selling price rather than description.
2 There should be an overall total cost at the bottom.
3 The costs should be displayed using the correct currency symbol, such as $.

Sorting the items by product description

> ➤ Open **custinvoiceRPT** in design view.
> ➤ Click on the **Group & Sort** button.
> ➤ Click on Add a Sort, which now appears under the report design. Data presented in reports is often sorted according to one or more database fields.

> ➤ When setting up the report in the first instance we displayed products ordered by Description.
>   o Select 'Group, Sort and Total' and then 'Add a Sort'.
>   o Select the Price field heading from the list of fields which appear on screen to now sort by SellingPrice instead.
>
> ➤ Display the report in Report View to see how this affects how the data is displayed.

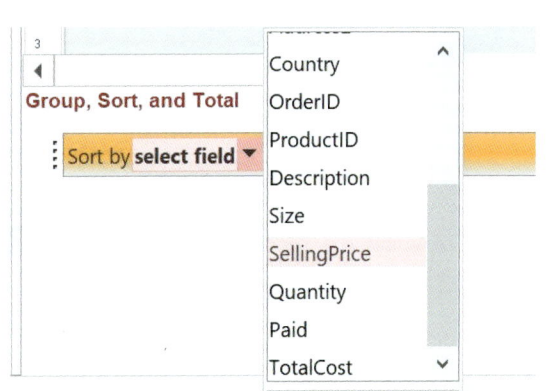

KEYWORD

Group & Sort: a feature available in *Microsoft Access* which allows data to be sorted and grouped in reports before display on screen

Adding overall total cost at the bottom

➤ Display the report in Layout View again.

➤ Right click on any of the Total Cost data items on the report and select Total TotalCost and Sum to add an overall total to the invoice:

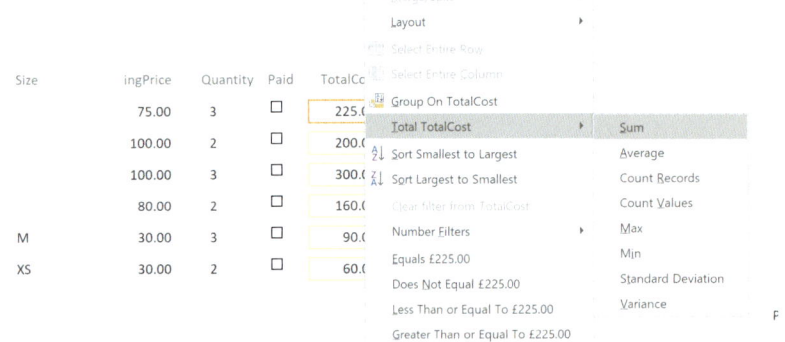

You have now learned how to amend how data can be displayed in a database report using the software wizard and the design tool.

Displaying monetary values with $ for currency

➤ Right click on any of the Total Cost values.

➤ Select Properties at the very bottom of the drop-down list that appears.

➤ Select Format and then select Currency and select an appropriate format for the currency values being displayed on the report.

➤ Save **custinvoiceRPT**.

➤ Close *Microsoft Access*.

Remember, you can also change the layout of a report by opening the report in design view.

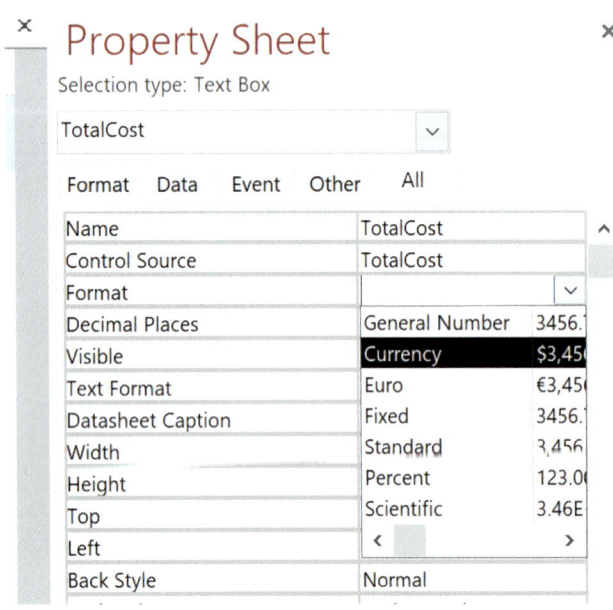

Go further

Large businesses often need to be able to send **mail-shots** out to large groups of customers. Using a process known as a **mail merge** the companies can create personalised letters for mass†mailing†of a standardised letter. Mail merges are usually carried out using a word processed document which contains a mixture of fixed text and variables or data items which are inserted from another application, such as a database application.

The owners of Gig-Well need to send a letter to all customers to give them information about parking on the day of the event. They have asked you to help them with this task.

KEYWORDS

mail-shot: a large scale distribution of a standard document, often for the purposes of displaying a message or for promotional reasons

mail merge: the process of automatically personalising documents through the insertion of individual recipients' contact details from a database application

Computational Thinking

Use generalisation to apply what you already know about letter presentation and content to complete the task below. In this task you will create a personalised letter for each customer to inform them of the parking plans for the Par-T event.

◆ Open a word processing application, in this instance we are using *Microsoft Word* and create a letter similar to this:

Gig-Well Part-T

Parking Plans for the Days

Dear

We are looking forward to seeing you at the Par-T event coming soon. We know some of you will drive to the venue on the day so we have made special parking plans for you.

When you arrive at the Par-T look for the signposts for Car-Park A and B. Your care will be secure here and we can provide buses back to your car at the end of the night.

Take this letter with you for free parking on the day!

Yours sincerely

Gig-Well
Concert Promoter and Event Production

◆ Save your letter as **Gig-WellParking**.
◆ In *Microsoft Word*, click on the Mailings Tab and then select Start Mail Merge and then Letters.

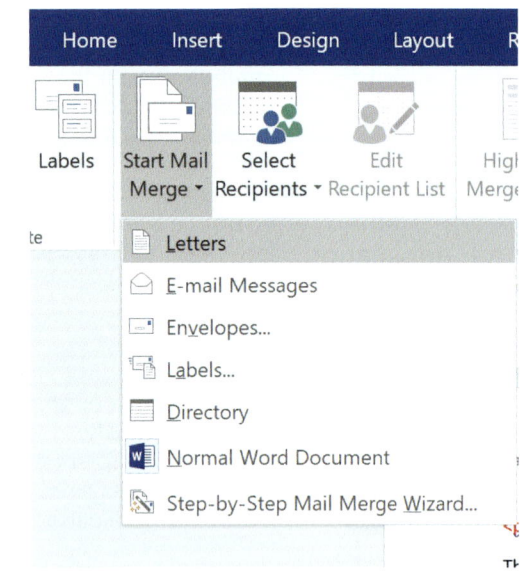

- Click on Select Recipients and then select Use Existing List.
- When the Select Data Source window appears browse to and then select the Gig-WellDB database.
- You will then be presented with a Select Table window – select custTBL.
- Add the name and address fields to the letter using Insert Merge Field.

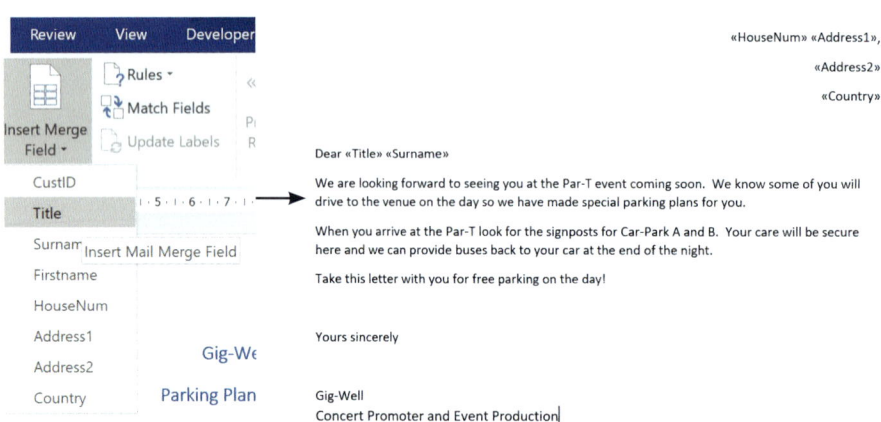

- Click close when all relevant fields have been added and remember to add spaces and commas in the correct places in between the name and address fields which will appear on the letter.
- Click on Finish and Merge and then Edit individual documents.
- Click on Select All to merge and then OK to merge the letter to a new document and include the names and addresses of all customers in each copy of the letter.
- Save the merged document as **Gig-WellParkingComplete** as evidence that you have completed the task successfully.
- Close *Microsoft Word*.

> Think about when the owners of Gig-Well might use this letter template again. Now that the customer's name and address has been inserted into the letter template, could this be reused to send out another letter to customers; for example, by changing the text in the letter?

Challenge yourself

The owners of Gig-Well have asked that you create some standard queries they can use that would allow them to extract useful data from the database.

They would like to use the database to produce a list of contact details for all customers from USA and Canada so they can write to them about visa requirements for their visit.

Computational Thinking

Use the process of abstraction to consider the fields, tables and criteria needed to create each of the queries described.

> You are searching for customers from two specific countries, think about how you will use the 'Criteria Row' and the 'Or' row in the query wizard.

➤ Create a query using custTBL which will display all of the contact details of customers from USA or Canada.

➤ Save the query as custUSAandCanadaQRY.

➤ Run the query to ensure the correct results are displayed.

The manager is concerned about how long it might take to process queries using the database; especially since over time the database is expected to become quite large.

All queries produced in *Microsoft Access* operate using a language called SQL (Structured Query Language). One of the ways developers increase the speed of processing in databases is by optimising the SQL which is automatically created by the software when the developer creates a query.

➤ View the SQL created by the custUSAandCanadaQRY by clicking on Home, the View tab and then SQL.

➤ Examine the SQL displayed.

```
SELECT custTBL.[CustID], custTBL.[Title], custTBL.[Surname], custTBL.[Firstname], custTBL.[HouseNum],
custTBL.[Address1], custTBL.[Address2], custTBL.[Country]
FROM custTBL;
```

Notice how custTBL. appears before each field in the SQL statement.

➤ Remove the table name and the '.' from before each of the field names in the SQL statement.

➤ Save the query and run it to ensure the same results are produced.

> Including the table name unnecessarily provides additional processing and can slow down the production of results when the query is executed.

The manager would also like to use the database to create a list of contact details of all customers who purchased a Gold Ticket so they can contact them to let them know of a special upgrade available to them.

➤ Create a query using data from the custTBL, orderTBL and productTBL which will allow the manager to view the contact details of all customers who have ordered a 'Gold Ticket'.

➤ Save this query as goldticketQRY.

➤ View the SQL created by the query called goldticketQRY.

| ◀ | 🔳 orderTBL | 🔳 custTBL | 🗗 custUSAandCanadaQRY | 🗗 **goldticketQRY** |

SELECT custTBL.CustID, custTBL.Title, custTBL.Surname, custTBL.Firstname, custTBL.HouseNum, custTBL.Address1, custTBL.Address2, custTBL.Country, orderTBL.ProductID, productTBL.Description
FROM productTBL INNER JOIN (custTBL INNER JOIN orderTBL ON custTBL.[CustID] = orderTBL.[CustID]) ON productTBL.[ProductID] = orderTBL.[ProductID]
WHERE (((productTBL.Description)="Gold Ticket"));

You can only remove references to table names from fields not used as part of relationships in the query structure.

For example, the highlighted fields in the SQL statement below are all used to form links between the three tables in the database; so, the table references cannot be removed here.

SELECT **custTBL.CustID**, custTBL.Title, custTBL.Surname, custTBL.Firstname, custTBL.HouseNum, custTBL.Address1, custTBL.Address2, custTBL.Country, **orderTBL.ProductID, productTBL.Description**

FROM productTBL INNER JOIN (**custTBL** INNER JOIN orderTBL ON custTBL.[CustID] = orderTBL.[CustID]) ON **productTBL.[ProductID] = orderTBL.[ProductID]**

WHERE (((**productTBL.Description**)="Gold Ticket"));

DID YOU KNOW?

Many websites use an alternative to SQL called MySQL to create web based databases. Scripting languages are then used to interact in real-time with the MySQL database to return information immediately to the user.

KEYWORDS

MySQL: an open-source tool which can be used to manage relational databases using SQL

real-time: when input data is processed and output provided almost immediately for the user; it is used, for example, in aircraft control systems where delays could have life-threatening implications

---

➤ Optimise this query using the same steps you applied to the custUSAandCanadaQRY.

➤ Save your optimised query and run it to ensure the correct results are displayed.

The owners of Gig-Well are concerned that some staff are not experts in the use of computer systems and they would like the system to have a user-friendly navigation system.

Bound forms can be used to enter data into linked tables in a database.

Unbound forms can be used to help users navigate around database applications. Using forms in this way can help provide a user-friendly interface for end users.

Create a form which is used to display macro buttons used to open other parts of the Gig-Well database. In this case the macro will be used to open the form called custFRM.

> Providing a user-friendly interface for the user will help ensure that the end user does not need to navigate the application at object level and it reduces the risk of them editing or deleting necessary objects in the application. (In other words the user does not need to use or access the tables, queries, forms or reports in design view so there is less change of them deleting something in error).

We will create a macro first of all which will automatically open the form custFRM when the macro is operated by the end user.

➤ Open *Microsoft Access* and the Gig-Well database.
➤ Click on the Create tab and click on Macro.

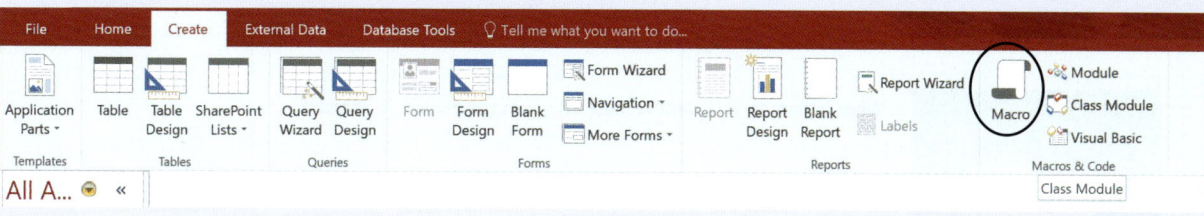

➤ Select the Open Form option from the drop down list.

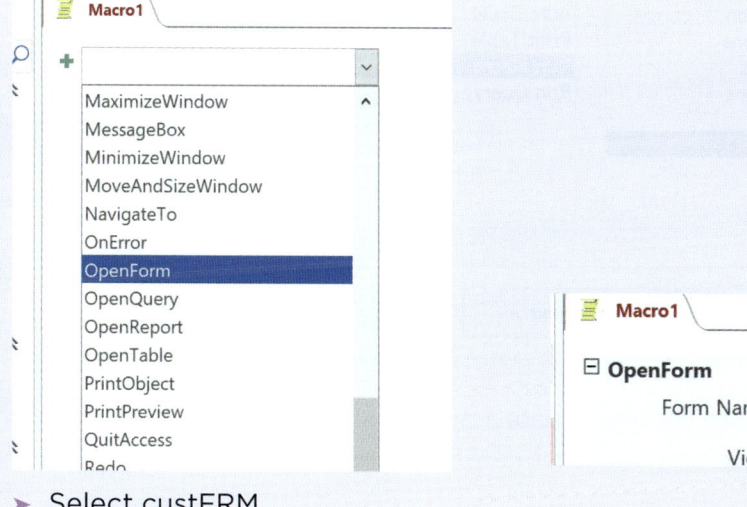

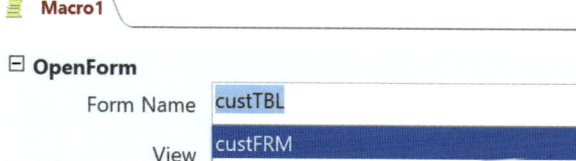

➤ Select custFRM.
➤ Close the Macro window by clicking on the X in the top right corner and name the macro opencustMCR.

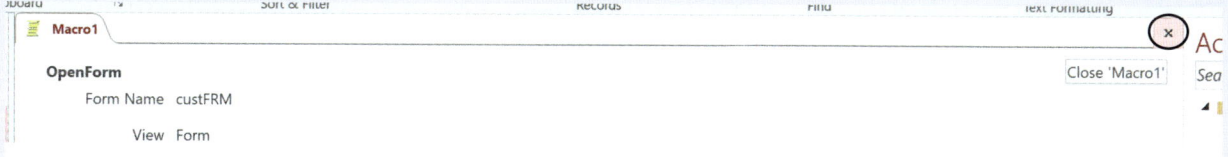

You will now create an unbound form which will operate as a menu for the end user. This form will eventually contain a number of buttons linked to macros used to automate operation of the Gig-Well database.

➤ Create a new blank form by clicking on the Create tab and clicking on Blank form.

➤ Save the form as menuFRM.

➤ Click on the icon for a new Button.

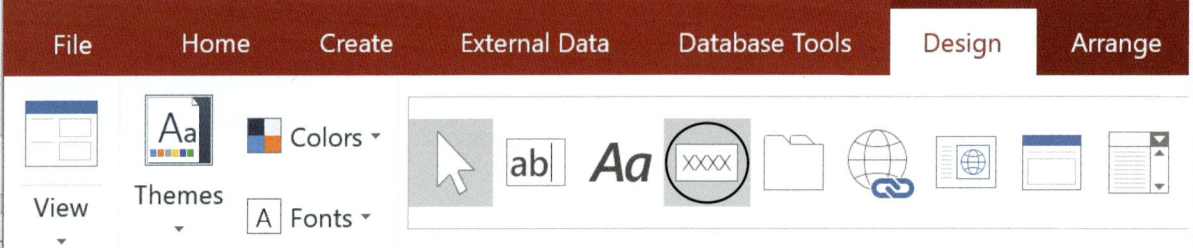

➤ Click and drag on the blank form to add a new button and start the Command Button Wizard. Select Miscellaneous and then Run Macro.

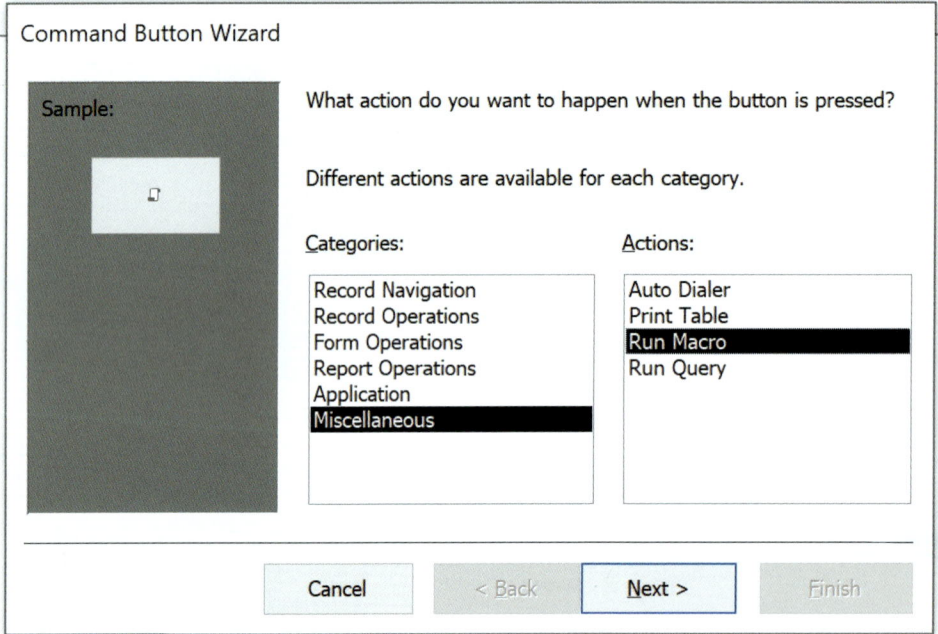

➤ Click Next and select the opencustMCR you created previously.

➤ Click Next and edit the text on the button to read Customer Form before clicking on Next.

Command Button Wizard

Sample:

> Customer
> Form

Do you want text or a picture on the button?

If you choose Text, you can type the text to display. If you choose Picture, you can click Browse to find a picture to display.

◉ T̲ext: Customer Form

◯ P̲icture: MS Access Macro   Browse...

☐ Show All Pictures

Cancel   < B̲ack   N̲ext >   F̲inish

➤ Give the command button a meaningful name such as opencustform and click Finish.

➤ Test your macro button by opening the form menuFRM in form view and click on the button. It should open custFRM.

Use your knowledge of the design tools in *Microsoft Access* to:

➤ add a text box to menuFRM to label the menu as Gig-Well Main Menu

➤ create macros to open each of the reports and forms you have created for the Gig-Well database so far

➤ add command buttons to menuFRM to link to each macro

➤ create a macro and a command button that can be added to each form and report to allow the user to navigate back to the menuFRM.

Final project part 1

Gig-Well has asked that you expand its database application to include the following.

➤ A report that produces a list of all tickets sold for the Par-T event, to include:

- a list of the names and addresses of the customers who purchased tickets, the ticket type they purchased
- the quantity of each ticket
- how much each customer spent on each ticket type
- an overall total at the bottom telling them how much money has been spent on tickets so far.

> Remember to create a query first of all to select the data you need from each table. Add a calculated field to this query before creating your report. Pages 190–193 can help you with this task.

➤ A query to allow the owners of Gig-Well to search for a customer by their Surname.

➤ A query which allows the owners of Gig-Well to search for customers by CustID.

➤ Each query should be optimised using the methods described on page 196.

➤ At the end of each day they would like to produce a detailed report telling them how many tickets they have sold for each zone, along with the total number of tickets sold overall.

➤ The database should have a macro button to allow the owner to open each query and report from the main menu form.

> Remember using groupings and sorts to sort data. You should also view your report in layout view and use the Total tool to help you view an overall total of tickets sold.

Unfortunately, Gig-Well has found out that the main attraction, the artist Ali-D, is unable to perform at the event. You need to produce a mail-merge letter which can be sent out to all customers to let them know. The letter should contain:

● the customer's name and address
● today's date
● the Gig-Well name and address (you can make this your school's address)
● an offer of a refund if the customer no longer wishes to attend the Par-T.

Evaluation

Ask a friend to test your database to make sure it meets all of the user requirements.

➤ Your friend should also evaluate your form and report layouts to determine how professional they are. You should discuss:
  o use of text style, size, font and colour
  o use of background colours
  o how well the field headings describe each attribute
  o use of special instructions to help the user.

➤ Write down any improvements your friend recommended and then describe in a short written report any changes you made to your database and why.

Spreadsheet applications: Modelling and decision making

Businesses use spreadsheet software to help make decisions. Spreadsheets can be used to create a **model** of real-life events and the relationships between events. By changing data items or formulas in a spreadsheet, the user can see how different values, which represent different events, depend on each other.

KEYWORD

model: a computer program that has been designed to predict the way another system works

Being able to change values in a spreadsheet model allows businesses to answer 'what if' questions. They can ask: what if I increase the price of this product by 2%? How will that impact on sales and profits?

Spreadsheets contain a range of tools that can be used by businesses when they are trying to make important decisions.

In this unit you will learn how to use:

→ VLOOKUPs to create links between data items in a spreadsheet model

→ pivot tables, charts, trend lines and goal seek to support decision making

→ templates, headers and footers to present data in a spreadsheet application.

DID YOU KNOW?

The first spreadsheet application called VisiCalc was developed for computers in 1979.

SCENARIO

Gig-Well is keen to make a success of its first big event. The Par-T is the largest event Gig-Well has organised so far. To make sure it is a success, its owners are trying to think ahead so they can make good decisions about ticket sales, stock levels for merchandise, ticket prices, and so on.

They have asked for your help setting up a spreadsheet that can help them make these decisions.

Do you remember?

Before starting this unit, you should be able to:

✔ use the relative and absolute cell references in a spreadsheet formula

✔ be able to apply conditional formatting and validation to cell contents

✔ be able to name cell ranges and use them in formulas

✔ use If statements and Lookup statements to support data modelling

✔ sort and filter spreadsheet content.

Spreadsheet solutions: Goal Seek

Learn

A powerful feature available in *Microsoft Excel* is Goal Seek. It can be used to help businesses make decisions.

Goal Seek uses a 'trial and error' approach to problem solving. It will allow the user to set their final goal (the value they want to reach) and it will experiment with the input values to work out which input values will allow the user to reach that final goal. Goal Seek is the main feature that helps businesses ask 'What if' questions. For example, a formula to work out income from the sale of T-shirts would multiply the number of T-shirts sold by the selling price. Using Goal Seek on this formula would allow you to work out how many T-shirts you need to sell to make $10 000.

KEYWORD

Goal Seek: a *Microsoft Excel* feature which supports what-if questioning by looking at the desired outcome

Algorithmic thinking

Spreadsheets can make use of complex formulas and existing data to help users analyse high volumes of data.

Combine your general understanding of mathematical rules with algorithmic thinking to help you produce appropriate formula for the tasks which follow. Remember, all formulas added to cells in a database application must start with an equal sign but also consider what other mathematical symbols and cell references you need to apply to formulas to help you complete the following tasks.

Practice

Gig-Well has created a spreadsheet to help analyse potential sales of tickets and merchandise. The data is based on

- how many tickets, T-shirts, sweatshirts, and so on, that Gig-Well thinks it will sell in advance of the event and during the event
- potential costs associated with running the event.

Gig-Well wants to use the spreadsheet to ask some 'What-if' style questions to see how many tickets, T-shirts and sweatshirts need to be sold to make a profit. You need to complete the formula.

- Open *Microsoft Excel*.
- Open the spreadsheet called Gig-WellSS provided by your teacher.
- The spreadsheet contains two shaded areas:
  o A22:B35 will be used as a price's lookup list.
  o F1:G3 will be used as a capacity lookup list.

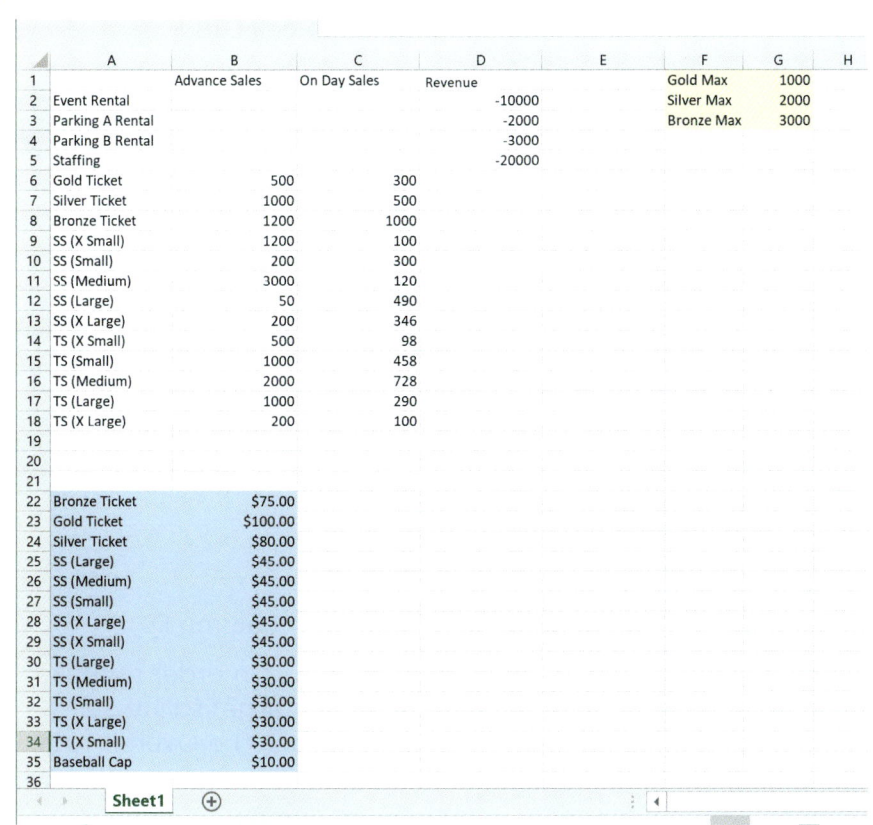

	A	B	C	D	E	F	G	H
1		Advance Sales	On Day Sales	Revenue		Gold Max	1000	
2	Event Rental			-10000		Silver Max	2000	
3	Parking A Rental			-2000		Bronze Max	3000	
4	Parking B Rental			-3000				
5	Staffing			-20000				
6	Gold Ticket	500	300					
7	Silver Ticket	1000	500					
8	Bronze Ticket	1200	1000					
9	SS (X Small)	1200	100					
10	SS (Small)	200	300					
11	SS (Medium)	3000	120					
12	SS (Large)	50	490					
13	SS (X Large)	200	346					
14	TS (X Small)	500	98					
15	TS (Small)	1000	458					
16	TS (Medium)	2000	728					
17	TS (Large)	1000	290					
18	TS (X Large)	200	100					
19								
20								
21								
22	Bronze Ticket	$75.00						
23	Gold Ticket	$100.00						
24	Silver Ticket	$80.00						
25	SS (Large)	$45.00						
26	SS (Medium)	$45.00						
27	SS (Small)	$45.00						
28	SS (X Large)	$45.00						
29	SS (X Small)	$45.00						
30	TS (Large)	$30.00						
31	TS (Medium)	$30.00						
32	TS (Small)	$30.00						
33	TS (X Large)	$30.00						
34	TS (X Small)	$30.00						
35	Baseball Cap	$10.00						
36								

Sheet1 ⊕

➤ Both of these areas will be used as look-up areas on the spreadsheet. In other words, they will be used to contain data which is accessed and used by other formulas in the database.

   o Highlight cells A22:B35, right click, select Define Name and name this area 'Prices'.

   o Highlight cells F1:G3 and using the same process name this area 'Capacity'.

➤ Insert a formula into D6 to show the total revenue from Gold Ticket sales. This is based on the number of Gold Tickets sold in advance and on the day and should be multiplied by the cost of a Gold Ticket

➤ With a friend discuss what will happen if you replicate this formula.

➤ Discuss how a VLOOKUP might allow Gig-Well to use the lookup table.

➤ Copy and complete this formula and insert this into cell D6.

=(___+_____)*(VLOOKUP(A6,prices,____))

> When Gig-Well spends money, a negative (−) value is recorded. When money is being paid to Gig-well, a positive (+) value is recorded.

> Some of the formulas accessing the two lookup areas will be complicated. It is good practice to apply names to cell ranges that are going to be used in this way as this can help make complex formulas easier to write and understand.

> Look carefully at the next two rows in the two parts of the spreadsheet, the next row down in the lookup list is Silver Ticket and then SS(Large). Does this match the data in the main part of the spreadsheet?

> The result produced should be $80 000.

➤ Once you are happy with your formula, copy the formula down to cell D18.

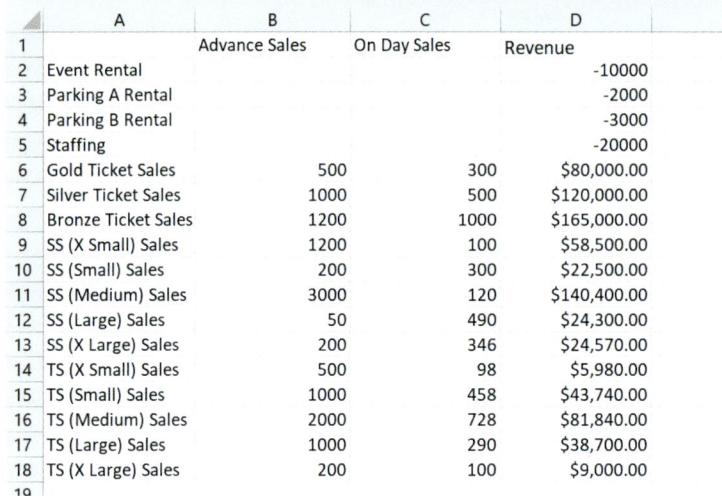

	A	B	C	D
1		Advance Sales	On Day Sales	Revenue
2	Event Rental			-10000
3	Parking A Rental			-2000
4	Parking B Rental			-3000
5	Staffing			-20000
6	Gold Ticket Sales	500	300	$80,000.00
7	Silver Ticket Sales	1000	500	$120,000.00
8	Bronze Ticket Sales	1200	1000	$165,000.00
9	SS (X Small) Sales	1200	100	$58,500.00
10	SS (Small) Sales	200	300	$22,500.00
11	SS (Medium) Sales	3000	120	$140,400.00
12	SS (Large) Sales	50	490	$24,300.00
13	SS (X Large) Sales	200	346	$24,570.00
14	TS (X Small) Sales	500	98	$5,980.00
15	TS (Small) Sales	1000	458	$43,740.00
16	TS (Medium) Sales	2000	728	$81,840.00
17	TS (Large) Sales	1000	290	$38,700.00
18	TS (X Large) Sales	200	100	$9,000.00
19				

➤ Add the label 'Overall Total' to cell A19.
➤ Add a formula to cell D19 to calculate the 'Overall Total Revenue' in column D.

Gig-Well has worked out it needs an Overall Total Revenue of $800 000 in order to make a profit from selling tickets and merchandise. There are a lot of TS (X Large) still to sell and so Gig-well wants to know how many more need to be sold to reach the Overall Total.

➤ Click on cell D18.
➤ Click on the Data Tab and Click on What-If Analysis and then Goal Seek.

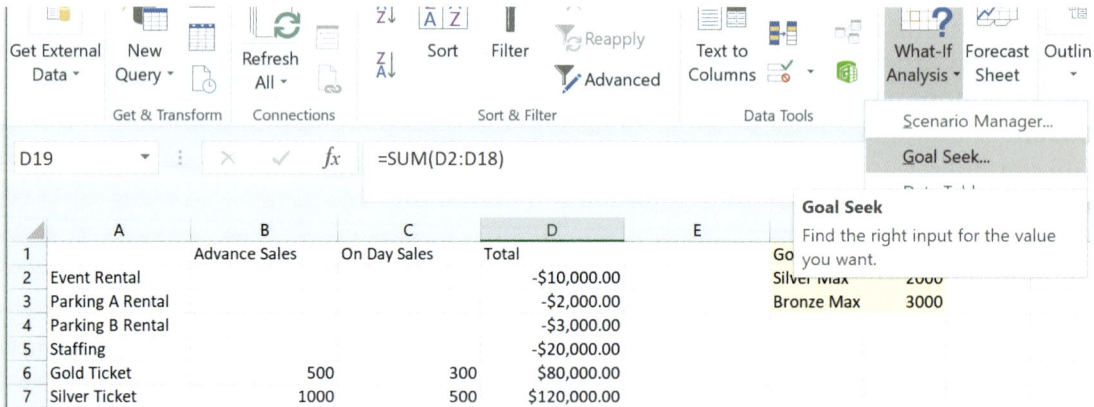

➤ Set the To value to the Overall Total they want to reach (800000) and set By changing cell to B18.

Your teacher will give you a copy of a worksheet called **Goal Seek Challenge**.

➤ Using the same process above for each item separately, complete the worksheet by recording how many of each item Gig-Well would need to sell (assuming the number of other items stayed the same) to reach their target Overall Total of $800 000.

➤ Which single product do they need to sell the least of to boost their Overall Total to $800 000?

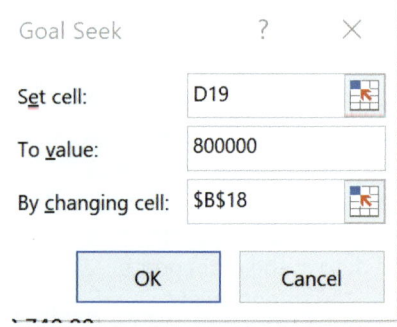

Spreadsheet solutions: Bucking the trend

Learn

Organisations often need to make decisions based on looking at previous patterns. For example, most supermarkets will know based[†]on previous experience that they need to increase their stock[†]of calendars and diaries towards the start of a new calendar year. However, the pattern in sales is not always that obvious. To help[†]organisations recognise those patterns *Microsoft Excel* provides[†]a very useful tool called a **trendline**. A trendline is also sometimes known as 'a line of best fit'. It is a line that is superimposed over the data included on an existing line graph and it[†]is used to show the general pattern or overall direction of the data.

KEYWORD

trendline: a line that is superimposed over the data included on an existing line graph and is used to show the general pattern or overall direction of the data

What are some other ways in which trendlines can be used?

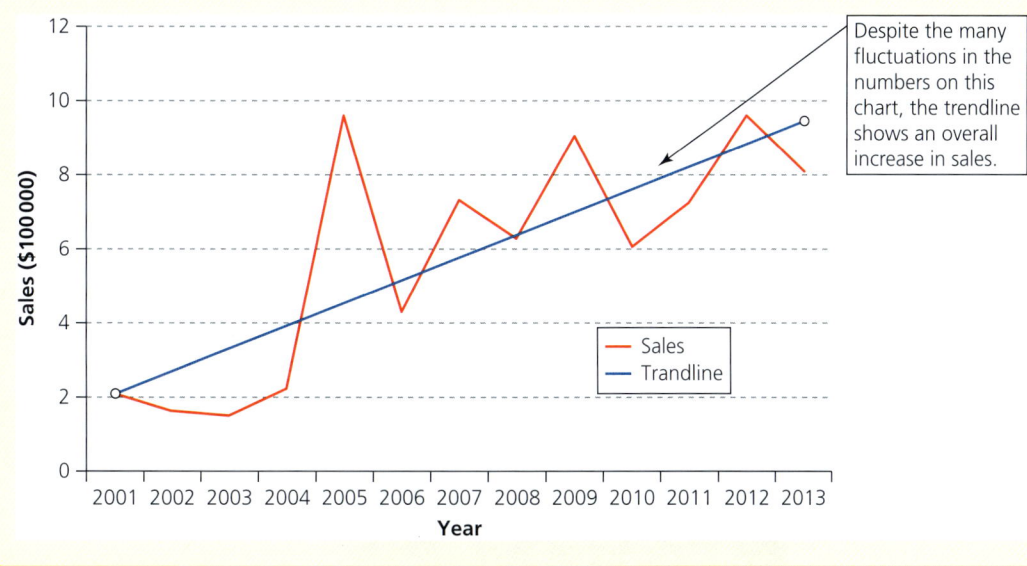

Despite the many fluctuations in the numbers on this chart, the trendline shows an overall increase in sales.

Practice

The owners of Gig-Well are concerned about their pre-event sales. They want to get an overall picture of the pattern of sales so they can decide if they need to increase advertising for the Par-T.

Sheet 2 on the **Gig-WellSS** spreadsheet includes details of advance ticket sales since they started selling them. They have asked you to help them produce a chart to analyse their sales.

To create your chart:

➤ Open *Microsoft Excel*.
➤ Open **Gig-WellSS** and click on Sheet 2.
➤ Highlight all of the data in Sheet 2, including the column headings.
➤ Click on the Insert Tab and select 2-D line shown to allow you to add a trendline.

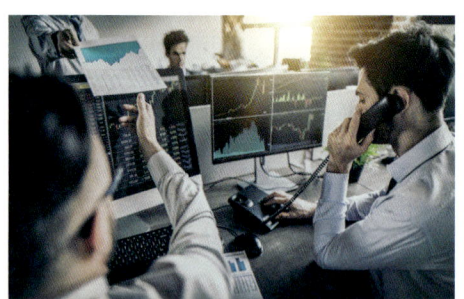

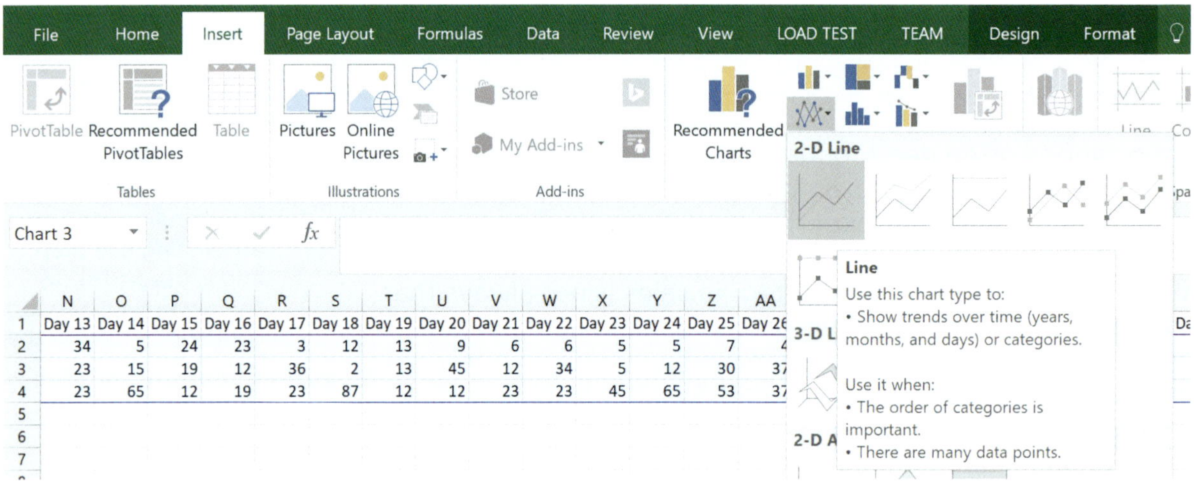
File
Home
Insert
Page Layout
Formulas
Data
Review
View
LOAD TEST
TEAM
Design
Format
PivotTable
Recommended PivotTables
Table
Tables
Pictures
Online Pictures
Illustrations
Store
My Add-ins
Add-ins
Recommended Charts
2-D Line
Chart 3
Line
Use this chart type to:
• Show trends over time (years, months, and days) or categories.
Use it when:
• The order of categories is important.
• There are many data points.
N O P Q R S T U V W X Y Z AA
1 Day 13 Day 14 Day 15 Day 16 Day 17 Day 18 Day 19 Day 20 Day 21 Day 22 Day 23 Day 24 Day 25 Day 26
2 34 5 24 23 3 12 13 9 6 6 5 5 7 4
3 23 15 19 12 36 2 13 45 12 34 5 12 30 37
4 23 65 12 19 23 87 12 12 23 23 45 65 53 37

➤ Right click on the line for the Gold Ticket and Select Add Trendline.

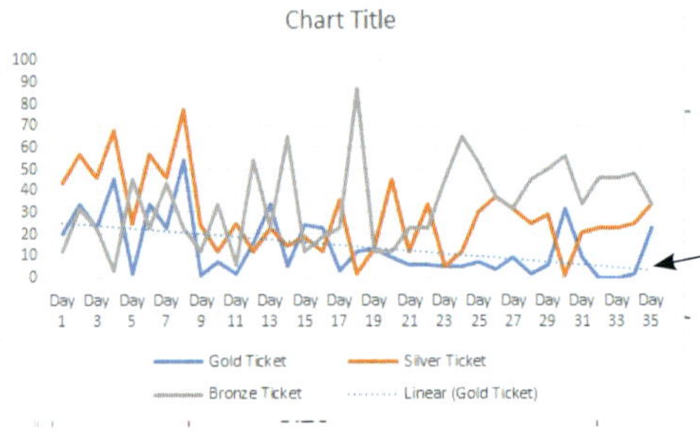
Chart Title
100
90
80
70
60
50
40
30
20
10
0
Day 1 Day 3 Day 5 Day 7 Day 9 Day 11 Day 13 Day 15 Day 17 Day 19 Day 21 Day 23 Day 25 Day 27 Day 29 Day 31 Day 33 Day 35
Gold Ticket
Silver Ticket
Bronze Ticket
Linear (Gold Ticket)

The trendline shows a downward trend in sales for the Gold Tickets.

Make your chart larger so you can see all of the lines more clearly.

DID YOU KNOW?

The trendline function uses complex mathematical statistical functions to work out the trend in sales and is often used by traders in the stock market. A trendline can be used to give a general idea of the general direction in the sales or value of a product. Traders can use trendlines to help them decide if they wish to keep or sell their stock.

Computational Thinking

Repeat this process to create a trendline for each of the other ticket types. Use the process of abstraction to identify one ticket type which has the greatest downward trend in sales and should perhaps be advertised more.

Challenge yourself

The owners of Gig-Well want to be able to analyse the sales data they have recorded in their *Microsoft Access* database but don't want to have to re-enter it all into the separate spreadsheet application. However, it is normally possible to import data from one to the other.

➤ Open *Microsoft Access* and open **Gig-WellDB**.

➤ Right click on the query called custinvoiceQRY and select Copy. A copy of the query will automatically be saved for you. Use this copy for the remainder of this task.

➤ Open this query in Design view and remove the prompt where the user is asked to enter the customer's ID number.

> Remember this query was used to create a query for one customer at a time, but for the purposes of the spreadsheet we would like to see all of the sales recorded in this database.

➤ Right click on Copy of custinvoiceQRY in the *Microsoft Access* objects.

➤ Select Export and then Excel.

➤ Select Export data with formatting and layout and Open the destination file after the export operation is complete.

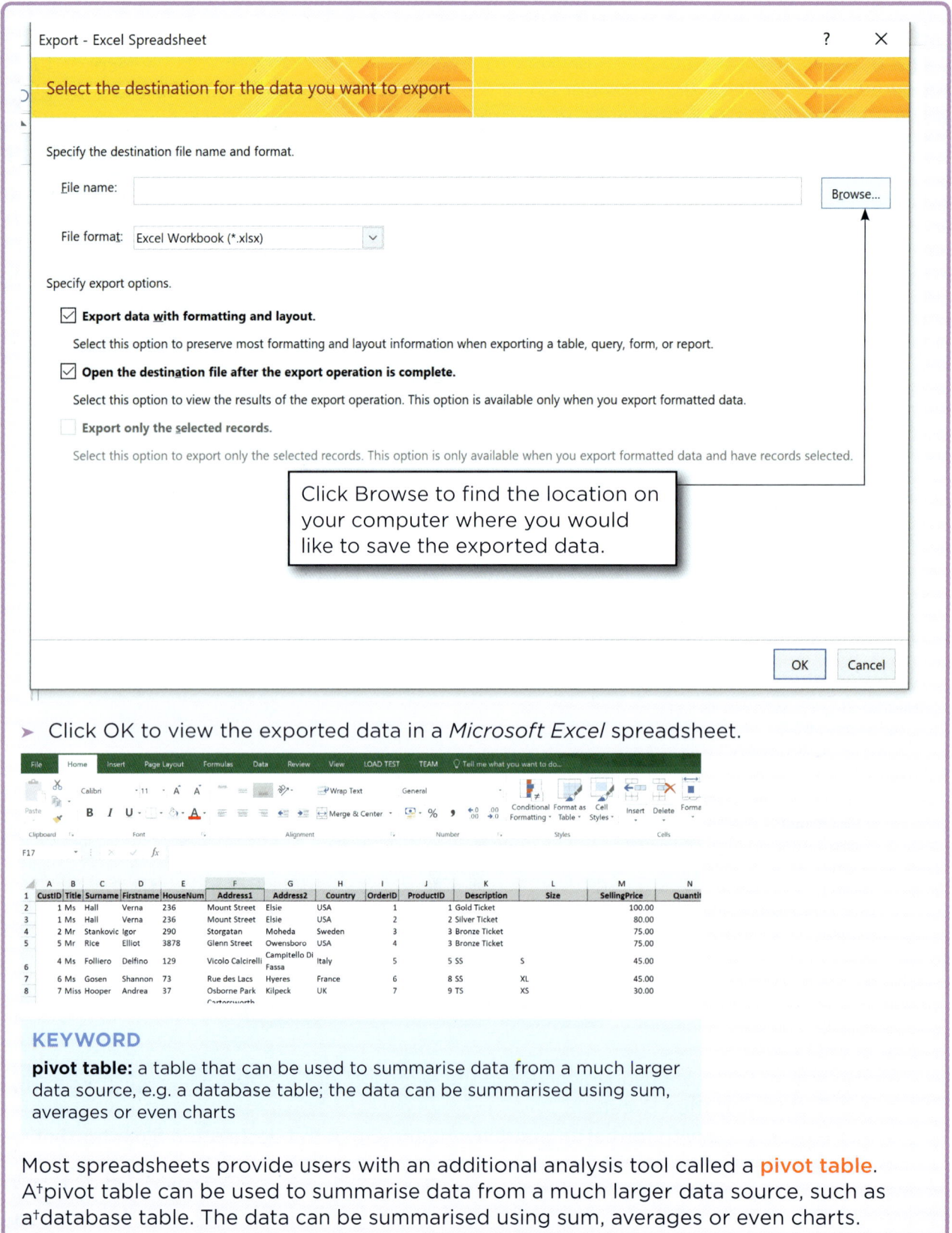

Click OK to view the exported data in a *Microsoft Excel* spreadsheet.

KEYWORD

pivot table: a table that can be used to summarise data from a much larger data source, e.g. a database table; the data can be summarised using sum, averages or even charts

Most spreadsheets provide users with an additional analysis tool called a **pivot table**. A†pivot table can be used to summarise data from a much larger data source, such as a†database table. The data can be summarised using sum, averages or even charts.

Gig-Well wants to use the pivot chart to create a graphic illustration of all of the sales of tickets and merchandise so far. The owners would like to group the data according to sales of Gold Tickets, Silver Tickets, Bronze Tickets, Sweatshirts (SS) and T-shirts (TS).

➤ Select all of the data in the worksheet and click on the Insert tab and select PivotChart and then select 'PivotChart & Pivot Table'.

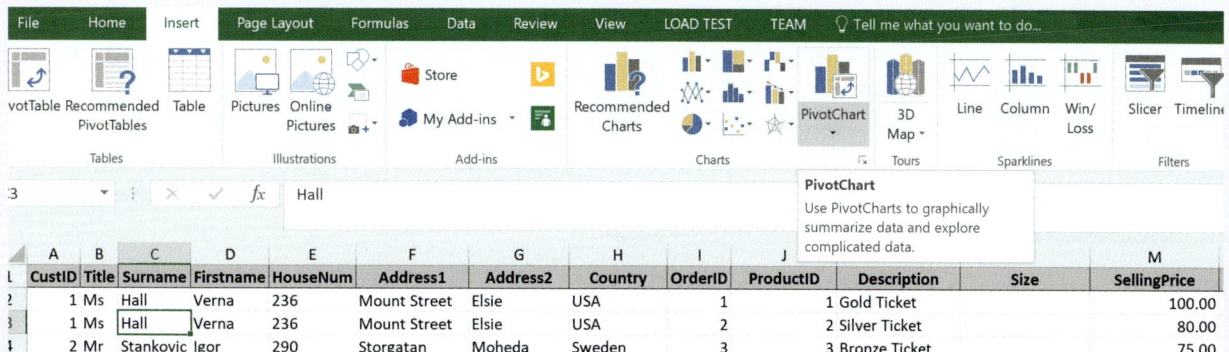

We want to see the total number of sales (the Quantity field) for each item (the Description field).

➤ On the right hand side you will see Pivot Chart Fields. First, select the Description field and drag and drop it into the AXIS (CATEGORIES) area at the bottom right.

➤ Then, select the Quantity field and drag and drop into the Σ VALUES area. The Quantity field represents the numerical data that we wish to analyse.

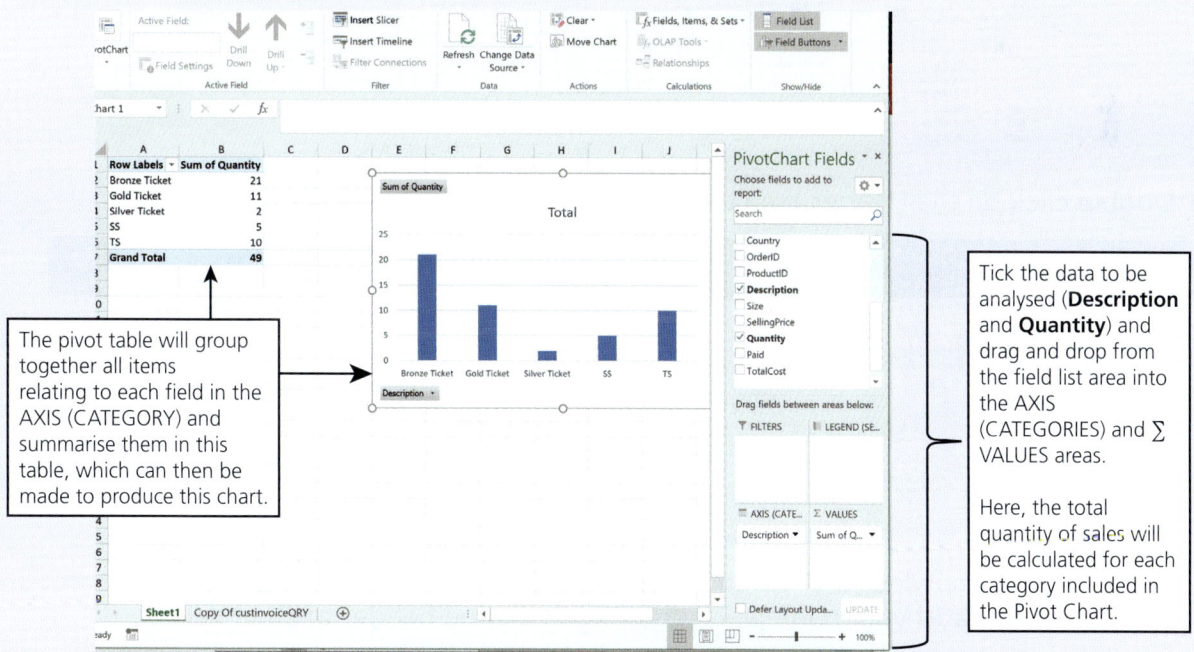

The pivot table will group together all items relating to each field in the AXIS (CATEGORY) and summarise them in this table, which can then be made to produce this chart.

Tick the data to be analysed (**Description** and **Quantity**) and drag and drop from the field list area into the AXIS (CATEGORIES) and Σ VALUES areas.

Here, the total quantity of sales will be calculated for each category included in the Pivot Chart.

You can see how the final Pivot Table groups together all data items relating to each category and calculates a total quantity for each category. The Pivot Table is then used to create the Pivot Chart shown.

➤ Save this spreadsheet as **Gig-WellPivot** and close *Microsoft Excel*.

Pivot tables are very powerful tools for organisations seeking to analyse large quantities of data. By changing only one field in the AXIS (CATEGORIES) area a very different type of data analysis can be carried out; for example,

➤ drag Description out of the AXIS (CATEGORIES) area

➤ replace it with the field Country.

Examine the data displayed in the new Pivot Chart and Pivot Table. What does this new analysis show the owner of Gig-Well?

Go further

Spreadsheets are used to present numerical data and are often used in professional situations where presentation is important. Many of the presentation skills developed through the use of word processing applications can also be applied to spreadsheet presentations. We can personalise the presentation of spreadsheet documents through the use of predefined themes, headers and footers and text-editing tools.

◆ Open *Microsoft Excel* and then open **Gig-WellSS**.

◆ Click on the Insert tab. Select the Text Tool and then select Header and Footer.

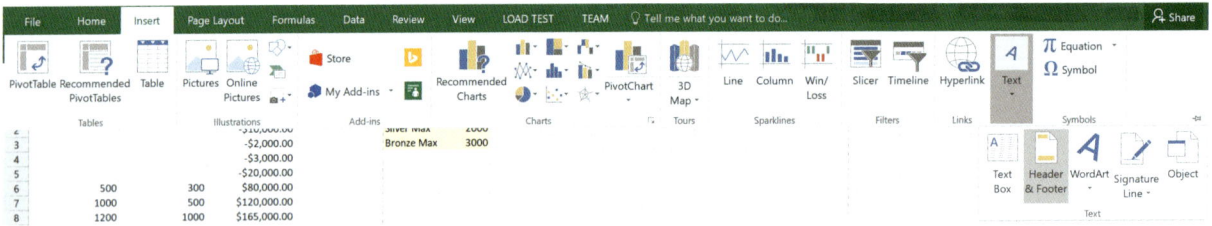

◆ Double click on the Header area to reveal the Design tool.

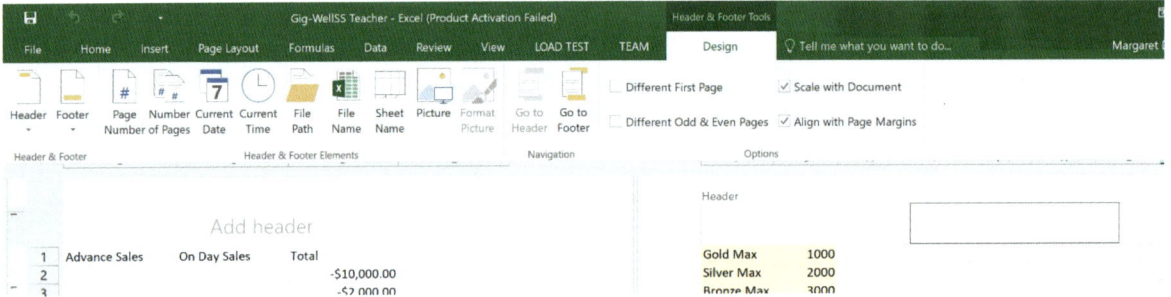

◆ Use your own knowledge of editing and formatting tools in word processing applications to add your name and today's date to the header of Gig-WellSS.

◆ Scroll down to the bottom of the page and use the available tools to add a page number to the footer of the spreadsheet.

◆ When you have finished adding a header and footer to the spreadsheet, click on the View tab and select Normal to continue editing the spreadsheet.

◆ Improve the general presentation of the spreadsheet by adding a theme, available by clicking on the Page Layout tab and selecting Themes.

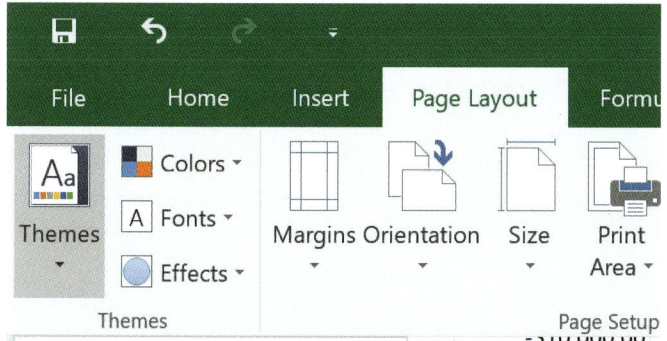

◆ Look carefully at the spreadsheet and consider what data items are most important. What formatting tools are available to help you ensure these data items are emphasised? Consider:

- ❏ increasing font size
- ❏ amending text styles or colours
- ❏ adding/changing borders and cell shading
- ❏ ensuring that all money-related values are displayed in currency format.

Final project

Gig-Well has asked you to help with further data analysis using its spreadsheets.

The company has recorded sales data for each size of sweatshirt and saved them on Sheet 3 of the **Gig-WellSS** file. You need to do the following:

➤ Create an additional chart and trendline to examine sales of the sweatshirts over the last 35 days.

- ● Use trendlines to gain an overall view of the sales recorded.
- ● Look at the trendlines and identify:
  - ● any items which are selling well that might need to be reordered
  - ● any items that are not selling well that they should not order any more of before the event.
- ● Save your chart and trendline on Sheet 3.
- ● Edit Sheet 3 to include:
  - ● a Theme
  - ● an appropriate header and footer
  - ● a text box including your recommendations from above about items to be reordered and those that should not be reordered.

Gig-Well has decided to give a special meet and greet prize to its customers who have made the most purchases.

➤ Create an additional Pivot Chart and Table using the data from Copy of **custinvoiceQRY** to help them make this decision. You used this query in the previous Challenge Yourself panel.

> In this Pivot Chart you should place the customer's name along the axis rather than the Description.

> ➤ Add a text box to the spreadsheet with the name of the winning customer inside. Which item do they need to advertise more, or perhaps drop the price of, to try and increase sales?

Now that you have completed your data analysis, there are some areas where Gig-Well could make changes to help ensure the $800 000 target is reached.

> ➤ Produce a short report, using a word processor, to advise Gig-Well of required changes to ticket allocation and sales, and the price of other merchandise.
> ➤ Use the trendlines, the pivot charts and additional Goal Seek analysis to support what you are saying.
> ➤ You should include at least two charts in your report. The report should help the owners of Gig-Well to consider:
>   ● what merchandise they should **not** stock
>   ● what merchandise they should stock more of
>   ● whether they should make any changes to their ticket prices.

Evaluation

Share your report and your reformatted Gig-Well spreadsheet with a friend. Ask them to read your report and comment on:
> ➤ how easy it was to understand
> ➤ how helpful your charts were in helping their understanding
> ➤ how well laid out your report was
> ➤ how well presented your Gig-Well spreadsheet is.

Based on their feedback make improvements to your report and spreadsheet to improve its readability.

Glossary

Key Term Definition

3Vs term used to explain the concept of big data (volume, velocity and variety)

5G fifth generation mobile networks providing high speed data transfer

abstract a representation that does not show all of the detail; the way a high-level programing language can be used to represent more than one machine code instruction

accumulator (ACC) a register which holds the intermediate results of processing carried out by the ALU

action attribute an HTML attribute which will provide details of where to send data from an input form when the submit button is clicked by the user

address bus carries details of an address location in memory which is being accessed so data can be written into it or read from it

algorithm a step by step representation of a solution written in pseudocode or using a flow chart

anchor a hyperlink which provides a link to content or headings further down a web page

AND gate a logic gate which accepts two inputs and will output a 1 (or TRUE) value only if both inputs equal 1

arithmetic logic unit (ALU) carries out all of the calculations needed during the execution of a program

arithmetic operators +, – , *, / and other symbols which can be used for arithmetic

array a data structure which holds items of data all of the same data type

artificial intelligence (AI) the use of computers to simulate intelligence displayed by humans

assembly language a low-level language which uses abbreviations using human type language structures to represent easily understood versions of each instruction in a CPU's instruction set

assignment statements a statement which assigns a variable a value; for example, x=3

asymmetric encryption a form of encryption that uses two keys, one for encrypting the data and another for decrypting the data

atbash cipher a very old method of encrypting which reverses the alphabet to create cipher text

backup a copy of data stored safely in case the original data is destroyed or damaged

big data refers to the large quantities of data that can be mined (analysed) for information by large organisations; big data can be described using the 3Vs

binary search a method of searching data which starts at the middle of a sorted list and reduces the number of items searched after each attempt

biometric the measurement of individuals' unique physical characteristics such as finger prints and facial recognition

biometric authorisation the use of biometric data to identify authorised users to an application and limit control to technology

black spot an area which is not covered by Wi-Fi

Bluetooth a short range technology used to connect devices together; it uses radio waves to communicate

bound form a form which is linked to a data source such as a table and which is then used to input, display or edit data directly into a table

bridge a network bridge joins two separate computer networks and enables communication between them

bubble sort a method of sorting data which compares adjacent items of data and swaps them if they are not in the correct order; this process is repeated until the data is sorted

built-in a function written as part of the Python language, such as print()

bus communication line used to transfer signals from one part of a digital device to another; for example, a set of wires used to transfer data around the inside of a computer

business critical data data that is vital to the operation of the business

cache high speed memory, close to the processor, normally on the same processor chip, used to store frequently used instructions so the processor can access them quickly.

Cascade Delete if an item is deleted from a linked lookup table, all related entries will be deleted from the table which uses the lookup table as a data source

central processing unit (CPU) contains all of the electronic circuitry a computer needs to carry out all of the instructions provided by the computer programs running on the device

channel the path along which data will travel on a particular network

cipher a method of encrypting text by replacing each letter with other symbols or letters

circuit board a thin plastic plate or unit which contains electronic components

class a CSS definition that combines a number of styles; the class selector/name starts with "." and they styles associated with that class are contained within { }; the class can then be applied to any HTML element that calls it

client the person for whom an application is being developed

client-side processing refers to the situation where a program or script is processed within the client's web browser; the code is often embedded in the HTML of the web page being viewed or it may be called as an external file; a common example of client-side processing is the validation of data entered into an online form before it is submitted by the user

client-side script a small program which runs on the user's computer

clock ticks a unit to measure time inside a computer system

combinational logic the use of more than one logic gate in a logic circuit to allow complex tasks to be carried out

comparison checking two data items against each other to determine their correct order

complex queries queries which extract data using more than one criterion, from more than one data source, and may also include calculations

computer viruses software designed to damage a computer

container class a CSS class which can be used to group HTML elements together so they can all be styled the same way

contiguous next to each other

control bus carries control signals to different parts of the digital device telling them what task they need to carry out next

control unit issues commands to all of the other hardware components to help ensure programs are carried out correctly

core an individual processing unit in the CPU; each processing unit can carry out its own set of instructions

corrective measures the actions taken by the programmer after testing to correct errors in the programs

current instruction register (CIR) stores instruction currently being executed by the CPU

cyber security protecting systems, data and software from digital attacks

data analytics the process of extracting meaningful information from raw data using automated processes and algorithms

data breaches the illegal viewing, accessing or modification of data perhaps by a hacker

data bus carries data signals around the inside of the device

data dictionary (programming) information about the data used in the program; usually presented in a table structure

data dictionary (databases) a document used to describe the tables used in a database

data requirements the data items required for the program

data source a table or query used to provide data for display or further processing

data structure a variable designed to hold a number of data items together

data subjects the people about which data is held; for example, an employee (or you!)

data theft when data has been acquired illegally without the permission of the company or individual to which it belongs

data types the type of data to be stored in a variable; for example, string and integer

deadline a date by which a particular task must be completed.

decode the process of working out what the instruction means, what it is telling the CPU to do

decrypt decode or unscramble data using the required key

digital divide the uneven distribution of access to modern technology

electronic circuit a physical device programmed to make decisions on (process) inputs in order to produce an output signal

element a data item identified by the array name and the position in the array; for example, runTimes[2] is the third element in the array

encryption a process which scrambles data making it unreadable; the data can only be read by someone who has the key to decode it

Enforce Referential Integrity an entry for an item with a foreign key field cannot be placed in a table if that item does not already exist in the linked lookup table

entities the people or things represented in a database application

entity relationship diagram (ERD) a diagram used to show how entities such as people, objects relate to each other within a system such as a database

event driven programming when a portion of a program is only executed when an event occurs when the application is running; for example, the user clicks a button on screen

execute the process of carring out the instruction

fault tolerant the capability of a computer network to continue operating if a problem occurs

fetch the process of collecting an instruction from another location

fetch–decode–execute cycle another name for the instruction cycle

file server the main computer on the network; it holds data and software and manages security and backup

firewall hardware or software designed to prevent or allow access to a private network; it can also prevent unauthorised internet users from accessing the network

form a database object containing labels, text boxes and buttons to help users input, view or edit data in a database

form element an HTML element which tells the browser that a form for data entry is to be displayed in a browser window

form mail script a specially written script file which is stored on a web server with a website; the script is linked to from within an HTML document and is used to collect data recorded on an HTML form before sending it to a specified email address

function a sub-program designed to perform a particular task; a named unit of code that can be called in a program

functionality the range of operations which can be carried out by a digital device or application

Gantt chart a bar chart that shows a project schedule.

General Data Protection Regulation (GDPR) a law which protects people's personal data and ensures that companies protect the data and use it appropriately

Goal Seek a *Microsoft Excel* feature which supports what-if questioning by looking at the desired outcome

Group & Sort a feature available in *Microsoft Access* which allows data to be sorted and grouped in reports before display on screen

hacker a person who has gained unauthorised access to a network or computer with intent to damage or destroy it

high-level language (HLL) a programming language, such as Python, that is closer to human language than the language a computer understands

hub computer hardware used to connect a number of computers together; they are similar to switches except they send all data to all connected computers; there are also USB hubs which are used to connect a number of devices to a computer

id attribute a method of applying a name or unique id to an HTML element

immersive creating an experience that makes the user feel they are part of the scene being projected

index can be used to refer to the position of an element in an array

insertion sort a method of sorting data in which the items of data are compared and swapped to their correct position one at a time

instruction cycle the cycle carried out by the CPU as it processes instructions

instruction set the set of all instructions in machine code that can be executed by a CPU

interactive website a website which allows two-way communication between the user and the application

internal clock (or system clock) a timer which is used to control the rate instructions are carried out

internet protocol (IP) address a unique address which identifies an individual device on the internet

JavaScript a programming language used to add interactive features to websites

layout the way data is presented or laid out on a screen or printed copy of a document

library a suite of programming procedures designed to carry out specific tasks and provided for use in the development of other applications

linear search a simple search method which checks every data item in a list when searching for an item

list a set of objects in Python which can be edited; a list can hold objects of different data types

Little Man Computer (LMC) an online CPU simulation program

logic circuit a combination of logic gates used to carry out complex operations

logic gate a physical device or circuit that carries out a logical operation

logical operations instructions carried out using logical operators such as >, <, >=, <>, where the result can only be TRUE or FALSE

low-level language (LLL) a programming language where the commands used link directly to the instructions the processor can carry out

machine code a computer programming language consisting of binary instructions that the computer can understand without a need to carry out translation

macro a small program written to complete a repetitive task automatically

mail merge the process of automatically personalising documents through the insertion of individual recipients' contact details from a database application

mail-shot a large scale distribution of a standard document, often for the purposes of displaying a message or for promotional reasons

mailto form HTML which allows the user to click on a submit button which then opens an email application

main memory another name for RAM, which is used to store the programs and data currently being operated on by the CPU

margins space around the top, right, bottom and left of an HTML element

megabits per second (Mbps) and gigabits per second (Gbps) the speed of data transfer; 1 Mbps means one million (1 000 000) bits are transmitted each second; 1 Gbps means one billion (1 000 000 000) bits are transmitted each second

memory address register (MAR) holds the address of the memory location being accessed either to read data from, or to write data to

memory data register (MDR) any data or instructions that pass into or out of main memory must pass through the MDR

memory location an address or physical space in computer memory for holding data

model a computer program that has been designed to predict the way another system works

motherboard a circuit board that houses the CPU and provides connections between the hardware components inside a computer

MySQL an open source tool which can be used to manage relational databases using SQL

navigation bar a section of an interface which provides users with a method of accessing other content or pages in an application

network cables generally copper cables used to link each computer in the network to the file server

network interface card an internal hardware device which enables a computer to connect to a network using a cable

NOT gate a logic gate which accepts one input and will output the opposite value to the input; for example, if the input value is 1, the output value will be 0 and vice versa

object the group of items which can be produced when creating a *Microsoft Access* database, including tables, forms, queries and reports

opcode an instruction to be carried out

operand a data item to be operated on or a location in memory where the data is stored

OR gate a logic gate which accepts two inputs and will output a 1 (or TRUE) value only if either of the input values equals 1

packet unit of data which travels along a network as a single package

padding provide space between any HTML element and any borders around it

parameters values or variables that are passed into a function from the main program; they are used in calculations and processing within the function

pass one complete run through the data items in the list or array

password a set of characters known only to the user which is used with the username to log on

physical security the protection of hardware, software, networks and data from the effects of a physical attack or event such as a flood

piconet a temporary network formed when two or more Bluetooth devices connect together

tic-tac-toe cipher a replacement cipher which uses grids and symbols to replace letters

pivot table a table that can be used to summarise data from a much larger data source, e.g. a database table; the data can be summarised using sum, averages or even charts

plagiarism taking someone else's work or ideas and passing them off as one's own

presence check a check to ensure a data entry field is not left blank

private IP address an IP address that is allocated to a networked device and is internal to the network

program counter (PC) stores the address of the next instruction waiting to be executed (carried out) by the CPU

project manager the person who is responsible for managing the scheduling, costing and timing of a project

pseudocode English-like phrases used to represent the solution to a problem

public IP address an IP address that is allocated to a device on the internet by the internet service provider; it is the main gateway through which data will enter a LAN from the internet

public key a key which is known that is used to encode or encrypt data

radio button a graphical control element used to provide users with options to choose from when entering data; only one option can be selected

real-time when input data is processed and output provided almost immediately for the user; used for example in aircraft control systems where delays could have life-threatening implications

register a memory location within the CPU itself, used for high speed access to data such as instructions, memory addresses or individual data items

repetition repeating program statements based on a condition, using a loop

reusable code code written so that it can be called and reused in different parts of the program

router a hardware device which connects networks together; for instance, a LAN and the internet

satellite dish a dish shaped aerial used to transmit and receive data

search space the number of items in the list that are currently being checked for the target value

security the protection of data and hardware on the network

selection selecting program statements to be executed based on a condition, using an IF-statement

server-side processing when a web page is posted back to the web server, the script is processed on the web server and returns feedback to the user's web page; a common example of server-side processing is saving data to a web based database, navigating to a new web page or validating a user's login to a website

server-side script a program which runs on a web server in response to input from the web page user

subform a form which has been inserted into another form

submit input type an HTML form element which provides users with a button to click when they have completed a data entry form

subnet mask divides an IP address into the network address and the host address and allows networks to be divided up for better performance

swaps swapping the position of two data items in the list or array

switch a device which is a connection point for a group of computers on a network; the device is then connected to the server; switches can send data to the correct computer on the network as each computer is connected to a switch

symmetric encryption a form of encryption that uses the same key for encrypting and decrypting data

syntax the spelling and grammar of the programming language

target value the number or value that is currently being searched for in the list

TCP/IP a combination of communications protocols which allows devices on the internet to connect and send and receive data

text-based hyperlink a word or words which have a hyperlink embedded to provide users with a link to additional content or pages in an application

transmission control protocol (TCP) a network communications protocol for sending data in packets over the internet

trendline a line that is superimposed over the data included on an existing line graph and is used to show the general pattern or overall direction of the data

truth table a table which shows all possible combinations of inputs and outputs for a logic gate

tuple similar to a list; a tuple is a list which cannot be edited or changed without creating a new list

unbound form a form which is not linked to any data sources but can be used to help users operate the database

user interface the means used to allow a user to communicate with a computer system

user requirements (programming) a list of tasks that the program should perform agreed between the user and the analyst

user requirements (databases) a document which specifies what the user expects the software to do

username a unique name given to a user on a network which can be used to log on

validation ensuring that data entered is acceptable or satisfies criteria

validation checks checks carried out automatically during data input to help ensure only appropriate data is entered

vehicle telematics information telecommunications from vehicles – this includes monitoring and broadcasting of vehicle location using GPS, engine status, and so on

virtual reality (VR) the use of technology to create an artificial environment that looks and feels realistic to the end user

w3-bar a class which groups HTML elements together and displays them across the screen in a web browser

w3-bar-item a class used to define the individual items which will appear inside a w3-bar container

w3-border class displays a border around an HTML element when it is displayed in a browser window

w3-button a w3 class used to define a button style element which can be used for navigation bars on web pages

w3-cell class displays blocks of HTML content side by side in a browser window as though presented inside a table

w3-circle class will display an HTML element inside a circle shape when it is presented in a browser window

w3-color class a css class predefined by w3schools which can be used to add colour to any HTML element

w3schools CSS a CSS library provided by w3schools which is free to use

w3-text-color class a css class predefined by w3schools which can be used to change the colour to any HTML text element

what-if questioning the process of making predictions about outcomes in a scenario by changing input values to see how they impact on related output

Wi-Fi the technology that allows a device to connect to the internet at high speed without the use of wires; the technology uses radio signals to transmit data

wireframe a layout diagram of a screen or web page

wireless access point (WAP) a hardware device that allows other Wi-Fi devices to connect to a wired network

wireless adapter the general term used for a device that can connect a laptop or computer to a wireless network

wireless enabled the capability to connect to a Wi-Fi network

wireless network interface card (WNIC) an internal hardware device that allows the computer to connect wirelessly to the network

wireless router combines the functions of a router and a wireless access point

XOR gate a logic gate which accepts two inputs and will output a 1 (or TRUE) value only if either of the input values equals 1, but not if both equal 1

Index

Numbers

3Vs, big data 171
5G 125

A

abstract representations 16
accumulator (ACC) 14, 21–2
action attributes 96
address bus 14–15
algorithms 140, 145–7
anchors 87–8
AND gates 28–30
arguments 158
arithmetic logic unit (ALU) 14
arithmetic operators 43
arrays 42, 43–4
artificial intelligence (AI) 9
  examples 34
assembly language 8, 16, 17
asymmetrical encryption 128–9
atbash cipher 128, 129

B

Babbage, Charles 108
backups 111
barcodes, check digits 136
big data 171
binary search 42, 65–7
  creating code for 68–9
biometric authorisation 10, 133
biometrics 10
black box testing 72, 163
black spots 117
Bluetooth 117
  advantages and disadvantages 116
  how it works 115–16
  range 116
  speed of data transmission 116
Boolean variables 27, 64
bound forms 182
bridges 112

bubble sort 42, 49–50, 55
  comparison with insertion sort 62–3
  creating code for 51–4
built-in functions 43
buses 9, 14–15
business critical data 133

C

cables 111
cache memory 12
Caesar's cipher 127–8, 129, 130
calculations, databases 187
cascade delete 181
Cascading Stylesheets (CSS) 82
  w3schools CSS classes library 82–7, 90–1
central processing unit (CPU) 8, 11–12
  accumulator 21–2
  components of 14–15
  fetch–decode–execute cycle 18–20, 25–7
  logic gates 27–33
channels 117
check digits 136–7
checksum 136
ciphers 127–8, 129, 130
circuit boards 11
classes, CSS 82–7, 90
clients 175
client-side processing 77
client-side script 98
clock ticks 11, 13
combinational logic 36
Command Prompt 123
communications satellites 116–17
comparisons 42
complex queries 185, 186–7
computer viruses 131, 132
container class 83
contiguous locations 44
control bus 14–15
control unit (CU) 14
copyright 131, 132
cores 12